Maritime Claims and Underwater Archaeology

The Law of the Sea

Volumes published in this Brill Research Perspectives title are listed at *brill.com/rpls*

Maritime Claims and Underwater Archaeology

When History Meets Politics

By

Mariano J. Aznar

BRILL

LEIDEN | BOSTON

This paperback book edition is simultaneously published as issue 4.1–2 of *Law of the Sea*, DOI:10.1163/24519359-12340010.

Library of Congress Control Number: 2021945639

Typeface for the Latin, Greek, and Cyrillic scripts: "Brill". See and download: brill.com/brill-typeface.

ISBN 978-90-04-50446-2 (paperback)
ISBN 978-90-04-50447-9 (e-book)

This book is printed on acid-free paper and produced in a sustainable manner.

Contents

Maritime Claims and Underwater Archaeology: When History Meets Politics

Mariano J. Aznar
Professor of Public International Law, Universitat Jaume I, Spain
maznar@uji.es

Abstract

Among other circumstances relevant to maritime delimitations, some States have recently used the protection of underwater cultural heritage (UCH) as grounds for advancing jurisdictional or sovereignty claims over different maritime areas. After identifying the contours of current international law governing that heritage, this book critically addresses: *first*, the generally limited use of archaeological heritage in territorial claims; *second*, the broad acceptance by States of 'archaeological maritime zones' that overlap with declared contiguous zones; and, *third*, the (mis)use of UCH and underwater archaeology in three still disputed maritime claims, namely, Canada's claim in Arctic waters, China's in the South China Sea, and Russia's in Crimea and its surrounding waters. Legal and ethical issues related to underwater archaeology are also discussed.

Keywords

law of the sea – maritime claims – underwater cultural heritage – maritime delimitations – historical evidence – codification and progressive development

 | DOI:10.1163/9789004504479_002

To my friends, for always being there

Abbreviations

Area	The seabed and ocean floor and subsoil thereof, beyond the limits of national jurisdiction
CTS	Consolidated Treaty Series
DOALOS	Division for Ocean Affairs and the Law of Sea
EEZ	Exclusive economic zone
ICJ	International Court of Justice
ICOMOS	International Council of Monuments and Sites
ICUCH	ICOMOS International Committee on Underwater Cultural Heritage
IDI	*Institut de Droit international*
ILA	International Law Association
ISA	International Seabed Authority
LOSC	United Nations Convention on the Law of the Sea
LNTS	*League of Nations Treaty Series*
MSR	Marine scientific research
NLCA	Nunavut Land Claims Agreement
NWP	Northwest Passage in the Arctic
STAB	Scientific and Technical Advisory Body of the Meeting of States Parties to the 2001 UNESCO Convention
UNRIAA	*United Nations Reports of International Arbitral Awards*
UNCLOS III	Third United Nations Conference on the Law of the Sea
UNESCO	United Nations Educational, Scientific and Cultural Organisation
UNTS	*United Nations Treaty Series*
VCLT	Vienna Convention on the Law of Treaties
WHC	Convention concerning the Protection of the World Cultural and Natural Heritage

> Who controls the past controls the future. Who controls the present controls the past
>
> G. ORWELL, *1984*

1 Introduction

Beginning in 1939 and over the course of several excavations conducted in occupied territories, Nazi Germany sought alleged evidence of *Germania* to support the National Socialist myth of Aryan supremacy. In doing so, the regime's archaeologists not only plundered museums and private collections in various countries but also looted and decontextualised numerous sites across Poland, Ukraine, and other places east of the Rhine. Just weeks before the Focke Museum in Bremen revisited these historical facts in an exhibition that opened in March 2013,[1] the Israel Museum in Jerusalem inaugurated another fascinating exhibition on Herod the Great, portraying the final journey of the king buried in Herodium, near Bethlehem.[2] From the outset, numerous voices expressed concerns about the archaeological origin of some of the exhibited pieces, accusing the museum of displaying objects excavated from occupied territories, particularly the West Bank.[3]

These two recent cases show how archaeological objects – and archaeology itself – can be, and are, used for political purposes. Although such politicisation has been widely criticised and re-assessed,[4] it remains a powerful tool in the hands of States and non-State entities alike when discussing their ideological support and sovereign pretentions.[5] Sometimes, they are simply seeking to destroy traces of history to justify their claims or demonstrate their power. In others cases, archaeology – along with the objects recovered from ancient sites – is used for an unstated purpose, not immediately disclosed, but with long-term effects for the defence of a State's sovereign claims. In a highly grotesque image, in 1973 and 1979, some Hong Kong newspapers reported the discovery of ancient remains (specifically, markings dating from the early

1 Focke Museum, *Graben für Germanien*, 10 March–8 September 2013 (source: <https://www.focke-museum.de/vorlage/akkordeon-graben-fuer-germanien/>).

2 The Israel Museum, *Herod the Great: The King's Final Journey*, 2 February 2013–4 Mar 2014 (source: <https://www.imj.org.il/en/exhibitions/herod-great>).

3 Examples of such criticism can be found in H. Naylord, 'King Herod exhibit "latest example of Israeli exploitation"', *The National*, 23 February 2013, at: <https://www.thenational.ae/world/mena/king-herod-exhibit-latest-example-of-israeli-exploitation-1.306231>; and J. Greenberg, 'Museum exhibit becomes front in Israeli-Palestinian struggle', *The Washington Post*, 13 February 2013, at: <https://www.washingtonpost.com/world/middleeast/museum-exhibit-becomes-front-in-israeli-palestinian-struggle/2013/02/13/dca47284-7614-11e2-95e4-6148e45d7adb story.html>.

4 See, generally, P. L. Kohl and C. Fawcett, *Nationalism, Politics and the Practice of Archaeology* (Cambridge University Press: Cambridge, 1996); P. L. Kohl, M. Kozelsky and N. Ben-Yehuda (eds), *Selective Remembrances: Archaeology in the Construction, Commemoration, and Consecration of National Pasts* (University of Chicago Press: Chicago, 2007). On how underwater archaeology can also be misused in general, see I. Gately and J. Benjamin, 'Archaeology Hijacked: Addressing the Historical Misappropriations of Maritime and Underwater Archaeology' (2018) 13(1) *Journal of Maritime Archaeology* 15–35.

5 That said, there are also cases in which "reasonably well-grounded archaeological interpretation can be shown to foster legitimate national pride, ethnic awareness, or communal solidarity". N. A. Silberman, 'Promised lands and chosen peoples: the politics and poetics of archaeological narrative', in Kohl and Fawcett (n. 4), at 251.

1900s) in the Paracel Islands in the South China Sea, which purportedly provided proof of China's historical presence there. It has since been revealed, and has not yet been contested, that the true story is rather different: that in June 1937, the head of Chinese military region number 9 was sent on a secret mission to the Paracels to determine whether there was Japanese activity on the islands – but that he was also given another task, recorded in a classified annex to the mission's report that was published in Chinese in 1987 by the Guangdong Province Committee of Place Names, according to which his boat was loaded with 30 milestones or markings, dated 1902, 1912, and 1921, and that the team buried two of the 1902 milestones and four from 1912 on North Island, one each from 1902, 1912, and 1921 on Lincoln Island, and two from 1921 on Woody Island, and finally, they deposited a single milestone, dated 1912, on Rocky Island. The milestones were then 'forgotten' until 1974, when they were suddenly (re)discovered.[6]

Akin to these cases on land, which can impact the sea, the oceans are subject to similar claims. Although today almost all States' land boundaries have generally been traced, their sea boundaries sometimes remain unclear, if not disputed. Rules and principles on how to trace these maritime boundaries have crystallised in the law of the sea, as part of international law. Most of them – clarified and applied *in casu* by international courts, particularly the International Court of Justice (ICJ) – were codified by the 1982 United Nations Convention on the Law of the Sea (LOSC),[7] widely ratified and generally accepted as the 'Constitution of the Oceans'. Beyond historical maritime disputes – both outstanding and settled[8] – new facts and arguments have been discussed as elements to consider when (re)tracing maritime boundaries. For example, unlike the right of indigenous peoples to have a say in the tracing of land or sea boundaries – which has largely been neglected[9] –, rising sea levels are gaining traction in the literature and public discourse because of

6 See all the data in F.-X. Bonnet, 'Archaeology and Patriotism: Long Term Chinese Strategies in the South China Sea', paper presented at the Southeast Asia Sea conference (Ateneo Law Center, Makati, 27 March 2015), available at: <http://www.imoa.ph/archeology-and-patriotism-long-term-chinese-strategies-in-the-south-china-sea/>. See also B. Hayton, 'When Good Lawyers Write Bad History: Unreliable Evidence and the South China Sea Territorial Dispute' (2017) 48(1) *Ocean Development & International Law* 17–34, at 24–25.

7 Adopted 10 December 1982, entered into force 16 November 1994, 1833 UNTS 3.

8 For an appraisal of the latter, see the collection *International Maritime Boundaries* edited for Brill by the American Society of International Law and C. G. Lathrop in various volumes, available at: <https://brill.com/view/serial/IMBO>.

9 See, for example, D. M. Schug, 'International maritime boundaries and indigenous people: The case of the Torres Strait' (1996) 20(3) *Marine Policy* 209–222; S. Atala, 'Indigenous archaeology and decolonizing practice' (2006) 30(3) *American Indian Quarterly* 280–310; or M. J. Aznar, 'The human factor in territorial disputes', in: M. G. Kohen and M. Hébié, *Research*

their "potential to impact significantly the spatial extent of national claims to maritime jurisdiction".[10] Perhaps less relevantly, but nevertheless increasingly, the use of maritime archaeological missions and the interpretations given to the historical objects found or recovered at sea are also fuelling various claims by different States around the world.

This book explores how some of these actions are being carried out, the legal basis for performing them, and the political goals driving all these scenarios. Here, as in most disputes, the questions of *what*, *how*, and *why* are entangled and cannot be answered separately. The following pages will attempt to address, in an orderly fashion, the most important points of the current debate over whether and how underwater archaeology and underwater cultural heritage can be a legal tool for diplomacy when States are claiming or negotiating the final drawing of a maritime boundary. To this end, this study will begin with a general *tour d'horizon* of the meaning of underwater cultural heritage and maritime archaeology[11] for the limited purposes of the theme of this book. Chapter 2 will then focus on how underwater cultural heritage came late to the law of the sea, discussing the gaps and achievements of this legal framework. It will also refer to the agreements reached – especially the 2001 UNESCO Convention on the Protection of the Underwater Cultural Heritage[12] – and the concerns still present in its regulation, as well as how they might influence maritime claims.

Chapter 3 moves on to the uses (and abuses, if any) of underwater archaeology in relation to maritime claims. It will review how archaeological remains and activities have had a (limited) impact on land delimitation and how this might be extended to the tracing of maritime boundaries. It will also examine other cases in which underwater archaeology has yielded evidence of improper claims. Finally, it will review how States are using archaeological grounds today to claim either jurisdiction or sovereignty in various maritime disputes.

The final part of the book offers some concluding remarks intended to address and assess the legal, political, and ethical limits of the use and abuse of underwater archaeology.

Handbook on Territorial Disputes in International Law (Edward Elgar: Cheltenham, 2018), 291–342.

10 D. Vidas, D. Freestone and J. McAdam (eds), *International Law and Sea Level Rise: Report of the International Law Association Committee on International Law and Sea Level Rise* (Brill: Leiden/Boston, 2019), at 16.

11 This book will essentially address maritime cultural heritage only, leaving aside underwater heritage located in inland waters such as rivers, lakes, and wetlands. The term *underwater* rather than *maritime* or *submarine* is used because of its general acceptance as a term of art and its inclusion in recent international and domestic legal texts.

12 Adopted 2 November 2001, entered into force 2 January 2009, 2562 UNTS 1 (hereinafter, 2001 UNESCO Convention).

2 The Underwater Cultural Heritage and the Law of the Sea

2.1 *The Late Arrival of UCH to UNCLOS III*

Current law of the sea is the typically complex product of a codification process. Originally consisting of venerable rules such as *jus naufragii*, *mare liberum*, or rules to combat piracy and slavery, it reached a turning point with the emergence of increasing technicalities and a more 'vertical' approach to maritime issues – deep-sea fishing, mining, submarine navigation – to round out the more 'horizontal' interests – police and port jurisdiction, defence, surface navigation – of which it had consisted until the 20th century. Since then, a lengthy but fruitful codification process, culminating in the Third United Nations Conference on the Law of the Sea (UNCLOS III), has forged the corpus of conventional and customary rules that governs the seas and oceans today.[13] Although the LOSC is the main final product, the process has once again been set in motion conventionally, with the negotiation of a new treaty on marine biological diversity[14] and, more importantly for the purposes of this book, the still remote extension of the 1972 Convention concerning the Protection of the World Cultural and Natural Heritage (WHC),[15] both of which are potentially applicable to areas beyond national jurisdiction. But this development is not only conventional: State practice, particularly that of States with a special interest, is also (re)shaping some aspects of rules of the law of the sea – some codified by the LOSC – through a customary process, as well as adapting certain universal regimes to these states' particular interests. To sum up then, current law of the sea is both conventional and customary, relative and general, never static but in motion.

---

13 See, among others, R. R. Churchill and A. V. Lowe, *The Law of the Sea*, 3rd edn (Manchester University Press: Manchester, 1999); D. R. Rothwell and T. Stephens, *The International Law of the Sea*, 2nd edn (Hart Publishing: Oxford, 2016); D. Rothwell, A. O. Elferink, K. Scott and T. Stephens (eds), *The Oxford Handbook of the Law of the Sea* (Oxford University Press: Oxford, 2015); J. R. Martínez Vargas and G. Vega Barbosa, *Tratado de Derecho del Mar* (Valencia: Tirant, 2016); and M. Forteau and J.-M. Thouvenin (eds), *Traité de droit international de la mer* (Editions A. Pedone: Paris, 2017).

14 In Resolution 72/249 of 24 December 2017, the UN General Assembly decided to convene an Intergovernmental Conference, under the auspices of the United Nations, to elaborate the text of an international legally binding instrument under the LOSC on the conservation and sustainable use of the marine biological diversity of areas beyond national jurisdiction. See: <https://www.un.org/bbnj/>.

15 Adopted 16 November 1972, entered into force 17 December 1975, 1037 UNTS 151. UNESCO has begun to discuss the possibility of negotiating an amendment (or a Protocol) to make it applicable to the high seas. See the report for UNESCO by D. Freestone, D. Laffoley, F. Douvere and T. Badman, *World Heritage in the High Seas: An Idea Whose Time Has Come* (2016), available at: <https://whc.unesco.org/en/news/1535/>.

This is not new. During UNCLOS III, the negotiating States were aware of the changing landscape; they were not only codifying existing law of the sea but also progressively developing this area of law, as the LOSC Preamble expressly recalls. However, within that process, little attention was paid to underwater cultural heritage, resulting in its neglect under the convention. There are several intertwined reasons for this, well described in the literature.[16] They could be summarised as stemming from the maritime powers' fear of opening new talks on the delicate balance of the jurisdictional mosaic achieved in the text negotiated at Montego Bay for the newly established exclusive economic zone (EEZ) regime and the revisited rights and duties of coastal States regarding their contiguous zone and continental shelf. The result was the presumption, based on a legal fiction, included in Article 303(2) LOSC, which provides as follows:

> In order to control traffic [in archaeological and historical objects], the coastal State may, in applying article 33, presume that their removal from the seabed in the zone referred to in that article without its approval would result in an infringement within its territory or territorial sea of the laws and regulations referred to in that article.

This article, which has been harshly criticised in the literature,[17] gave coastal States only a limited jurisdictional right to protect underwater cultural heritage

---

16 See S. Dromgoole, *Underwater Cultural Heritage and International Law* (Cambridge University Press: Cambridge, 2013); M. They, *La protection internationale du patrimoine culturel de la mer. Les compétences de l'État sur les biens culturels submergés* (Brill/Martinus Nijhoff: Leiden/Dordrecht, 2018); R. Garabello, *La Convenzione UNESCO sulla protezione del patrimonio culturale subacqueo* (Giuffrè Editore: Milan, 2004); J. L. Bonifácio Ramos, *O achatamento de bens culturais subaquáticos* (Livraia Petrony: Lisbon, 2008); and M. J. Aznar, *La protección del patrimonio cultural subacuático* (Tirant: Valencia, 2004). See also G. Bass, 'The Development of Maritime Archaeology', in: B. Ford, D. L. Hamilton and A. Catsambis (eds), *The Oxford Handbook of Maritime Archaeology*, available at: <https://www.oxfordhandbooks.com/view/10.1093/oxfordhb/9780199336005.001.0001/oxfordhb-9780199336005-e-0?print=pdf>; J. P. Delgado (ed.), *Encyclopaedia of Underwater and Maritime Archaeology* (British Museum Press: London, 1997); and A. Hafner, H. Öniz, L. Semaan and Ch.J. Underwood, *Heritage at Risk. Threats-Challenges-Solutions* (ICOMOS/ICUCH, 2020), available at: <https://openarchive.icomos.org/id/eprint/2488/>.

17 See, among others, A. C. Arend, 'Archaeological and Historical Objects: The International Legal Implications of UNCLOS III' (1982) 22 *Virginia Journal of International Law* 777–803; B. H. Oxman, 'Marine Archaeology and the International Law of the Sea' (1988) 12 *Columbia-VLA Journal of Law & the Arts* 353–372; C. Lund, 'Protection of the Under-Water Cultural Heritage', in: U. Leanza (ed.), *Il regime giuridico internazionale del Mare Mediterraneo* (Editoriale Scientifica: Naples, 1987), 351–354; T. Scovazzi, 'A Contradictory

up to the outer limit of their contiguous zone, when declared.[18] Beyond that limit and up to the outer limit of the EEZ and, most particularly, the continental shelves, activities directed at the underwater cultural heritage (or activities that might incidentally affect it) were not regulated but rather subordinated to the rights and duties related to the exploration and exploitation of these zones' natural resources.

A different, albeit unsatisfactory, regime for underwater cultural heritage located in the Area was outlined under Article 149 LOSC, which, with a likewise confusing wording, establishes that:

> All objects of an archaeological and historical nature found in the Area shall be preserved or disposed of for the benefit of mankind as a whole, particular regard being paid to the preferential rights of the State or country of origin, or the State of cultural origin, or the State of historical and archaeological origin.

The failure to define the States or 'countries' of origin and to specify the hierarchy of these 'preferential rights' among them and in relation to 'the benefit of mankind as a whole' for the preservation or disposal of objects of an archaeological or historical nature found in the Area, render this proviso "of little practical value ... a leftover provision that has lost is original thrust".[19] Article 149 LOSC provides no clear guidance on how to manage the finding of archaeological objects in the course of activities currently performed in the Area, nor is the 'Mining Code' adopted by the International Seabed Authority (ISA) particularly helpful in this regard.[20]

---

and Counterproductive Regime', in: R. Garabello and T. Scovazzi (eds), *The Protection of the Underwater Cultural Heritage: Before and After the 2001 UNESCO Convention* (Brill: Leiden/Boston, 2003), 3–18; and A. Strati, 'Protection of the underwater cultural heritage: from shortcomings of the UN Convention on the Law of the Sea to the Compromises of the UNESCO Convention', in: A. Strati (ed.), *Unresolved Issues and the New Challenges to the Law of the Sea* (Brill: Leiden/Boston, 2006), 21–62.

18 Notwithstanding the legal nature of this seabed as part of the continental shelf, for the purposes of the activities directed at the underwater cultural heritage, the concept of contiguous zone includes this seabed. For a discussion of these rights, see M. J. Aznar, 'The contiguous zone as an archaeological maritime zone' (2014) 29 *The International Journal of Marine and Coastal Law* 1–51.

19 Arend (n. 17), at 800.

20 For an appraisal, see the documents and literature assessed in M. J. Aznar, 'Exporting Environmental Standards to the Protection of Underwater Cultural Heritage in the Area', in: J. Crawford, A. G. Koroma, S. Mahmoudi and A. Pellet (eds), *The International Legal Order: Current Needs and Possible Responses – Essays in Honour of Djamchid Momtaz* (Brill: Leiden/Boston, 2017), 255–273. Sadly, the protection of the underwater cultural

Aside from the *horror jurisdictionis* and the inconclusive regime for the Area, two more factors may shed light on why underwater cultural heritage and its preservation were neglected by the LOSC. Because recognition of marine archaeology as an independent scientific discipline was still limited in the 1970s and marine research was mainly concerned with the natural environment and resources, marine archaeology was not considered marine scientific research (MSR) during UNCLOS III.[21] Admittedly not a 'resource',[22] underwater cultural heritage was regulated as simply another type of 'object' that could be found at sea. As such, and due in part to the influence of the powerful treasure-hunter lobby, which was backed by some States at UNCLOS III, it could be considered a 'commodity' and was thus subject to the *venerable* maritime laws of finds and/or salvage. Consequently, for that lobby and the States that supported it, nothing should impede the commercialisation of underwater cultural heritage as a mere tradeable type of artefact.[23] This was, for example, the view traditionally taken by the US admiralty courts since the 1980's.[24] But the

heritage in the Area has been (and continues to be) neglected by the literature and case law. See, for example, the otherwise fascinating recent book edited by Catherine Banet (ed.), *The Law of the Seabed* (Brill: Leiden/Boston, 2020), which mentions this heritage only twice and without further elaboration (at 223 and 257); or the Advisory Opinion rendered by the Seabed Disputes Chamber of the International Tribunal of the Law of the Sea (ITLOS), which did not mention, even tangentially, any obligation or duty of States regarding the general protection of UCH in the Area as provided for under Articles 149 and 303 LOSC (*Responsibilities and obligations of States with respect to activities in the Area*, Advisory Opinion, 1 February 2011, *ITLOS Reports* 2011).

21 See, among others, A. Soons, *Marine Scientific Research and the Law of the Sea* (TMC Asser Instituut: The Hague, 1982), at 275. It has been plausibly argued that contemporary marine archaeology is a full scientific discipline perfectly aligned with the concept of MSR. See S. Dromgoole, 'Revisiting the relationship between marine scientific research and the underwater cultural heritage' (2010) 25 *The International Journal of Marine and Coastal Law* 33–61.

22 Quite early on, the International Law Commission considered that "[i]t is clearly understood that the rights of the coastal State do not cover objects such as wrecked ships and their cargoes (including bullion) lying in the seabed or covered by sand in the subsoil". *Yearbook of the International Law Commission*, vol. II, 1956, at 289.

23 For different views, see, among others, S. Dromgoole and N. Gaskell, 'Who has a right to historic wrecks and wreckage?' (1993) 2 *International Journal of Cultural Property* 217–273; D. Bederman, 'The UNESCO Draft Convention on Underwater Cultural Heritage: A Critique and Counter-Proposal' (1999) 30 *Journal of Maritime Law & Commerce* 331–354; V. Vadi, 'Investing in culture: underwater cultural heritage and international investment law' (2009) 42 *Vanderbilt Journal of Transnational Law* 853–904; and O. Varmer and C. M. Blanco, 'The case for using the law of salvage to preserve underwater cultural heritage: The integrated marriage of the law of salvage and historic preservation' (2018) 49 *Journal of Maritime Law & Commerce* 401–424.

24 A general and critical overview of the evolving application of 'treasure' salvage can be found in T. J. Schoenbaum, *Admiralty and Maritime Law*, 6th edn (West Academic: St Paul,

acceptance by these courts, first, of a different legal regime for sunken State vessels (in the Spanish frigate saga)[25] and, later, of the historical importance of any sunken vessel above and beyond any monetary considerations (in the *Titanic* case)[26] has made them an uncomfortable forum for treasure-hunters and salvage litigation today.

Yet this change has costed a lot of time and effort by archaeologists, historians, curators, lawyers, and, eventually, diplomats. It was not the *weltgeist* at UNCLOS III, except among certain delegations (particularly those from Greece, Turkey, Italy, Cape Verde, Malta, Portugal, Tunisia, and former Yugoslavia). Hence, the text of Article 303(3) ultimately embedded those private interests in the LOSC, safeguarding "the rights of identifiable owners, the law of salvage or other rules of admiralty, or laws and practices with respect to cultural exchanges".

The regime thus created by Articles 149 and 303(2) and (3) LOSC leaves a series of unfortunate gaps in the international legal protection of the underwater cultural heritage. However, even before the 1982 Convention's entry into force, several scientific institutions had begun to call attention to these lacunae and to prepare a new legal text; and in 1994, they sent to UNESCO a draft of what would eventually be adopted as the 2001 UNESCO Convention.[27]

2.2 *(De)constructing Ambiguities: The 2001 UNESCO Convention*

The 2001 UNESCO Convention was negotiated for the main purpose of solving the caveats left unresolved by the LOSC and creating a new international

---

MN, 2018), at 786–813. See also N. Gaskell and C. Forrest, *The Law of Wreck* (Routledge: London, 2019), 325–355.

25 See M. J. Aznar, 'Treasure hunters, sunken State vessels and the 2001 UNESCO Convention on the Protection of Underwater Cultural Heritage' (2010) 25 *The International Journal of Marine and Coastal Law* 209–236; and T. Scovazzi, 'Sunken Spanish Ships before American Courts' (2018) 34 *The International Journal of Marine and Coastal Law* 245–290.

26 The final judicial fate of the RMS *Titanic* is self-explanatory. See *R.M.S. Titanic, Inc. v. Wrecked & Abandoned Vessel*, 804 F. Supp. 2d 508 (E.D. Va. 2011), which subjects any title "to the covenants and conditions that the United States, through the United States Attorney, negotiated and finalized with RMST and the court (the 'Revised Covenants and Condition')". These "Covenants and Conditions" are attached as Exhibit A to a previous decision by the same court dated 12 August 2010 (742 F. Supp. 2d (E.D. Va. 2010) at 809–824). Surprisingly enough, they mirror the basic rules annexed to the 2001 UNESCO Convention, which the US accepts as best practice but has not ratified. See further J. Nafziger, 'The UNESCO Convention on the Protection of the Underwater Cultural Heritage: Its Growing Influence' (2018) 49 *Journal of Maritime Law & Commerce* 371–400.

27 For these initial efforts of the International Law Association (ILA) and the International Council on Monuments and Sites (ICOMOS), see P. O'Keefe and J. Nafziger, 'The Draft Convention on Underwater Cultural Heritage' (1994) 25 *Ocean Development & International Law* 391–418.

cooperation regime for the protection of the underwater cultural heritage according to generally accepted scientific standards. It focusses on activities rather than on the objects themselves, and on how States Parties should conduct their activities directed at the underwater cultural heritage in the different maritime zones or that might incidentally affect it. Although not universally ratified,[28] the 2001 UNESCO Convention has attracted growing interest around the world, notwithstanding the existence of 'reticent' and 'opposing' States. 'Reticent' States are those not vehemently opposed to the Convention but with strong concerns about its compatibility with the LOSC and, especially, with their policies regarding the legal status of sunken State vessels. This is the case of the US and the UK, which nevertheless accept the Convention's main principles and archaeological protocols as best practice.[29] Other States, such as China, Germany, the Netherlands, Australia, and Canada, are less reticent and have initiated (with varying degrees of intensity and celerity) domestic discussions on possible adherence to the Convention. In contrast, there are two types of 'opposing' States: those like Russia or Norway, which have declared they will not ratify the Convention, claiming that it plainly contradicts the LOSC; and those like Colombia, Turkey, or Venezuela, which will not ratify a Convention that they consider subordinate to the LOSC, to which they are not parties.[30]

28 As of 1 July 2021, there are 72 States Parties to the Convention: Albania, Algeria, Antigua and Barbuda, Argentina, Bahrain, Barbados, Belgium, Benin, Bolivia, Bosnia and Herzegovina, Bulgaria, Cabo Verde, Cambodia, Costa Rica, Croatia, Cuba, DR Congo, Dominican Republic, Ecuador, Egypt, Estonia, France, Gabon, Ghana, Granada, Guatemala, Guinea, Guinea-Bissau, Guyana, Haiti, Honduras, Hungary, Iran, Iraq, Italy, Jamaica, Jordan, Kuwait, Lebanon, Libya, Lithuania, Madagascar, Mali, Malta, Mexico, Micronesia, Montenegro, Morocco, Namibia, Nigeria, Niue, Oman, Palestine, Panama, Paraguay, Poland, Portugal, Romania, Saint Kitts and Nevis, Saint Lucia, Saint Vincent and the Grenadines, Saudi Arabia, Senegal, Slovakia, Slovenia, South Africa, Spain, Switzerland, Togo, Trinidad and Tobago, Tunisia, and Ukraine. Source: UNESCO website.

29 For the UK, see *Hansard*, House of Commons, Written Answers for 24 January 2005, Col. 46W (available at: <https://publications.parliament.uk/pa/cm200405/cmhansrd/vo050124/text/50124w13.htm#50124w13.html_sbhd5>). See also H. Roberts, 'The British Ratification of the Underwater Heritage Convention: Problems and Prospects' (2018) 67(4) *International and Comparative Law Quarterly* 833–865. For the US, see n. 26 above and O. Varmer, 'Closing the Gaps in the Law Protecting Underwater Cultural Heritage on the Outer Continental Shelf' (2014) 33(2) *Stanford Environmental Law Journal* 251–286. For US practice and its position prior to the adoption of the UNESCO Convention, see R. Elia, 'US Protection of Underwater Cultural Heritage Beyond the Territorial Sea: Problems and Prospects' (2000) 29 *The International Journal of Nautical Archaeology* 43–56.

30 See M. J. Aznar, 'La Convention UNESCO pour la protection du patrimoine culturel subaquatique: une évaluation dix ans après son entrée en vigueur' (2018) 23 *Annuaire du droit de la mer* 197–211.

As the product of a political negotiation, the 2001 UNESCO Convention was inevitably subject to diplomatic bargaining – in some ways inherited from UNCLOS III. To be adopted, it had to include what has been called 'constructive ambiguities'.[31] These ambiguities mainly concern the legal status of sunken State vessels and the Convention's jurisdictional impact. The latter points to the core subject of this book and will be discussed separately (section 2.2.2 below); the former has been discussed at length in the literature and will be only briefly reviewed in the following sub-section (2.2.1), along with other responses given by the Convention.

2.2.1 Main Features of the 2001 UNESCO Convention

The Convention departs from the mandate given in Article 303(1) LOSC whereby "States have the duty to protect objects of an archaeological and historical nature found at sea and shall cooperate for this purpose". In accordance with Article 2, the Convention "aims to ensure and strengthen the protection of underwater cultural heritage" (paragraph 1), to which end the "States Parties shall cooperate in the protection of underwater cultural heritage" (paragraph 2).

Unlike some other UNESCO conventions, the 2001 text does not focus mainly on the object being protected, but on the activities directed at it. It gives a broad definition of underwater cultural heritage without assigning title to it.[32] This was the result of a serious debate settled early on, in the first pre-UNESCO drafts: in discussing whether the Convention should apply only to abandoned objects, the talks soon and obsessively came about to sunken State vessels. It was ultimately decided not to include any property proviso but rather a *renvoi* to general international law.[33] Hence, Article 2(8) of the Convention provides:

---

31 See C. Forrest, 'A New International Regime for the Protection of Underwater Cultural Heritage' (2002) 51 *International and Comparative Law Quarterly* 511–554; M. Rau, 'The UNESCO Convention on Underwater Cultural Heritage and the International Law of the Sea' (2002) 6 *Max Planck Yearbook of United Nations Law* 387–472; G. Carducci, 'New Developments in the Law of the Sea: The UNESCO Convention on the Protection of Underwater Cultural Heritage' (2002) 96(2) *The American Journal of International Law* 419–434; and A. González, 'Negotiating the Convention on Underwater Cultural Heritage: Myths and Reality', in: Garabello and Scovazzi (n. 17), 83–88.

32 Under Art. 1(1)(a) of the Convention, underwater cultural heritage means "all traces of human existence having a cultural, historical or archaeological character which have been partially or totally under water, periodically or continuously, for at least 100 years such as: (i) sites, structures, buildings, artefacts and human remains, together with their archaeological and natural context; (ii) vessels, aircraft, other vehicles or any part thereof, their cargo or other contents, together with their archaeological and natural context; and (iii) objects of prehistoric character".

33 See *Report of the Meeting of Governmental Experts on the Draft Convention for the Protection of the Underwater Cultural Heritage*, UNESCO Doc. CLT-98/CONF.202/7, para. 13.

> Consistent with State practice and international law, including the United Nations Convention on the Law of the Sea, nothing in this Convention shall be interpreted as modifying the rules of international law and State practice pertaining to sovereign immunities, nor any State's rights with respect to its State vessels and aircraft.

However, the concern stemmed from Article 7(3) of the 2001 UNESCO Convention, which provides:

> Within their archipelagic waters and territorial sea, in the exercise of their sovereignty and in recognition of general practice among States, States Parties, with a view to cooperating on the best methods of protecting State vessels and aircraft, *should* inform the flag State Party to this Convention and, if applicable, other States with a verifiable link, especially a cultural, historical or archaeological link, with respect to the discovery of such identifiable State vessels and aircraft. [*emphasis added*]

The decision to use the recommendatory 'should' rather than the mandatory 'shall' was the result of two opposing views during the negotiating process. The latter term was defended by historical and current maritime powers, which held that a coastal State *must* respect a foreign State's ownership and sovereign immunity and communicate the discovery of a sunken State vessel in its territorial sea (or archipelagic waters) to its flag State. In contrast, quite a few coastal States maintained that nothing in international law obliges a State to inform another State of any circumstance occurring within its territory unless otherwise agreed or imposed by a rule of international law.[34]

---

34 Arguably, the conflicting relationship between sovereignty and property was behind the disagreement. To some States – especially the Latin American States – the location of the wreck was tantamount to recognition of the title of the coastal State to them. For example, Latin American and Caribbean countries asserted that underwater cultural heritage "is the property of the State in which it is found and through this it is the heritage of the Humanity". See 'Santo Domingo Declaration', 16 June 1998, which resulted from the First Meeting of the Technical Commission on Underwater Cultural Heritage of the Forum of Ministers of Culture and Officials Responsible for Cultural Policy in Latin America and the Caribbean, reprinted in UNESCO, *Background Materials on the Protection of the Underwater Cultural Heritage*, vol. II (UNESCO: Paris, 2000), at 341–2. However, some Latin American States have changed their position. For example, in 2014, Mexico amended its 1972 *Ley Federal de Monumentos y Zonas Arqueológicos, Artísticos e Históricos*, including a new Art. 28*ter* under which the sovereign immunity of foreign sunken State vessels shall be respected. See the text of the law (in Spanish) at <http://www.diputados.gob.mx/LeyesBiblio/ref/lfmzaah.htm>.

In keeping with the LOSC, Article 7(1) of the 2001 UNESCO Convention provides, "States Parties, in the exercise of their sovereignty, have the exclusive right to regulate and authorize activities directed at underwater cultural heritage in their internal waters, archipelagic waters and territorial sea." But this provision concerns only the regulation and authorisation of *activities* directed at wrecks *within a coastal State's territory* and does not automatically convey title to them to the coastal State.[35] Nor does it change the flag State's interest in its underwater cultural heritage under the LOSC or otherwise. An exception to the rule laid out in Article 7(1) of the 2001 UNESCO Convention – the coastal State's exclusive right to regulate and authorise activities directed at underwater cultural heritage in its internal waters, archipelagic waters, and territorial sea[36] – is the immunity of sunken warships. This exception is allowed under Article 2(8) of the Convention and has been confirmed by State practice and *opinio juris*.[37] The logic of this approach is likewise on display in how the Convention addresses sunken State vessels located in the EEZ, on the continental shelf, or in the Area. In the first two cases, Article 10(7) simply states that "no activity directed at State vessels and aircraft shall be conducted without the agreement

35 For example, under the agreement regarding the CSS *Alabama*, France recognised and respected the continued ownership, sovereign immunity, and interest of the United States in its Civil War wreck, whilst the US recognised the jurisdiction of France to regulate all activities directed at this wreck in the territorial sea of France (see Agreement between the Government of the United States of America and the Government of the French Republic concerning the Wreck of the CSS *Alabama*, of 8 March 1995, in (1992) 20 *Law of the Sea Bulletin*, at 26–27). Both States responded analogously in the case of the wreck of *La Belle*, a French warship sunk in US waters (see Agreement between the Government of the French Republic and the Government of the United States of America Regarding the Wreck of "La Belle", adopted 31 March 2003, entered into force 31 March 2003, 2238 UNTS 413). This was also the position sustained, for example, by Spain concerning the legal title to the HMS *Sussex*, a British warship sunk in Spanish waters in 1694. When problems arose with its recovery in 2007 by a private US company acting under the authorisation of the British Ministry of Defence, Spain did not assert title over the wreck but simply required that Spanish archaeological law be applied to operations directed at it as an archaeological site located in Spanish waters (see Note by the Spanish Ministry of Foreign Affairs and Cooperation of 23 March 2007 (on file with the author)). On the *Sussex* case, see S. Dromgoole, 'Murky waters for government policy: the case of a seventeenth century British warship and ten tonnes of gold coins' (2004) 28 *Marine Policy* 189–198.

36 States have 'exclusive competence' regarding their own territory (*Isla de Palmas*, UNRIAA, vol. 2, 1928, 829, at 838), including the maritime spaces within those territories (*Military and Paramilitary Activities in and against Nicaragua* (*Nicaragua v. United States of America*), Merits, Judgment, ICJ Reports 1986, 14, at 111, para. 212).

37 See, among others, the Resolution on 'The Legal Regime of Wrecks of Warships and Other State-owned Ships in International Law', adopted by the *Institut de Droit international* on 29 August 2015, Tallinn Session, available at: <http://www.justitiaetpace.org/idiE/resolutionsE/2015Tallinn09en.pdf>.

of the flag State". However, even without the flag State's consent, coastal States may take: (i) urgent measures to protect the wreck (including measures against its unauthorised salvage)[38] and (ii) sovereign measures relating to the safety of navigation, which could damage the wreck. As for wrecks located in the Area, Article 12(7) provides: "No State Party shall undertake or authorize activities directed at State vessels and aircraft in the Area without the consent of the flag State." The recognition of the flag State's interest is therefore not diminished, but reinforced. Furthermore, nothing in the 2001 UNESCO Convention – which must be interpreted contextually – implies that the legal status of sunken State vessels changes simply because they are located in the internal waters, archipelagic waters, or territorial seas of a coastal State instead of on the continental shelf or in the Area.[39] The principles of sovereignty and immunity thus radiate contextually throughout the Convention; these tenets of international law are (and must be) carefully balanced with the protection of sunken State vessels when considered underwater cultural heritage in accordance with the definition provided in Article 1 of the Convention.

Leaving aside this bitter debate over the legal status of sunken State vessels – which has prominently focussed attention and wasted so much time – it should be noted that, in line with other UNESCO conventions, the 2001 Convention embodies a form of scientific cooperation built around three main ideas: (i) the performance of any activity directed at the underwater cultural heritage in keeping with widely recognised scientific standards; (ii) the avoidance of any commercial approach to that heritage; and (iii) the creation of a collaborative framework among the States Parties.

First, adopted at UNESCO, the Convention inevitably bears the imprint of archaeologists and historians, who had a strong influence during its drafting. States were also willing to include as general principles those rules already adopted by the international scientific community.[40] These included: the *in situ* preservation of underwater cultural heritage as the first option; the minimum-

38 Art. 10(4) of the 2001 UNESCO Convention.

39 As Craig Forrest has noted, "The actual regime for State owned vessels in the Convention reflects the resulting compromise between flag States and coastal States. Rather than focusing on the rights of the flag State, it was agreed that a balance would be drawn between the right of the flag State and the coastal State." Forrest (n. 31), at 528–29.

40 These principles are enumerated in Art. 2 of the Convention and Rules 1–8 of its Annex. In 1996, ICOMOS adopted its 'Charter on the Protection and Management of Underwater Cultural Heritage' (available at: <https://www.icomos.org/18thapril/underwater-eng.pdf>), which details these main principles for the protection of and the activities directed at that heritage. The text of the Charter was adapted and adopted as the Annex of the 2001 UNESCO Convention. Its 36 rules form an integral part of the Convention and, unless expressly provided otherwise, a reference to the Convention includes a reference to the Rules, as expressed in Art. 33 of the Convention.

impact rule and the preferred use of non-destructive techniques; the deposition, recording, conservation, and management of the heritage to ensure its long-term preservation and non-dispersal; its non-commercialisation (as will be discussed below); the non-disturbance of human remains and venerated sites; and responsible public access to underwater heritage compatible with these rules, among others. The Convention's Preamble thus considers that "survey, excavation and protection of underwater cultural heritage necessitate the availability and application of special scientific methods and the use of suitable techniques and equipment as well as a high degree of professional specialization, all of which indicate a need for uniform governing criteria".

Second, the Convention assumes the concern for the increasing commercial exploitation of underwater cultural heritage, particularly by means of certain activities aimed at the sale, acquisition, or barter of this heritage. Article 2(7) outlaws such activities, providing that underwater cultural heritage "shall not be commercially exploited".[41] However, the Convention goes even further by also limiting the applicability of the law of salvage (and the law of finds), the legal cover habitually used for such commercialisation. Hence, Article 4 – drafted as an exception to the general rule and with cumulative conditions – states:

> Any activity relating to underwater cultural heritage to which this Convention applies *shall not* be subject to the law of salvage or law of finds, unless it: (a) is authorized by the competent authorities, *and* (b) is in full conformity with this Convention, *and* (c) ensures that any recovery of the underwater cultural heritage achieves its maximum protection [*emphases added*].

To some extent this is in line with the practice of several States Parties to the 1989 International Convention on Salvage.[42] Article 30(1)(d) of that Convention provides that a State Party may reserve the right not to apply the provisions of the Convention "when the property involved is maritime cultural

41 Rule 2 of the Annex provides: "The commercial exploitation of underwater cultural heritage for trade or speculation or its irretrievable dispersal is fundamentally incompatible with the protection and proper management of underwater cultural heritage. Underwater cultural heritage shall not be traded, sold, bought or bartered as commercial goods."

42 Adopted 28 April 1989, entered into force 14 July 1996, 1953 UNTS 165 (hereinafter, '1989 Salvage Convention'). According to the preparatory works, a related IMO convention – the Nairobi International Convention on the Removal of Wrecks (adopted 18 May 2007, entered into force 14 April 2015, 46 ILM 694) – does not apply to historical wrecks.

property of prehistoric, archaeological or historical interest and is situated on the sea-bed".[43]

Finally, the Convention tries to organise a cooperative scheme among the States Parties based on a shared information mechanism that varies in intensity depending on the maritime zone where the activities are to be performed. As noted, in internal waters, archipelagic waters, and the territorial sea, coastal States have the exclusive right to regulate and authorise activities directed at underwater cultural heritage in the exercise of their sovereignty (Article 2(1) of the 2001 Convention). In the contiguous zone, where declared, States Parties have a somewhat increased jurisdiction over underwater cultural heritage, which, as will be seen below, seems to have crystallised a change in Articles 33 and 303(2) LOSC, giving new rights to coastal States (Article 8 of the 2001 Convention). In the EEZ and on the continental shelf, Article 9 of the 2001 Convention establishes a reporting and notification system among States Parties (through the Director-General of UNESCO) for activities directed at the underwater cultural heritage located in these zones. This system is based on the concept of 'interested States', i.e., a State party interested in being consulted on how to ensure the effective protection of that underwater cultural heritage.[44] These States will cooperate under the coordination of the so-called 'coordinating State' (normally the coastal State unless otherwise decided by that State and the rest of the interested States),[45] which shall act on behalf of the States Parties as a whole and not in its own interest (Article 10(6) of the

43 As of 1 July 2021, this reservation has been made by 25 of the 74 States Parties, including States especially interested in underwater cultural heritage, such as Australia, Bulgaria, Canada, China, Croatia, Ecuador, Estonia, Finland, France, Germany, Iran, Jamaica, Mexico, the Netherlands, New Zealand, Norway, Poland, the Russian Federation, Saudi Arabia, Spain, Sweden, Tunisia, Turkey, Ukraine, and the United Kingdom. Source: IMO website.

44 The interest should be based on a verifiable link, especially a cultural, historical, or archaeological one, to the underwater cultural heritage concerned (Art. 9(5) of the Convention). In 2015, the States Parties to the Convention adopted its Operative Guidelines under which the interest is to be demonstrated by (a) the results of scientific expertise, (b) historical documentation, or (c) any other adequate documentation. Doc. UNESCO CLT/HER/CHP/OG 1/REV, August 2015, at 9 (available at: <http://unesdoc.unesco.org/images/0023/002341/234177E.pdf>). On the notion of 'interest' in the Convention, see M. J. Aznar, 'The notions of "preferential right" and "interest" of states in the protection of the underwater cultural heritage' (2019) 38 *Revista Electrónica de Estudios Internacionales* 1–37. On the question of 'verifiable link', see T. J. Maarleveld, 'The Notion of "Verifiable Links" in the 2001 UNESCO Convention on the Protection of the Underwater Cultural Heritage' (2014) 19 *Art Antiquity and Law* 101–119.

45 Art. 10(3)(b) provides, "Where there is a discovery of underwater cultural heritage or it is intended that activity shall be directed at underwater cultural heritage in a State Party's exclusive economic zone or on its continental shelf, that State Party shall [...] coordinate such consultations as 'Coordinating State', unless it expressly declares that it does not

2001 Convention). This cooperation may entail the performance of preliminary research, the authorisation of archaeological activities, or the adoption of urgent and preventive measures. Finally, Articles 11 and 12 mirror the system created for the EEZ and the continental shelf, adapting it to the Area, introducing the participation of the International Seabed Authority through its Secretary-General, who shall be informed and participate in the consultations with the interested States. Given that activities are to be performed in the Area, a principle is introduced whereby the State selected from among the interested States as the coordinating State "shall act for the benefit of humanity as a whole, on behalf of all States Parties", paying particular regard "to the preferential rights of States of cultural, historical or archaeological origin in respect of the underwater cultural heritage concerned" (Article 12(6) of the Convention). The *spirit* of Article 149 LOSC is thus maintained.

Aside from these three main features, the 2001 UNESCO Convention calls for implementing control measures, both in general terms (Articles 5 and 16) and with regard to the surveillance of specific border and maritime facilities (Articles 14 and 15), as well as adapting the domestic sanction and seizure regime to possible violations of the Convention, including illicit traffic (Articles 17 and 18). Further, measures for general collaboration and information sharing (Article 19), public awareness (Article 20), and training in underwater archaeology (Article 21) are also encouraged.[46] Disputes between parties to the Convention concerning its interpretation or application shall be subject to negotiations in good faith or other peaceful means of settlement of their choice, possible mediation by UNESCO, or, if they cannot be thus settled, the provisions relating to dispute settlement set out in Part XV of the LOSC, to be applied *mutatis mutandis*, whether or not the parties to the dispute are also parties to the LOSC (Article 25).

2.2.2 The 2001 UNESCO Convention and Creeping Jurisdiction

The concern sparked by the 2001 UNESCO Convention regarding possible creeping jurisdiction persists. There are two main reasons for it, both related to the rights and duties that the Convention assigns to the States Parties in

wish to do so, in which case the States Parties which have declared an interest under Article 9, paragraph 5, shall appoint a Coordinating State."

46 The Convention establishes an institutional framework based on the Meeting of the States Parties, which has established a Scientific and Technical Advisory Body (STAB) that assists the Meeting in questions of a scientific or technical nature regarding the implementation of the Rules (Art. 23), as well as a Secretariat (Art. 24).

relation to activities performed in the EEZ or on the continental shelf, which it attempts to solve with its 'constructive ambiguities'.[47]

The first reason stems from the text of Article 9(1), under which, in the case of discovery or engagement in an activity directed at underwater cultural heritage in these zones, States Parties shall require their national or the master of the vessel to report that discovery or activity to them and to the coastal State. Alternatively, the State Party shall require the national or master of the vessel to report the discovery or activity to it and shall ensure the rapid and effective transmission of that report to all other States Parties. For some States, this proviso would grant the coastal State the right to impose an obligation on non-nationals and on masters of vessels flying a foreign flag to report such activities and discoveries. However, this outcome could simply be seen as the application of the principle whereby a State is recognised by international law as having the power to impose reporting obligations on its nationals and on vessels flying its flag wherever they may be. Nothing in the provision indicates that it is an extension of coastal States' jurisdiction over underwater cultural heritage. Even if a coastal State were to implement laws under the 2001 Convention to require foreign vessels and nationals to report finds of underwater cultural heritage within its EEZ and on its continental shelf, it could only enforce those laws against foreign vessels and nationals of States that have consented to this requirement under the Convention or other international law. Such a coastal State law would not apply to foreign vessels and nationals of a State that is not a party to the 2001 UNESCO Convention or did not consent to the requirement under some other law.[48]

A second set of jurisdictional concerns arises from the role of the 'coordinating State'. Under the 2001 Convention, the coordinating State will be the focal point in consultations with "all other States Parties which have declared an interest under Article 9(5), on how best to protect the underwater cultural heritage".[49] The coordinating State – and this is the most controversial point – may further "take all practicable measures, and/or issue any necessary authorizations in conformity with this Convention and, if necessary prior to

47 For Russia, however, "[t]he ambiguity and vagueness of some articles of the Convention are, in our view, bound to give rise to conflict situations". UNESCO, *Records of the General Conference, Proceedings of the 31st session*, 2 November 2001, vol. 2, at 562 (available at: <http://unesdoc.unesco.org/images/0012/001289/128966m.pdf>).

48 In fact, States Parties that have indicated which reporting procedure they prefer under Art. 9 of the Convention have chosen the second option – that of sub-paragraph (b)(ii) – which is more consistent with the LOSC. This is the case of Argentina, Cuba, Italy, Mexico, Portugal, Saudi Arabia, and Ukraine. The rest remain silent.

49 See Art. 10(3)(a) of the 2001 UNESCO Convention.

consultations, to prevent any immediate danger to the underwater cultural heritage, whether arising from human activities or any other cause, including looting".[50] It shall also implement measures of protection agreed by the consulting States, shall issue all necessary authorisations for such agreed measures, may conduct any necessary preliminary research on the underwater cultural heritage, and shall issue all necessary authorisations to that end.[51]

However, these provisions are not necessarily inconsistent with the LOSC and do not upset the delicate jurisdictional balance between flag State jurisdiction and coastal State jurisdiction under it. This is true for four main reasons:

(i) The 2001 UNESCO Convention plainly excludes any such effect insofar as Article 2(11) provides that "[n]o act or activity undertaken on the basis of this Convention shall constitute grounds for claiming, contending or disputing any claim to national sovereignty or jurisdiction";[52]

(ii) Article 3 of the 2001 UNESCO Convention states that nothing in it "shall prejudice the rights, jurisdiction and duties of States under international law, including the United Nations Convention on the Law of the Sea" and that it "shall be interpreted and applied in the context of and in a manner consistent with international law, including the United Nations Convention on the Law of the Sea";[53]

---

50 See Art. 10(4). Russia, for example, considered that this proviso may "be interpreted as broadening, beyond the limits laid down by the 1982 United Nations Convention on the Law of the Sea, the rights and jurisdiction of a coastal State over adjacent maritime areas. It can be regarded as offering a coastal State the right, unilaterally and at its own discretion, to take any measures, not excluding the use of force, on the pretext of protecting the underwater cultural heritage." UNESCO, *Records of the General Conference* ... (n. 47), at 562.

51 Art. 10(5).

52 Moreover, in accordance with Art. 10(2) of the 2001 Convention, "[a] State Party in whose exclusive economic zone or on whose continental shelf underwater cultural heritage is located has the right to prohibit or authorize any activity directed at such heritage to prevent interference with its sovereign rights or jurisdiction as provided for by international law including the United Nations Convention on the Law of the Sea."

53 As a matter of interpretation under Art. 31 of the 1969 Vienna Convention on the Law of Treaties (adopted 23 May 1969, entered into force 27 January 1980, 1155 UNTS 331; hereinafter, VCLT), the Preamble of the 2001 UNESCO Convention recalls that the negotiating States realised "the need to codify and progressively develop rules relating to the protection and preservation of underwater cultural heritage *in conformity with international law and practice, including* the UNESCO Convention on the Means of Prohibiting and Preventing the Illicit Import, Export and Transfer of Ownership of Cultural Property of 14 November 1970, the UNESCO Convention for the Protection of the World Cultural and Natural Heritage of 16 November 1972 and *the United Nations Convention on the Law of the Sea of 10 December 1982* [...]" [*emphases added*].

(iii) With regard to the coordinating State's allegedly extensive powers, Article 10(6) of the 2001 Convention recalls that any decision taken by that State in accordance with the Convention "shall not in itself constitute a basis for the assertion of any preferential or jurisdictional rights not provided for in international law, including the United Nations Convention on the Law of the Sea"; and
(iv) In any case, as a general rule of the law of treaties, the Convention applies only to its States Parties and does not create obligations for them without their express and written consent.[54]

In short, the Convention establishes sufficient firewalls against any kind of creeping jurisdiction. The activities regulated in its provisions cannot be used as a legal argument to expand or reinforce current jurisdictional or sovereign rights as recognised by the LOSC. The sole creeping jurisdiction included in the 2001 Convention – unchallenged and generally accepted – can be found in its Article 8, regarding the contiguous zone, according to which States Parties may *regulate* and *authorise* activities directed at the underwater cultural heritage.[55] This question will be examined in more detail below.[56]

3 The (Ab)Uses of Underwater Archaeology and the Law of the Sea

3.1 *The Limited Use of Archaeology in International Law*

International courts and tribunals have rarely relied on archaeological activities or remains to find evidence (or a lack thereof) to support claims of jurisdiction or sovereignty or for the tracing of boundaries.[57] At most, they have

---

54 As codified in Arts. 34 and 35 VCLT.

55 It should again be recalled that Art. 303(2) LOSC only says that the removal of historical and archaeological objects from the seabed in this zone without the approval of the coastal State would result in an infringement within its territory or territorial sea of the laws and regulations referred to in Art. 33 LOSC, and only for the purpose of controlling traffic in such objects.

56 See section 3.2.1.

57 This was the case, for example, of the Palestine Mandate. During the Ottoman period, Palestine was never a political unit but rather several sub-provinces of Ottoman Syria. As has been noted elsewhere, "[I]n the 1870s, the British Palestine Exploration Fund mounted an ambitious mapping project in which the Fund's explorer delineated a precise territorial unit that encompassed the traditional 'Land of the Bible', from Dan in the north to Aqaba in the south, and that archaeological map served as the basis for territorial division and colonial administration at the Versailles Conference after World War I." N. A. Silberman, 'If I forget thee, O Jerusalem: archaeology, religious commemoration and nationalism in a disputed city, 1801–2001' (2001) 7(4) *Nations and Nationalism* 487–514, at 495. See further U. Ra'anan, *The Frontiers of a Nation* (Hyperion Press: Westport, CT, 1976).

simply made observations such as "there is no historical record of any battle ever having been fought in this field".[58] Sometimes, the parties to a case have sought to discuss archaeological proof. In the *Eritrea/Yemen* case, for example, Yemen alleged "the existence of anchorages and settlements on the Islands bearing distinctly Yemeni Arabic names" and that "the Islands are home to a number of Yemeni holy sites and shrines, including the tombs of several venerated holy men".[59] However, neither of these arguments was fully considered by the arbitrators.[60] In the *Abyei Area* case, one of the parties argued that oral tradition should be used "in conjunction with writings, archaeology, linguistic or even ethnographic evidence".[61] However, the final award did not elaborate on this idea. In other cases, the parties have precluded the discussion of archaeological data, sometimes simply by not submitting historical evidence to the judges. "The Parties", reads one award, "provided no further details when questioned regarding historical navigation."[62] But in other cases – which will be discussed later in this book[63] – an arbitral award left the door open for archaeological arguments should the parties so decide. In the *South China Sea Award* of 2016, when discussing whether sustaining human habitation or economic life of its own is enough for a marine feature to be characterised as an island under Article 121(3) LOSC, the Tribunal suggested that

> historical evidence of human habitation and economic life in the past may be relevant for establishing a feature's capacity. If a known feature proximate to a populated land mass was never inhabited and never sustained an economic life, this may be consistent with an explanation that it is uninhabitable. Conversely, positive evidence that humans historically

58 *The Indo-Pakistan Western Boundary (Rann of Kutch) between India and Pakistan (India, Pakistan)*, UNRIAA, vol. 17, 1968, 1, at 24.

59 *Territorial Sovereignty and Scope of the Dispute (Eritrea and Yemen)*, UNRIAA, vol. 22, 1998, 209, at 223–224, para. 37–38.

60 Nor others related to intangible cultural heritage, such as that recounted in paragraph 39 of the same award: "In addition, Yemen points out that the Islands fall within the jurisdiction of a traditional system of resolving disputes between fishermen, in which a kind of arbitrator may 'ride the circuit' along the coast and among the Islands, in order to insure access to justice for those fishermen who are unable to travel." Ibid., at 224.

61 *Award in the Arbitration regarding the delimitation of the Abyei Area between the Government of Sudan and the Sudan People's Liberation Movement/Army*, UNRIAA, vol. 30, 2009, 145, at 293, para. 379.

62 *In the Matter of the Bay of Bengal Maritime Boundary Arbitration (The People's Republic of Bangladesh/The Republic of India)*, Award of 7 July 2014, at 48, para. 168 (available at: <https://www.pcacases.com/web/sendAttach/383>).

63 See section 3.2.2 below, in reference to China and the South China Sea.

> lived on a feature or that the feature was the site of economic activity could constitute relevant evidence of a feature's capacity.[64]

However, in most of these cases, the context of the decision focusses more on documentary evidence and maps than on archaeological objects. Only in two cases, both argued before the ICJ and discussed below, has there been further discussion of the impact of archaeological activities and remains when adjudicating territories.

3.1.1 Remains *vs* Archaeology: The *Temple of Preah Vihear* and *Qatar* v. *Bahrain* Cases

The first case concerns the dispute between Cambodia and Thailand over the ownership of the Preah Vihear temple. Only because of the Counter-Memorial submitted by Thailand were archaeological aspects even touched upon in the parties' arguments. Part of the dispute stemmed from the fact that the Cambodian authorities had accumulated a better collection of evidence, which Thailand argued was possible due to the more advanced study carried out by French archaeologists during their administration of that country.[65] However, in Annex 40 (a) of its Counter-Memorial, Thailand pointed to the existence (among other things) of the archaeological site of Preah Vihear on the mountain that divided the then-French territory (Cambodia) from what was then Siam (Thailand).[66] It also cited various instances of official correspondence making reference to the Temple (Annexes 40 (b) and (c)), referring to the history of the temple's construction[67] and to the need to register certain archaeological objects and monasteries (Annexes 41 (a) and (b)), as well as promulgate the necessary regulations to protect these sites, to which end it had decided to send an archaeological mission.[68]

For Cambodia, however, "the Preah Vihear temple is considered by all – archaeologists and historians alike – a foundation of the Kings of Angkor. The collected inscriptions leave no room for doubt. Thailand cannot seriously dispute this point." Cambodia thus emphasised "the temple's authentically Khmer

64 *The South China Sea Arbitration* (*The Republic of Philippines* v. *The People's Republic of China*), Award of 12 July 2016, para. 484 (available at: <https://pcacases.com/web/sendAttach/2086>).

65 *Case concerning the Temple of Preah Vihear* (*Cambodia v. Thailand*), *Counter-Memorial of Thailand*, at 186, para. 54.

66 Ibid., at 406.

67 Ibid., at 409–410.

68 Ibid., at 411–412.

character. These political, historical, religious, artistic, and archaeological ties are an additional reason for the temple to have been placed on the Cambodian side of the border when it was drawn in 1904–1907, without eliciting any protest or reservation from the Siamese Government or its representatives."[69] Cambodia also cited certain documents of the 'Indochina Archaeological Commission' of 1912 – which placed the temple in Cambodian territory[70] – several scientific missions, and various archaeological publications pointing to the temple's Cambodian nature, as well as legislative acts declaring it a historical monument of Cambodia without any record of this having sparked any protests from Thailand.[71]

In its Rejoinder, Thailand decried the archaeological activity carried out by Cambodia, although without weighing in on the archaeological value of the evidence.[72] The dispute thus focussed on archaeological activities – as acts of sovereignty – rather than on archaeological evidence – as proof of historical presence. This was again apparent in the case's oral phase,[73] and the Court, whilst noting all this – "[t]he Parties [had] also relied on other arguments of a physical, historical, religious and archaeological character" – nevertheless concluded that it was unable "to regard them as legally decisive".[74]

In the second case – between Qatar and Bahrain – both sides also submitted archaeological arguments, although Bahrain did so more explicitly. In discussing who had the better claim to Al Zubarah – a coastal archaeological site in the north-west of the Qatar Peninsula and one of the main issues being litigated

69 *Case concerning the Temple of Preah Vihear (Cambodia v. Thailand), Réplique cambodgienne*, at 439, para. 4. Author's translation of the original French: "[l]e temple de Préah Vihéar est considéré par tous, archéologues et historiens, comme une fondation des Rois d'Angkor. Les inscriptions recueillies ne laissent aucun doute. La Thaïlande ne peut soulever sur ce point de contestation sérieuse"; and "le caractère authentiquement khmer du temple. Ces liens politiques, historiques, religieux, artistiques et archéologiques sont un motif supplémentaire pour que, lors de la délimitation de la frontière en 1904–1907, le temple ait été placé du côté cambodgien, sans qu'aucune protestation ni réserve n'ait été faite par le Gouvernement siamois ou par ses représentants."

70 Ibid., at 467, para. 60. Reproduced as annexes to the *Réplique*.

71 Ibid., at 469, para. 65–66.

72 "Archaeological activity, even when it is undertaken by a semi-official body such as the École française d'Extrême-Orient, is not in the ordinary sense an example of the exercise by a government of its sovereign powers" (*Case concerning the Temple of Preah Vihear (Cambodia v. Thailand), Rejoinder of Thailand*, at 584, para. 83).

73 *Case concerning the Temple of Preah Vihear (Cambodia v. Thailand)*, ICJ Pleadings, Oral Arguments, Documents (vol. II, 1962).

74 *Case concerning the Temple of Preah Vihear (Cambodia v. Thailand)*, Judgment, *ICJ Reports* 1962, 6, at 15.

before the ICJ – Qatar argued not only that it was an archaeological site at the time of the proceedings, but also that it had been declared part of the public domain and was protected by Qatari legislation.[75] In 1944, Qatar alleged, both parties agreed to recognise that the archaeological site's special status should not be altered, as the historical remains at Al Zubarah offered proof of the existence of a population in the area prior to the arrival of the predecessors of the ruling families of Bahrain.[76] However, Bahrain placed more emphasis on the arguments concerning the archaeological evidence: in relation to Al Zubarah, it presented the scientific results of a Danish archaeological mission from 1956; in relation to the Hawar Islands, it presented a report on the existence of ancient cisterns by an Italian archaeological mission from 1995.[77] In its Reply of 30 May 1999, as well as in the oral phase before the Court, Bahrain reiterated the first point,[78] noting, "The antiquity, stability and permanence of the settlement is illustrated by physical evidence on the Hawar Islands."[79]

However, in its judgment of 16 March 2001, the Court merely echoed the aforementioned 1944 agreement on Al Zubarah concluded by the parties, without making reference to any archaeological aspects.[80] As for the Hawar Islands, it recalled in passing some of the historical-archaeological arguments put forward by Bahrain,[81] as well as references to historical vestiges linked to Bahrain made by the British during the delimitation process carried out in 1939, considered binding by the ICJ.[82]

75 *Memorial Submitted by the State of Qatar* (*Merits*), vol. I, 30 September 1996, para. 8.4 (the 'Highlighted Version' of the Pleadings has been used, given the confusing deletion by Qatar of some of the documentation it initially submitted to the Court).

76 Ibid., para. 8.46. This argument was repeated during the oral phase with a similar wording (Doc CR 2000/9, at 28–29).

77 *Counter-Memorial Submitted by the State of Bahrain* (*Merits*), vol. I, 31 December 1997, at 29, para. 64; and 83, para. 185, respectively.

78 "Both Arab and Western historians agree, and archaeological evidence confirms", argued Bahrein, "that the city of Zubarah was founded around the middle of the eighteenth century by the Al-Khalifa [the *Ruler* of Bahrein]" (*Reply Submitted by the State of Bahrain* (Merits), vol. I, 30 May 1999, para. 193, footnotes omitted).

79 Doc. CR 2000/13, at 15, para. 32. Bahrein stated that, according to the Italian archaeological report, the following was found: "[...] three ancient villages and houses [...] six cemeteries, including the children's cemetery [...] many dams and water cisterns, the animal-powered millstones, the pottery shards, games carved into the rocks [...] the gypsum quarries and the ancient mosques and prayer walls [and] the grazing pastures used by the Hawar islanders [...]" (ibid.)

80 *Maritime Delimitation and Territorial Questions between Qatar and Bahrain* (*Qatar* v. *Bahrain*), Merits, Judgment, *ICJ Reports* 2001, 40, at 60, para. 59.

81 Ibid., at 71–72, para. 102.

82 Ibid., at 80, para. 128.

These ICJ rulings show that archaeological vestiges, insofar as they may be considered possible evidence of an ancient presence in a territory, have not generally been considered in parties' arguments or, therefore, in the assessments of the courts charged with delimiting areas, which assign them only a secondary probative value.[83] At most, they have been used to materially corroborate the existence of a given historical title, but even then they have been cited more as possible anthropological evidence (social uses, tribal submissions, suzerainties, etc.) than archaeological evidence.[84]

3.1.2 Underwater Archaeology and 'Covert Affairs': The *Corfu Channel* Case

Underwater archaeology has helped clarify at least one case involving maritime claims based on dubious facts and documents, namely, the *Corfu Channel* case. This case arose in October 1946 when exploding mines damaged British warships and injured or killed numerous sailors as they passed through the Corfu Channel in a part of Albanian waters. The United Kingdom claimed that the channel – a narrow seaway separating the island of Corfu from the Albanian coast – was an international strait subject to innocent passage, a legal status challenged by the Albanian government.

Specifically, the blasts severely damaged two British Royal Navy destroyers – the HMS *Saumarez* and HMS *Volage* – killing 44 crew members and wounding another 42. The bow of the *Volage* was blown off and sank, taking several men to the bottom of the sea with it. Following a recommendation by the UN Security Council,[85] in 1947 the United Kingdom seized the ICJ, accusing Albania of having laid or allowed a third State to lay the mines.[86] After

83 Other cases offer some room for archaeological arguments. For example, Spain cited the damage caused to its underwater cultural heritage in the *M/V 'Louisa'* case before ITLOS (*Saint Vincent and the Grenadines* v. *Kingdom of Spain*), Judgment, *ITLOS Reports* 2013. Archaeologists have also appeared before the International Criminal Tribunal for the Former Yugoslavia (e.g. in the *Srebrenica* and *Karadžić* cases). See, K. Juhl, 'The Contribution by (Forensic) Archaeologists to Human Rights Investigations of Mass Graves' (2005) 5 *Am-Profil* (available at: <https://am.uis.no/getfile.php/13201047/Arkeologisk%20museum/2015/Store%20bilder%20til%20ny%20nettsider/amprofil-5.pdf>). See also S. Blau and M. Skinner, 'The use of forensic archaeology in the investigation of human rights abuse: Unearthing the past in East Timor' (2005) 9 *The International Journal of Human Rights* 449–463.

84 The first phase of the case between Eritrea and Yemen also points in this direction (*Territorial Sovereignty …* (n. 59), at 244–245, para. 127–130).

85 UN Doc. S/Res/22 (1947), 9 April 1947.

86 It was later confirmed by the Court that the sea-mines had been laid by Albania in the aftermath of World War II.

discussing the questions of jurisdiction and admissibility, decided by an order of 1948,[87] the Court rendered its decision on the Merits in 1949.[88]

Albania claimed that, by sending its warship to the Channel, the UK had violated Albanian sovereignty in its territorial waters. However, the Court found that the British warships were exercising their right of *innocent* passage through an international strait and that Albania was responsible under international law for the explosions that had taken place in Albanian waters and for the damage and loss of life that ensued.[89]

During the case, the UK denied permission to disclose certain sensitive British Admiralty documents that would have revealed the exact place where the Royal Navy destroyers hit the Albanian mines.[90] However, these doubts were put to rest in 2009 by an underwater archaeological expedition of RPM Nautical Foundation in collaboration with the Albanian government.[91] The *Volage* bow does not rest in the channel, but in the Bay of Sarande, just outside the port of the eponymous Albanian city. This raises the question of how close the British warships were ordered to 'the line' to test – or perhaps provoke – the Albanian government in 1946. It also raises the question of how honestly the British government acted towards the Court in denying access to the sensitive Admiralty documents that might have revealed the exact position of the Royal Navy destroyers in 1946.

This case shows how independent underwater archaeology can yield critical information for the assessment of maritime claims. In the *Corfu Channel* case, the UK was not claiming its national rights as such but a right – innocent passage through an international strait – to be enjoyed by the entire international

87 *Corfu Channel case* (*UK v Albania*), Preliminary Objections, Judgment, *ICJ Reports* 1948, 15.

88 *Corfu Channel case* (*UK v Albania*), Merits, Judgment, *ICJ Reports* 1949, 4. A third decision by the Court, rendered in 1949, assessed the amount of reparation owed to the United Kingdom and ordered Albania to pay £844,000 (*ICJ Reports* 1949, 244).

89 *Corfu Channel* (n. 87), at 28. The judgment placed this word in italics, as it was the terminology used in that time. The Court also found that the British mine clearance after the incident had violated Albanian sovereignty, because it had been carried out against the will of the Albanian Government.

90 On this affair before the ICJ, see A. Carty, 'The Corfu Channel Case – and the Missing Admiralty Orders' (2004) 3 *The Law and Practice of International Courts and Tribunals* 1–35; and W. M. Reisman and C. Skinner, *Fraudulent Evidence before Public International Tribunals: The Dirty Stories of International Law* (Cambridge University Press: Cambridge, 2014), 54–77.

91 See J. P. Delgado, J. Royal and A. Anastasi, 'Revisiting an Early Naval Incident of the Cold War: Archaeological Identification of the Bow of HMS *Volage* Sunk During the Corfu Channel Incident of October 22, 1946' (available at: <https://rpmnautical.org/wp-content/uploads/2016/10/rpm_publications-2010-volage.pdf>).

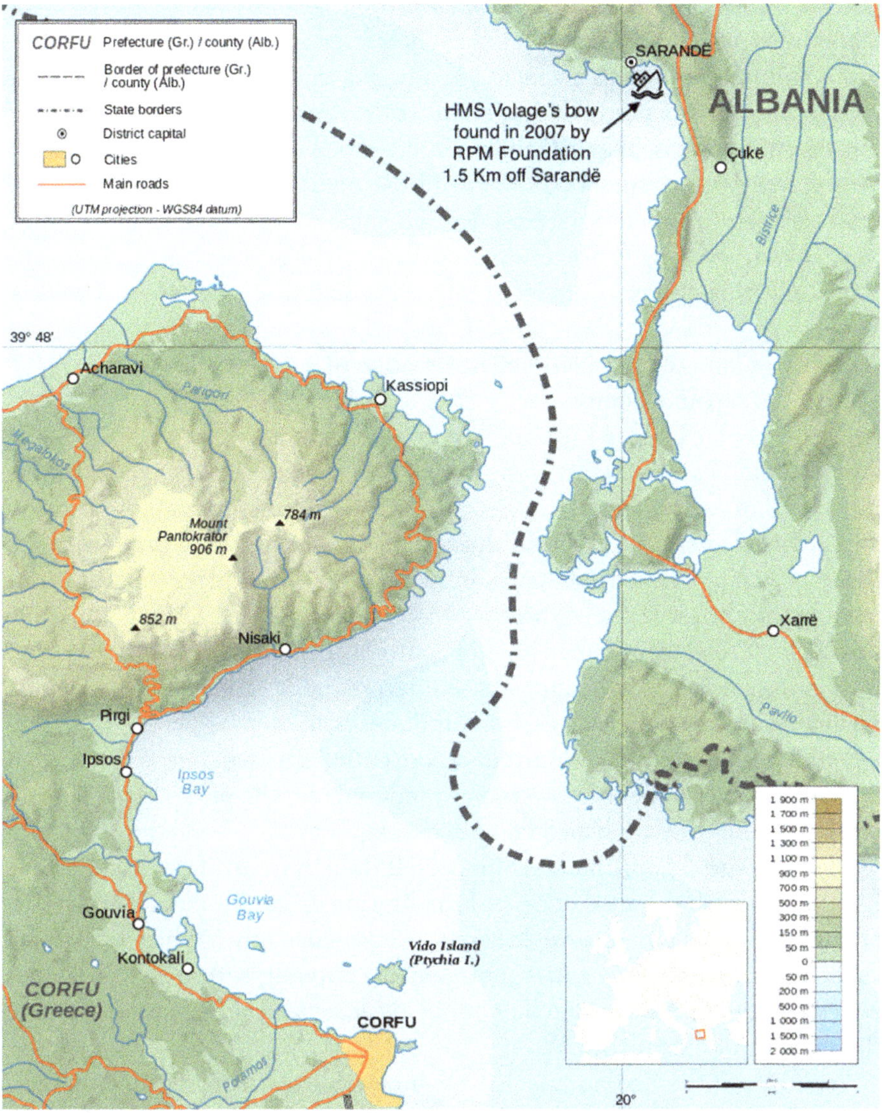

FIGURE 1 The Corfu Channel incident
SOURCE: ERIC SABA / AUTHOR'S ELABORATION (HTTPS://UPLOAD.WIKIMEDIA.ORG/WIKIPEDIA/COMMONS/D/D9/CORFU_TOPOGRAPHIC_MAP-EN.SVG)

community and, thus, the Albanian government's *erga omnes* obligation to tolerate that passage.[92]

92 The impact of this case on the codification process of the law of the sea is well known. Whilst the 1930 Hague Conference reached no consensus as to whether the right to

3.2 *Underwater Archaeology and Maritime Claims*

State practice shows a tendency to use the protection or regulation of underwater cultural heritage as an excuse to advance the limits of States' maritime jurisdiction. This is particularly evident with regard to the contiguous zone, but also, in some cases, up to the outer limit of the EEZ or the continental shelf. This practice seems intended to expand the maritime areas in which States exercise their jurisdiction (see section 3.2.1 below). However, in other cases, States claim sovereignty over enormous expanses of seas or strategic maritime routes, eliciting protests from other interested States (see section 3.2.2 below).

3.2.1 Claims of Jurisdiction: The Creation of Archaeological Maritime Zones

As we have seen, beyond the outer limit of the territorial sea – over which the coastal State has sovereignty – the law of the sea limits States' powers to the provisions of Article 303(2) LOSC, which states that the removal of historical and archaeological objects from the seabed in the contiguous zone without the approval of the coastal State would result in an infringement within its territory or territorial sea of the laws and regulations referred to in Article 33 LOSC, albeit solely for the purposes of controlling traffic in such objects.

This regime was soon qualified as counterproductive and plainly inefficient. Its nuances were challenged early on by States that, even before the LOSC was adopted, undertook a legislative and conventional practice to expand their jurisdiction to include the governance – not only for the purposes of controlling traffic – of the underwater cultural heritage located beyond the outer limit of their territorial seas. The exact model followed by these States differs: some have declared their jurisdiction in broad terms up to the outer limit of the continental shelf; others have declared the existence of what has been called 'archaeological maritime zones', normally overlapping with their contiguous zones; still others have declared or implicitly accepted this expansion through their conventional practice.[93]

With regard the first approach – i.e. broad declarations made via domestic legislation – several States have used general cultural laws to declare the extension of their licensing, authorisation, or protective domestic legislation on cultural heritage to their contiguous zone (or even their continental

innocent passage through territorial seas existed for warships, the *Corfu Channel* case heralded a change in this regime.

93 This section follows and updates the author's previous study cited in n. 18 above.

shelf or EEZ). Examples include Australia,[94] Barbados,[95] Bermuda,[96] Brazil,[97] Canada,[98] Cape Verde,[99] China,[100] Colombia,[101] Denmark,[102] the Dominican Republic,[103] Greece,[104] Ireland,[105] Italy,[106] Madagascar,[107] the Netherlands,[108] Spain,[109] Suriname,[110] the United States,[111] Venezuela,[112] and Vietnam,[113] among others.[114]

The second approach, consisting of creating a 'maritime archaeological zone', normally coinciding spatially with the State's respective contiguous zone, has been pursued by South Africa and Mauritius. South Africa created a proper

94 *Underwater Cultural Heritage Act 2018* (Underwater Heritage Act), 24 August 2018, *passim.*

95 *Coastal Zone Management Act* (1 May 2000), Sec. 15.1 and 16(a).

96 *Historic Wrecks Act 2001* (as amended 2004), 27 December 2001, Sec. 2, Interpretation.

97 *Law No. 7.542* (as amended by *Law No. 10.166* of 2000), 26 September 1986, Art. 20.

98 *Canada National Marine Conservation Areas Act 2002*, 13 June 2002, Secs. 5 and 16(1)(b).

99 *Law No. 60/IV/92*, 21 December 1992, Art. 28.

100 *Regulations Concerning the Management and Protection of Underwater Cultural Relics*, 20 October 1989 (as amended in 2002), Art. 2(2).

101 *Ley nº 26 Normas sobre antigüedades y valores náufragas*, 24 January 1986, Art. 4. See also *Ley 1675 por medio de la cual se reglamentan los artículos 63, 70 y 72 de la Constitución Política de Colombia en lo relativo al Patrimonio Cultural Sumergido*, of 30 July 2013.

102 *Act No. 749 of 2007, Act on Nature Conservation*, 21 June 2007.

103 *Act 66–77*, 22 May 2007, Art. 16 (additional paragraph *in fine*).

104 *Law 3028/2002 on the Protection of Antiquities and the Cultural Heritage in General*, 28 June 2002, Art. 1 (2).

105 *National Monuments (Amendment) Act, 1987*, 22 July 1987, Sec. 3.

106 *Law 61 on the Establishment of an Ecological Protection Zone Beyond the Outer Limit of the Territorial Sea*, 8 February 2006.

107 *Loi Nº 99-028, portant refonte du Code Maritime*, 3 February 2000, Ch. 5.

108 *Kingdom Act of 28 April 2005 (Contiguous Zone (Establishment) Act) and Decree of 14 June 2006 (Contiguous Zone (Outer Limits) Decree)*. These must be read in connection with the *Monuments and Historic Buildings Act of 1988*, as explained in the 'Explanatory Memorandum' added to the publication of the Act and reproduced in (2006) 62 *Law of the Sea Bulletin* 159, at 160–162. Furthermore, the *2007 Monuments Act* governs the excavation licences in the contiguous zone (Arts. 10 and 12) and the compulsory reporting system established for that zone (Arts. 8, 9, and 10).

109 *Law 16/1985, of 25 June, on the Spanish Historical Heritage*, Art. 41.

110 *Maritime Zones Act* (7 Abril 2017), Art. 8(3).

111 *National Marine Sanctuaries Act* (NMSA) (2000), 16 USC s. 1431 *et seq.* and *Sunken Military Craft Act* (SMCA) (2004), 10 U.S.C. 113 note.

112 *Aquatic Areas Organic Act* (17 November 2014), Arts. 67 and 68.

113 *Decree No 92/2002/ND-CP, on detailed regulations to implement some articles of the Law on Cultural Heritage*, 11 November 2002.

114 For the case of Taiwan, see the 1998 *Law on the Territorial Sea and Contiguous Zone of the Republic of China*, 21 January 1998, Art. 16.

'maritime cultural zone', which overlaps with its contiguous zone. Section 6 of the *Maritime Zones Act 1994*[115] reads as follows:

> (1) The sea beyond the territorial waters referred to in section 4, but within a distance of twenty-four nautical miles from the baselines, shall be the maritime cultural zone of the Republic.[[116]]
> (2) Subject to any other law the Republic shall have, in respect of objects of an archaeological or historical nature found in the maritime cultural zone, the same rights and powers as it has in respect of its territorial waters.

Mauritius took a very similar approach in 2005, creating a 'maritime cultural zone' defined as "an area coincident with the contiguous zone" with regard to which Mauritius's Prime Minister "may make regulations to regulate and authorise activities directed at underwater cultural heritage within [that] maritime cultural zone".[117]

But it may be States' conventional practice that offers the best array of declarations and positions, explaining how parties to different treaties – especially the LOSC – have expanded their jurisdiction to include the governance of underwater cultural heritage beyond the outer limit of their respective territorial seas. States pursue this practice with varying levels of *intensity* when extending this new space for jurisdiction. Perhaps the most *basic* level can be found in some of the declarations made upon acceding to the LOSC. For instance, four States – Bangladesh, Cape Verde, Malaysia, and Portugal – each declared, using virtually identical wording, that:

> without prejudice to article 303 of the Convention on the Law of the Sea, [...] any objects of an archaeological and historical nature found within

115 *Maritime Zones Act No. 15 1994*, 11 November 1994. The *National Heritage Resources Act No. 25 1999*, 28 April 1999, also applies to these 'maritime cultural zones'.

116 Previously, Section 5 of the Act creates the contiguous zone as follows: "(1) The sea beyond the territorial waters referred to in section 4, but within a distance of twenty-four nautical miles from the baselines, shall be the contiguous zone of the Republic. (2) Within the contiguous zone and the airspace above it, the Republic shall have the right to exercise all the powers which may be considered necessary to prevent contravention of any fiscal law or any customs, emigration, immigration or sanitary law and to make such contravention punishable."

117 *Maritime Zones Act No. 2 of 2005*, 1 April 2005, Sect. 25. Furthermore, Section 26 provides, "The Prime Minister may, notwithstanding any other enactment, make regulations to prohibit or authorise any activity directed at underwater cultural heritage in the EEZ or the continental shelf to prevent interference with the sovereign rights and jurisdiction of Mauritius."

> the maritime areas over which it exercises sovereignty or jurisdiction shall not be removed, without its prior notification and consent.[118]

However, this practice is not conclusive as such, despite the clear expansion of jurisdiction declared by each of those States. For them, underwater cultural heritage found in their contiguous zone cannot be removed "without [their] prior notification and consent" or, in the Portuguese wording, "only after prior notice to and subject to the consent of the competent Portuguese authorities".

Other States expressly referred to Article 303 LOSC or to archaeological or historical objects as such when declaring their maritime zones under the LOSC. Algeria declared that its right to exercise control within its contiguous zone should be exercised "[i]n accordance with articles 33 and 303 of the [LOSC]".[119] Mozambique declared that its government may regulate, in accordance with international law, "[a] protecção de objectos de carácter arqueológico no mar" [the protection of archaeological objects in the sea].[120] Some States issued a simple reminder of what was at stake. In the case of Norway, it was declared that "[l]egislation on the removal of objects of an archaeological or historical nature applying to the territorial sea is also applicable to the contiguous zone",[121] whilst the US declaration simply stated that "[t]his extension is an important step in preventing the removal of cultural heritage found within 24 nautical miles of the baseline".[122] Still other States went further.[123] Cyprus declared that within its contiguous zone not only may it exercise "the control

118 Text of Bangladesh's instrument of ratification (2001), like those of Cape Verde (1987) and Malaysia (1996). Upon ratification in 1997, Portugal declared that, "without prejudice to the provisions of Art. 303 of the United Nations Convention on the Law of the Sea and to the application of other legal instruments of international law regarding the protection of the underwater archaeological heritage, any objects of a historical or archaeological nature found in the maritime zones under its sovereignty or jurisdiction may be removed only after prior notice to and subject to the consent of the competent Portuguese authorities". All these declarations may be found in the Division for Ocean Affairs and the Law of the Sea (DOALOS, at: <http://www.un.org/Depts/los/index.htm>), which includes references to the *Law of the Sea Bulletin* when needed (at: <https://www.un.org/Depts/los/doalospublications/losbult.htm>).

119 *Presidential Decree No. 04-344, establishing a Zone Contiguous to the Territorial Sea*, 6 November 2004.

120 *Law nº 4/96*, 4 January 1996, Art. 34(d).

121 *Act No. 57 relating to Norway's territorial waters and contiguous zone*, 27 June 2003.

122 *Contiguous Zone of the United States – Proclamation by the President of the United States of America*, 2 September 1999.

123 This was also the case of the former Yugoslavia which, in its *Act concerning the Coastal Sea and the Continental Shelf* (23 July 1987), Art. 24, declared that it "shall exercise sovereign rights over the continental shelf relating to the exploration and exploitation of the natural resources and other resources of the shelf", where "other resources" refers to "archaeological and other buried articles"'. Although its successor States have followed

necessary to [...] control traffic of objects of an archaeological and historical nature found in this zone",[124] but it may also issue regulations for the purpose of adopting:

> preventive measures aim[ed at] the control, the avoidance or prevention of traffic of objects of an archaeological and historical nature found in [the contiguous zone] and [at] the licensing procedures for their removal.[125]

Cuba's declaration goes even further by affirming that the State shall exercise the control measures necessary to prevent any infringement of the laws and regulations relating to 'cultural heritage' committed not only in the Cuban contiguous zone but in its 'economic zone' and on its continental shelf.[126] It additionally states:

> Maritime cultural assets consisting of deposits, remains, vestiges or in general any asset of prehistoric, archaeological or historical interest situated within the contiguous zone, on the seabed subsoil of the contiguous zone, shall be the property of the Cuban State.[127]

Finally, Vanuatu asserted its "jurisdiction and control in the exclusive economic zone, in respect of: [...] the authorization, regulation and control of scientific research and the recovery of archaeological or historical objects [...]".[128]

Several States included 'all resources', 'any research', or 'all activities' clauses in their declarations of different maritime zones (particularly EEZs and continental

different legislative paths since the dissolution of the former Yugoslavia, all that are coastal States to the Adriatic Sea – Bosnia and Herzegovina, Croatia, Montenegro, and Slovenia – are parties to the 2001 UNESCO Convention.

124 *A Law to Provide for the Proclamation of the Contiguous Zone by the Republic of Cyprus*, 2 April 2004, sec. 4(b). This paragraph continues: "It is presumed that their removal from the sea-bed in this zone without the approval of the Republic, would result in an infringement within its territory or territorial sea of the law and regulations in accordance with Art. 303 of the Convention."

125 Ibid., sec. 5(2)(b).

126 *Legislative Decree No. 158, Contiguous Zone*, 12 April 1995, Art. 3(a).

127 Ibid., Arts. 4 and 5 add: "Cuba may engage in hot pursuit in its contiguous zone whenever it has reliable grounds for believing that a vessel has committed an infringement of the laws and regulations of the State, especially those mentioned in article 3 of this Legislative Decree, and whenever it has reasonable grounds for suspecting that the vessel is engaged in [...] illicit trafficking in [...] cultural assets [...]."

128 *Maritime Zones Act No 6 of 2010* (18 June 2010), Art. 10(2)(b).

shelves), including:[129] Barbados,[130] Guyana,[131] Iceland,[132] North Korea,[133] South Korea,[134] Malaysia,[135] Pakistan,[136] the Philippines,[137] and Tanzania.[138] However, apart from the cases dealing with the regulation of 'excavations' (Guyana, North Korea, Malaysia, the Philippines, and Tanzania), as noted earlier, the term 'resources' could not be interpreted as including underwater cultural heritage.[139] Finally, one more State – Papua New Guinea – could be added here, not because of its domestic legislation, but due to a delimitation agreement signed with Australia.[140] Article 9(1) of this treaty provides: "Wrecks of vessels and aircraft which lie on, in or under the seabed jurisdiction of a Party [i.e. the continental shelf] shall be subject to the jurisdiction of that Party."

In addition to this conventional practice relating to the LOSC, another such practice, this time related to the 2001 UNESCO Convention, should also be considered relevant to the matter at hand given its specific object and purpose. The first assumption that can be deduced is the States Parties' agreement on the content of Article 8 of the 2001 Convention, which reads as follows:

> Without prejudice to and in addition to Articles 9 and 10, and in accordance with Article 303, paragraph 2, of the United Nations Convention on the Law of the Sea, States Parties may regulate and authorize activities directed at underwater cultural heritage within their contiguous zone. In so doing, they shall require that the Rules be applied.[141]

---

129 Some of them, however, have abandoned this type of clause, e.g. Seychelles (*cf.* its Maritime Zones Acts of 1977 and 1999).

130 *Marine Boundaries and Jurisdiction Act of 1978* (25 February 1978), Art. 6(1)(a).

131 *Maritime Boundaries Act 1977* (30 June 1977), Arts. 10(1)(a) and 17.

132 *Law No. 41 concerning the Territorial Sea, the Economic Zone and the Continental Shelf* (1 June 1979), Art. 4.

133 *Decree by the Central People's Committee establishing the Economic Zone of the People's Democratic Republic of Korea* (21 June 1977).

134 *Territorial Sea and Contiguous Zone Act* (as amended 21 March 2017), Art. 5.

135 *Exclusive Economic Zone Act 1984* (no date), Sec. 5(a) and (b).

136 *Territorial Waters and Maritime Zones Act 1976* (22 December 1976), Secs. 5 and 6.

137 *Presidential Decree No. 1599 of 11 June 1978 establishing an Exclusive Economic Zone and for other purposes* (11 June 1978), Art. 3(a) and (b).

138 *Territorial Sea and Exclusive Economic Zone Act, 1989* (no date), Secs. 10(a) and (b).

139 See n. 22 above.

140 Treaty between Australia and the Independent State of Papua New Guinea concerning sovereignty and maritime boundaries in the area between the two countries, including the area known as Torres Strait, and related matters (adopted 18 December 1978, entered into force 15 February 1985, 1429 UNTS 207), Art. 9(1).

141 Arts. 9 and 10 of the Convention refer to the reporting, notification, and protection system established in the Convention for activities directed at the underwater cultural heritage located in the EEZ and on the continental shelf.

This implies that, according to this article and its interpretation in current State practice, States not only have the power to sanction the unauthorised removal of underwater cultural heritage in their declared contiguous zones, but also to regulate any activity directed at this heritage in that zone. In practical terms, this means applying the coastal State's heritage legislation not only to its territorial sea based on sovereignty arguments but also up to the outer limit of its contiguous zone, when declared, based on jurisdictional arguments. As we have seen, this Convention is presently ratified by 72 States.[142] But when it was adopted, no State – except for Turkey[143] – opposed this particular instance of creeping jurisdiction (where applicable).[144] On the contrary, some States (e.g. Canada) applauded the fact that activities directed at underwater cultural heritage could not be carried out in the contiguous zone unless they had been authorised under the Convention; others, whether critical (Netherlands, Norway, Russia, the United Kingdom, and the United States) or not (Turkey) of the creeping jurisdiction that the Convention allegedly endorsed, only and explicitly referred to jurisdiction affecting the EEZ and the continental shelf, not the contiguous zone, and nothing in their declarations suggests that they subsumed the contiguous zone within the other two areas.[145] Among others

142 See n. 28 above. Among those States, some had or have since enacted domestic legislation extending their jurisdiction over their contiguous zone, the EEZ, or the continental shelf for the protection of underwater cultural heritage. See Aznar (n. 18), at 21.

143 Mainly due to its location on the Aegean Sea and its maritime disputes regarding Greek islands close to the Turkish mainland and Cyprus. As argued during the negotiating process of the 2001 UNESCO Convention, "Turkey [wanted] to underline that to declare a contiguous zone for the purpose of controlling the traffic of underwater cultural heritage that lies on or under its continental shelf, not only falls contrary to State practice and to customary rules of international law in this field, but also means to reduce the area of jurisdiction and to confine the coastal State powers." Turkey's views on Art. 5 of the Draft Convention on the Protection of Underwater Cultural Heritage, quoted in Garabello (n. 16), at 171.

144 See the text of these declarations in Garabello and Scovazzi (n. 17), at 241–253.

145 This is particularly the case of the United States. US jurisdictional concerns refer to Arts. 9 and 10, not to Art. 8 (see Statement by Robert C. Blumberg, US Observer Delegate to the 31st UNESCO General Conference, to Commission IV of the General Conference, regarding the US views on the 2001 UNESCO Convention on the Protection of Underwater Cultural Heritage, 29 October 2001, Paris, France, available at: <http://www.gc.noaa.gov/documents/gcilheritage2blumberg.pdf>). As stated by authoritative commentators on the US position, "The seaward limit of coastal State jurisdiction over such UCH is 24 nautical miles from the baseline from which the Territorial Sea is measured, which corresponds with the seaward limit of the Contiguous Zone [art. 303(2)]." O. Varmer, J. Gray and D. Alberg, 'United States: Responses to the 2001 UNESCO Convention on the Protection of the Underwater Cultural Heritage' (2010) 5 *Journal of Maritime Archaeology* 129–141, at 131. See further S. Dromgoole, 'Reflections on the Position of the Major Maritime Powers

voting in favour, only one State (Greece) criticised the confusion between Article 8 and Articles 9 and 10;[146] others, such as Denmark or Japan, found no inconsistencies between the Convention and the LOSC.[147] Meanwhile, abstaining States, such as Sweden, welcomed "the fact that the legal content of the rules concerning the mandate of the coastal State in its declared contiguous zone is clarified in the Convention and regards this clarification as an indication of the present status of customary law".[148] With the entry into force of the 2001 UNESCO Convention, it must be assumed that its States Parties already accept as the legal regime for their contiguous zone that provided for under Article 8.[149]

---

with Respect to the UNESCO Convention on the Protection of the Underwater Cultural Heritage 2001' (2013) 38 *Marine Policy* 116–123.

146 Greece accompanied its vote with the following explanation: "The reference in article 8 to articles 9 and 10 *should be deleted* as it diminishes the rights, which the coastal State already enjoys in this area under article 303(2) of the LOS Convention." See Garabello and Scovazzi (n. 17), at 247.

147 It is significant that, during the drafting of the Convention, Japan maintained "that international customary law recognises the coastal State's rights to exercise jurisdiction over underwater cultural heritage in its territorial waters by sovereignty, and in its contiguous zone by using Article 302(2) [LOSC] in respect of archaeological and historical objects. It considers that seaward from the contiguous zone, no State has general jurisdiction over underwater cultural heritage. Therefore, it would treat in different ways, these two groups of maritime zones, for example in specifying that in the internal waters, territorial sea and contiguous zone [sic]." See Synoptic Report of Comments on the Draft Convention on the Protection of the Underwater Cultural Heritage, UNESCO Doc. CLT-99/CONF.204/5, April 1999, at 2.

148 Quoted in Garabello and Scovazzi (n. 17), at 250.

149 It may be further argued that non-parties that nevertheless voted in favour of the Convention must abide by the mild obligation imposed by Art. 18 VCLT, including the recognition of these new jurisdictional powers of the coastal State over its contiguous zone. Although this article refers to the "signature" of a treaty, the purpose of the interim obligation embodied in it is to preserve the negotiated agreement and the legitimate expectations of the other negotiating States as a manifestation of the general principle of good faith. In the case of conventions adopted in the UNESCO General Conference – such as the 2001 Convention, and analogously to the similar process at the International Labour Organisation – the vote in favour of the final adoption of a convention, in absence of any other conventional act before its ratification, might be assimilated to the signature of a treaty for the purposes of Art. 18 VCLT. See L. Boisson de Chazournes, A-M. La Rosa and M. M. Mbengue, 'Art. 18 Convention of 1969', in: O. Corten and P. Klein (eds), *The Vienna Contention on the Law of Treaties. A Commentary* (Oxford University Press: Oxford, 2011), 369–403, at 390–392. See also O. Dörr and K. Schmalenbach, 'Article 18. Obligation not to defeat the object and purpose of a treaty prior to its entry into force'. In: O. Dörr and K. Schmalenbach (eds), *Vienna Convention on the Law of Treaties* (Springer: Berlin/Heidelberg, 2012).

Based on this practice, it can be assumed that an important change has occurred in Article 303(2) LOSC as a result of a customary process and that coastal States may acquire new jurisdictional powers over their contiguous zones where declared. This has happened over the last few decades (beginning even before the entry into force of the LOSC in 1994) through both conventional and unilateral practice and the crystallisation of a new rule with the adoption of Article 8 of the 2001 UNESCO Convention. It is therefore not merely a new understanding of the meaning of the LOSC terms, but an intention to create a new legal regime governing coastal States' archaeological rights in their contiguous zones, supplementing the original, limited, and controversial enforcement rights with more extensive legislative rights over any and all activities directed to underwater cultural heritage located in that maritime zone.

It should be stressed, however, that this process does not seem to be affected by the jurisdictional firewall included in Article 2(11) of the UNESCO Convention, whereby "[n]o act or activity undertaken on the basis of this Convention shall constitute grounds for claiming, contending or disputing any claim to national sovereignty or jurisdiction". As much as it has been accepted by different States Parties, their acceptance of that new jurisdiction up to the outer limit of the contiguous zone has not been legally justified based on the Convention, which simply helped crystallise the new jurisdictional right.

3.2.2 Claims of Sovereignty or Jurisdiction: Canada, China, and Russia

Aside from these various claims of maritime jurisdiction, there are several cases in which underwater archaeology and the underwater cultural heritage are the basis for claiming sovereignty over disputed areas. Some are minor and their impact has not yet reached the threshold to be of serious political concern. This would be the case, for example, of the dispute between Spain and the UK and their respective claims to the maritime waters around Gibraltar[150] or Turkey's claims in the eastern Mediterranean in relation to a 16th-century Ottoman vessel.[151]

150 In 2009, Spain declared the Algeciras Bay (including disputed waters) an 'Archaeological Reserved Zone' (*zona de servidumbre arqueológica*). See, generally, J. Verdú Baeza, 'El patrimonio cultural subacuático y el Estrecho de Gibraltar. El caso de la Bahía de Algeciras/Gibraltar', (2016–2017) 2 *Cuadernos de Gibraltar – Gibraltar Reports*.

151 Reportedly, the cargo of this vessel included artefacts from 14 cultures and civilisations, including the earliest Chinese porcelain retrieved from a Mediterranean wreck, painted jugs from Italy, and peppercorns from India, perhaps revealing a previously unknown maritime silk and spice route running from China to Persia, the Red Sea, and into the eastern Mediterranean. For an overview, see: D. Alberge, 'Mediterranean shipwrecks reveal "birth of globalization" in trade', *The Guardian*, 18 April 2020, at: <https://www.theguardian.com/science/2020/apr/18/mediterranean-shipwrecks-reveal-birth-of

But in addition to these two low-profile cases, three major maritime claims are currently being disputed in the Arctic, the South China Sea, and the Black Sea.

3.2.2.1 *Canada and the Arctic's Northwest Passage*

Arctic waters have particularities with regard to historical titles that are sometimes merged with indigenous rights, myriad special delimitation circumstances, and, more recently, problems related to melting ice, rising sea levels, and new transit routes, as well as renewed sources of pollution, deep scrutiny with regard to their natural resources, and revisited military uses. The Arctic is thus today a cold place governed by hot rules.[152]

Particularly due to the impact of climate change and ice melt, traditionally ice-covered spaces in the Arctic region are progressively shrinking, facilitating the clearance of new maritime routes.[153] As Figure 2 shows, in the west lies the Northwest Passage (NWP), a passageway through the waters of the Canadian Arctic Archipelago – between the Davis Strait and Baffin Bay in the east and the Bering Strait in the west – that especially affects Canada's tentative maritime claims in Arctic waters.[154] These claims are well known and must be considered bearing in mind: (1) the aforementioned consequences of the melting ice; (2) Canada's general policy towards the Arctic and its participation in the Arctic Council; and (3) the special situation and rights of the indigenous groups in these cold spaces.

-globalisation-in-trade>; N. Theodoulou, 'Wrecks found between Cyprus and Lebanon "equivalent to finding new planet"', *Cyprus Mail*, 21 April 2020, at: <https://cyprus-mail.com/2020/04/21/wrecks-found-between-cyprus-and-lebanon-equivalent-to-finding-new-planet/>; and A. Rakoczy, 'Battle over shipwreck treasure: "Cultural heritage is not ours to sell"', *Cyprus Mail*, 10 May 2020, at: <https://cyprus-mail.com/2020/05/10/battle-over-shipwreck-treasure-cultural-heritage-is-not-ours-to-sell/>.

152 For a complete analysis of most of these factors, see M. Byers, *International Law and the Arctic* (Cambridge University Press: Cambridge, 2013). See also the bibliography compiled by E. Conde and M. Scopelliti for Oxford Bibliographies, available at: <https://www.oxfordbibliographies.com/view/document/obo-9780199796953/obo-9780199796953-0090.xml>.

153 L. Millan, 'First Arctic Navigation in February Sends a Worrying Climate Signal', 22 February 2021, *Bloomberg* at: <https://www.bloomberg.com/news/articles/2021-02-22/first-arctic-navigation-in-february-sends-a-worrying-climate-signal>. See, generally, L. C. Smith and S. R. Stephenson, 'New Trans-Arctic shipping routes navigable by midcentury' (2013) 110(13) *PNAS* E1191–1195 (available at: <https://www.pnas.org/content/pnas/110/13/E1191.full.pdf>). For a recent assessment of the impact of climate change on Arctic waters, see the various Arctic Climate Impact Assessments available at: <https://acia.amap.no>.

154 See M. Byers and S. Lalonde, 'Who Controls the Northwest Passage?' (2009) 42 *Vanderbilt Journal of Transnational Law* 1133–1210.

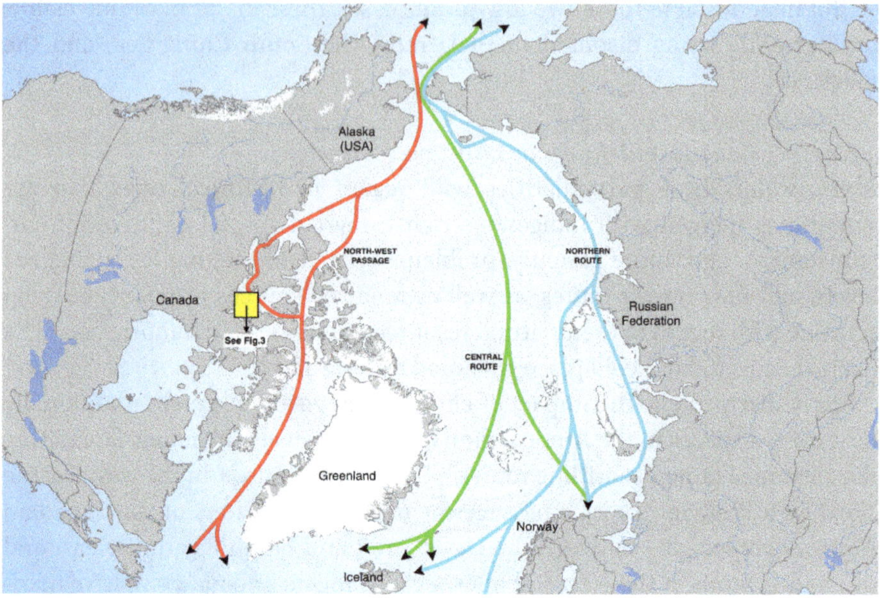

FIGURE 2 The Arctic routes
SOURCE: MALTE HUMPERT / THE ARCTIC INSTITUTE / AUTHOR'S ELABORATION

A renewed version of Canada's Arctic and Northern Policy Framework has recently been published.[155] It endorses the legal and historical basis for Canada's sovereignty over the Arctic as addressed over the last decades.[156] The expression of this sovereignty is based on a discourse of historical continuity:

155 'Canada's Arctic and Northern Policy Framework', 10 September 2019 (source: <https://www.rcaanc-cirnac.gc.ca/eng/1560523306861/1560523330587>). It replaces Canada's 2009 Northern Strategy and 2010 Statement on Canada's Arctic Foreign Policy.

156 For a pre-LOSC appraisal, see W. Smith, 'Sovereign in the North: The Canadian Aspect of an International Problem', in R. S. J. MacDonald (ed.), *The Arctic Frontier* (University of Toronto Press: Toronto, 1966), 195–211; D. Pharand, 'Historic Waters in International Law with Special Reference to the Arctic' (1971) 21(1) *The University of Toronto Law Journal* 1–14; or R. S. Reid, 'The Canadian Claim to Sovereignty Over the Waters of the Arctic' (1974) 12 *Canadian Yearbook of International Law* 111–136. For a more recent review, see, among others, D. Pharand, 'The Arctic Waters and the Northwest Passage: A Final Revisit' (2007) 38(1–2) *Ocean Development & International Law* 3–69; D. L. Van der Zwaag, 'Canada and the Governance of the Northwest Passage: Rough Waters, Cooperative Currents, Sea of Challenges', in: D. D. Caron and N. Oral (eds), *Navigating Straits: Challenges for International Law* (Brill/Nijhoff: Leiden/Boston, 2013), 87–121; and Chapter 4 ('Who owns the Northwest Passage?') in D. C. Burke, *International Disputes and Cultural Ideas in the Canadian Arctic* (Palgrave Macmillan: London, 2018), 155–195.

> Through the wide range of activities undertaken by the Government of Canada, its partners and local communities, Canada's enduring sovereignty over its Arctic and northern lands and waters is continually expressed. Canada's sovereignty over the region is long-standing, well-established and based on historic title, and founded in part on the presence of Inuit and First Nations since time immemorial.[157]

The historical continuity of Canadian sovereignty over the high Arctic Archipelago is based, first, on the UK's 1880 transfer to Canada of the title to territories not already included within the Dominion of Canada,[158] a title acquired through British discovery in previous decades, particularly by the expeditions discussed later in this chapter. As for the historical land rights of the Inuit people to that vast zone, under the 1993 Nunavut Land Claims Agreement (NLCA), the Inuit people surrendered aboriginal title to their lands and waters in Canada.[159] Article 15 NLCA, dealing with marine areas, establishes that "Canada's sovereignty over the waters of the Arctic Archipelago is supported by Inuit use and occupancy".

The new Arctic Policy is declared a key opportunity to clarify Canada's Arctic boundaries, including by defining the outer limits of Canada's continental shelf in the Arctic Ocean[160] and seeking appropriate opportunities to

---

157 'Canada's Arctic and Northern Policy Framework' (n. 155).

158 Imperial Order in Council (July 31, 1880), in C.O.42, Vol. 764, at 329; *The Canada Gazette*, Vol. XIV, No. 15 (Oct. 9, 1880), at 38. The exact text says: "From and after September 1, 1880, all British territories and possessions in North America, not already included within the Dominion of Canada, and all islands adjacent to any of such territories or possessions, shall (with the exception of the Colony of Newfoundland and its dependencies) become and be annexed to and form part of the said Dominion of Canada; and become and be subject to the laws for the time being in force in the said Dominion, in so far as such laws may be applicable thereto." See G. W. Smith, 'The Transfer of Arctic territories from Great Britain to Canada in 1880, and some related matters, as seen in official correspondence' (1961) 14 *Arctic* 53–73.

159 Signed on 25 May 1993 (source: <https://nlca.tunngavik.com>). Under Art. 2.7.1(a), the Inuit people "cede, release and surrender to Her Majesty The Queen in Right of Canada, all their aboriginal claims, rights, title and interests, if any, in and to lands and waters anywhere within Canada and adjacent offshore areas within the sovereignty or jurisdiction of Canada". The Inuit have negotiated four comprehensive land claims agreements covering northern Quebec (1975), the Beaufort Sea region (1984), Nunavut (1993), and northern Labrador (2004). All support Canada's Arctic sovereignty generally, but only the NLCA explicitly addresses it. See G. Christie, 'Indigeneity and sovereignty in Canada's far north: The Arctic and Inuit sovereignty' (2011) 110 *The South Atlantic Quarterly* 330–346.

160 In accordance with Art. 78(8) LOSC, on 23 May 2019 Canada filed a partial submission to the Commission on the Limits of the Continental Shelf with information on its continental shelf beyond 200 nm from the baselines from which the breadth of the territorial

resolve outstanding boundary issues under international rules and institutions. With regard to the NWP, Canada has declared that the passage forms part of Canada's historical internal waters. Under the law of the sea as codified by the LOSC,[161] this would mean that Canada's rights are sovereignty rights; Canada would thus exercise complete control, and its domestic legislation would be fully applicable to the route, including the right of passage through it.

This was previously challenged by the US during the 1969 incident in which the oil-tanker SS *Manhattan* – escorted by a US Coast Guard icebreaker – transited the NWP without seeking authorisation from Canada. This case sparked a longstanding dispute between the US and Canada over the respective rights to the passage and the regulation of its navigation.[162] The signing of an agreement on Arctic cooperation between Canada and the US in 1988 did not settle the dispute, but rather simply *froze* it.[163]

Arguably, the legal dispute originated in Canada's implementation of straight baselines in 1985,[164] which enclosed large areas of waters landward from these lines around the Canadian Arctic Archipelago. This legal assertion – to some extent in line with the ICJ ruling on the 1951 Anglo-Norwegian *Fisheries Case*[165] – has been specifically challenged by the US in light of another ICJ

---

sea is measured in the Arctic Ocean. This follows a decade of scientific and legal work to determine the limits of Canada's undersea landmass in the Arctic. For more information, see the DOALOS webpage at: <https://www.un.org/Depts/los/clcsnew/submissionsfiles/submissioncan1842019.html>.

161 The LOSC entered into force for Canada on 7 December 2003.

162 For an early discussion of the US and Canadian positions, see D. R. Rothwell, 'The Canadian-U.S. Northwest Passage Dispute: A Reassessment' (1993) 26(2) *Cornell International Law Journal* 331–372. More recently, see S. Lalonde and F. Lasserre, 'The Position of the United States on the Northwest Passage: Is the Fear of Creating a Precedent Warranted?' (2013) 44 *Ocean Development & International Law* 28–72; and D. R. Rothwell, *Arctic Ocean Shipping: Navigation, Security and Sovereignty in the North American Arctic*, Brill Research Perspectives in the Law of the Sea (Brill: Leiden/Boston, 2018).

163 'Agreement Between the Government of Canada and the Government of the United States of America on Arctic Cooperation' (signed 11 January 1988, entered into force 11 January 1988, 1852 UNTS 59). Section 3 *in fine* states, "The Government of the United States pledges that all navigation by U.S. icebreakers within waters claimed by Canada to be internal will be undertaken with the consent of the Government of Canada", whilst Section 4 provides, "Nothing in this agreement of cooperative endeavour between Arctic neighbours and friends nor any practice thereunder affects the respective positions of the Governments of the United States and of Canada on the Law of the Sea in this or other maritime areas or their respective positions regarding third parties."

164 'Order Respecting Geographical Coordinates of Points from which Baselines May Be Determined (Territorial Sea Geographical Coordinates (Area 7) Order)', 10 September 1985 (source: <https://laws-lois.justice.gc.ca/PDF/SOR-85-872.pdf>).

165 *Fisheries* case (*United Kingdom* v. *Norway*), *ICJ Reports* 1951, 116.

ruling, namely, the 1949 *Corfu Channel* case.[166] The US supports the NWP's legal status as a strait used for international navigation between one part of the high seas or an EEZ and another part of the high seas or an EEZ and thus argues that the transit passage provided for under Article 37 LOSC applies.[167] However, the US legal position is somewhat paradoxical. On the one hand, its traditional position on the freedom of the seas purports to maintain a solid argument regarding not only the NWP but also other straits such as those of Taiwan (Formosa), Ormuz, or Melaka. However, it takes the opposite stance in relation to, for example, the increasingly complex case of the Unimak Pass in Alaska. As Michael Byers has said,

> A more meaningful step would be for the United States to rethink its position on international straits, where historically it has pressed for maximum freedom of navigation, and to work with countries such as Canada and Russia to strengthen multilateral standards and coastal state powers.[168]

China has also allegedly challenged the Canadian claim when declaring its general position regarding the navigational rights and freedoms in the Arctic. Although respecting "the legislative, enforcement and adjudicatory powers of the Arctic States in the waters subject to their jurisdiction", China maintains that "the management of the Arctic shipping routes should be conducted in accordance with treaties including the [LOSC] and general international law and that the freedom of navigation enjoyed by all countries in accordance with the law and their rights to use the Arctic shipping routes should be ensured".[169] Meanwhile, Russia, with an eye to its own claim to the Northeast Passage, from the Bering Strait to the Barents Sea, allegedly supports Canada's position. In 1985, Russia also adopted straight baselines in its Arctic coastline and publicly expressed that "[w]hether it is the Northwest Passage or the Northeast Passage does not matter. Our position is based on provisions of international law.

---

166 *Corfu Channel* case (*UK v Albania*), Merits, Judgment, *ICJ Reports* 1949, 4.

167 See Lalonde and Lasserre (n. 162), passim.

168 Byers (n. 152), at 161. The Unimak Pass is a narrow strait through Alaska's Aleutian Islands chain and part of the Alaska Maritime National Wildlife Refuge. It is used annually by around 5,000 ships.

169 'China's Arctic Policy', White Paper published on 26 January 2018 (available at: <http://english.www.gov.cn/archive/whitepaper/2018/01/26/content281476026660336.htm>). The Paper continues, "China maintains that disputes over the Arctic shipping routes should be properly settled in accordance with international law." However, it has been argued that this position could be counter-productive for China and its legal interest in the Quionzhou Strait. See M. Byers and E. Lodge, "China and the Northwest Passage" (2019) 18 *Chinese Journal of International Law* 57–90.

The waters around islands belonging to a country are the internal waters of that country."[170] The European Union – still building a comprehensive Arctic policy[171] – has remained mostly silent,[172] although the European Commission arguably joined the US State Department in protesting Canada's drawing of straight baselines around its Arctic islands in 1985.[173]

Interestingly enough for the rationale of this book, the NWP is a sea route that once doomed a British expedition led by Sir John Franklin and his ships – the HMS *Erebus* and HMS *Terror* – in 1845. The expedition was seeking access through Arctic waters to riches it hoped to find in Asia. However, after several early fatalities, the two vessels became icebound in the Victoria Strait, near King William Island, in what today is the territory of the Nunavut indigenous people. The entire expedition, comprising 129 men, including Franklin, vanished.[174]

---

170 Quoted in Byers (n. 152), at 151. On the Russian policy, see E. Franckx, 'The legal regime of navigation in the Russian Arctic' (2009) 18(2) *Journal of Transnational Law & Policy* 327–342; and A. A. Todorov, 'The Russia-USA legal dispute over the straits of the Northern Sea Route and similar case of the Northwest Passage' (2017) 29 *Arctic and North* 63–75.

171 In July 2020, the European Commission and the European External Action Service launched a public consultation with a view to updating its policy. Closed on 10 November 2020, the consultation helped to reflect more broadly on the new challenges and opportunities in the Arctic region, in light of the EU's objectives under the "European Green Deal" and the EU's International Ocean Governance agenda. See the summary of results at: <https://op.europa.eu/en/publication-detail/-/publication/497bfd35-5f8a-11eb-b487-01aa75ed71a1>.

172 Its Joint Communication to the European Parliament and the Council on 'An integrated European Union policy for the Arctic' does not even mention the dispute (EU Doc. JOIN (2016) 21 final, 27 April 2016 (available at: <http://eeas.europa.eu/archives/docs/arcticregion/docs/160427joint-communication-an-integrated-european-union-policy-for-the-arcticen.pdf>)). Since its 2008 proposal for a regime for the Arctic akin to that provided for under the 1959 Antarctic Treaty, and the bitter reaction it elicited from the five main actors – Canada, Denmark, Norway, Russia, and the US, defending the plain application of the law of the sea to the frozen polar waters – the EU has moderated its position. See E. Conde, 'El régimen de los espacios polares el espacio ártico' in F. M. Mariño (ed.), *Instrumentos y regímenes de cooperación internacional*, 2nd ed. (Trotta: Madrid, 2017), 407–426.

173 Through the British High Commission Note No. 90/86, 9 July 1986. See US Department of State, *Limits in the Seas No. 112: US Responses to Excessive National Maritime Claims*, 9 March 1992 at 29–30 (available at: <https://www.state.gov/wp-content/uploads/2019/12/LIS-112.pdf>).

174 While finishing this book, the first member of the 1845 Franklin expedition whose identity has been confirmed through DNA and genealogical analyses was reported. See D. Stenton, S. Fratpietro, A. Keenleyside and R. Park, 'DNA identification of a sailor from the 1845 Franklin northwest passage expedition' (2021) 57 *Polar Record* E14 [doi: 10.1017/S0032247421000061].

Numerous contemporaneous expeditions were sent to find the remains of the 1845 mission.[175] Some ended in disaster, such as that of the HMS *Investigator*, which also became icebound and was abandoned by her crew in 1853, although not before they had documented the actual existence of the NWP in 1850.[176] From 1981 onwards, several land excavations and wreck search expeditions were sent to find the remains of the Royal Navy vessels in the Canadian Arctic. But it was not until September 2014 that they met with success, first, with the find of several items in the Queen Maud Gulf near Nunavut's King William Island and, later, with the location of the HMS *Erebus* wreck.[177] Two years later, the Arctic Research Foundation located the remains of the HMS *Terror*, south of King William Island in Terror Bay.[178] Unlike the *Erebus* – which had deteriorated considerably – the wreck of the *Terror* was found in pristine conditions.

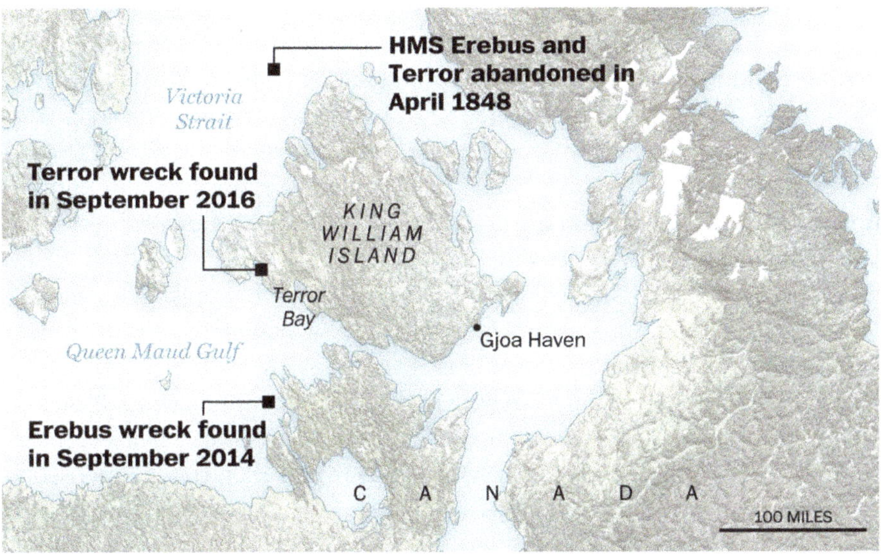

FIGURE 3 Location of the HMS *Erebus* and HMS *Terror*
SOURCE: MAPS4NEWS/HERE / THE WASHINGTON POST

175 See R. A. Potter, *Finding Franklin: The Untold Story of a 165-Year Search* (McGill-Queen's University Press: Montreal, 2016).

176 See L. Hodgetts, 'The rediscovery of HMS *Investigator*: Archaeology, sovereignty and the colonial legacy in Canada's Arctic' (2012) 13(1) *Journal of Social Archaeology* 80–100.

177 All the information about 'The 2014 Victoria Strait Expedition' can be found on Parks Canada's website at: <https://web.archive.org/web/20151004010237/http://www.pc.gc.ca/eng/culture/franklin/recherche-search/exp2014.aspx>.

178 P. Watson, 'Ship found in Arctic 168 years after doomed Northwest Passage attempt', *The Guardian*, 12 September 2016, at: <https://www.theguardian.com/world/2016/sep/12/hms-terror-wreck-found-arctic-nearly-170-years-northwest-passage-attempt>.

From the start of the search expeditions, the question of the title to the two Royal Navy vessels hovered in the background. On 5 August 1997, Canada and the UK signed a Memorandum of Understanding (MoU), which, once it was decided "to ensure the commemorative integrity of the wrecks through the orderly and scientific exploration, recovery and disposition of the wrecks and their contents", recognised the UK "as the owner of the wrecks" but "assign[ed] custody and control of the wrecks and their contents to the Government of Canada, and acknowledge[d] Canada as its agent for purposes of this Understanding".[179] The MoU goes further, stating

> Britain does not waive ownership or sovereign immunity with respect to the wrecks or their contents while they are on the seabed, but accepts that any site investigation, excavation or recovery of either of the wrecks or their contents will be under Canada's control.

However, in 1999, shortly after the MoU was signed, Canada created the new territory of Nunavut through the NLCA, previously concluded in 1993 with the Inuit people.[180] Article 17.1.2(d) of the NLCA states that Inuit Owned Lands are expected to include "areas of archaeological, historical or cultural importance". But the wrecks of the *Erebus* and *Terror* are actually located on federally owned lands, under the administration of what is now Public Services and Procurements Canada, subsequently transferred to Parks Canada.[181] Article 33(7)(1) of the NLCA provides for joint ownership by the Canadian Government and the Inuit Heritage Trust. In May 2016, following the discoveries of the *Erebus* and *Terror* between 2014 and 2016, negotiations on their ownership began between Canada and the UK but were temporarily paused. In the meantime, the Inuit claimed their rights to the original artefacts – as opposed to

179 'Memorandum of Understanding Between the Governments of Great Britain and Canada Pertaining to the Shipwrecks of the *HMS Erebus* and *HMS Terror*', 5 August 1997 (available at: <https://assets.publishing.service.gov.uk/government/uploads/system/uploads/attachmentdata/file/458500/MOUFOI0286-15.pdf>).

180 Nunavut is Canada's largest and most northerly territory, created on 1 April 1999 through the Nunavut Act (S.C. 1993, c.28) (available at: <https://laws-lois.justice.gc.ca/PDF/N-28.6.pdf>).

181 Originally protected, from 1992 on, by the Historic Sites and Monuments Act (R.S.C., 1985, c. H-4) as a National Historic Site of Canada (source: <https://www.lieuxpatrimoniaux.ca/en/rep-reg/place-lieu.aspx?id=19683>), since their actual discoveries, in 2014 and 2016, respectively, the *Erebus* and the *Terror* have been protected by the Canada National Parks Act (S.C. 2000, c. 32) (source: <https://www.canada.ca/en/parks-canada/news/2017/12/hmsterroraddedtothewrecksofhmserebusandhmsterrornationalhistor.html>).

the reproductions received – and the wrecks,[182] associated with Inuit intangible heritage.[183] Finally, in October 2017, an agreement was announced whereby the UK would transfer ownership of the *Erebus* and *Terror* wrecks (but not of the *Investigator*'s) and of any future recovered artefacts to the Government of Canada – to be treated as co-owned by the Inuit – but would keep the 65 items already recovered from the *Erebus*.[184] On 26 April 2018, a 'Deed of Gift and Memorandum of Understanding' between Canada and the UK was signed.[185] The first nine artefacts recovered thereafter, jointly owned by the Government of Canada and the Inuit, were recovered from the *Erebus* in the summer of 2018.[186] On 16 April 2019, the Government of Canada and the Inuit Heritage Trust signed an MoU detailing how the two institutions would work together to protect, study, conserve, and share the artefacts gifted by the UK.[187]

A change of ownership thus occurred between 1997, when the UK was still the owner, and 2018, when the title was transferred by gift to Canada and the

182 D. Beeby, 'Inuit press claim for co-ownership of Franklin artifacts', *CBC News*, 24 July 2016, at: <https://www.cbc.ca/news/politics/franklin-hms-erebus-inuit-parks-canada-hms-terror-1.3689503>.

183 See P.-L. Têtu, F. Lasserre, S. Pelletier, and J. Dawson, '"Sovereignty" over submerged cultural heritage in the Canadian Arctic waters: case study from the Franklin expedition wrecks (1845–48)' (2019) 42(2) *Polar Geography* 71–88.

184 See the Press Release of the UK Government, published 26 April 2018, at: <https://www.gov.uk/government/news/uk-gifts-historic-shipwrecks-to-canada>. Under the previous 1997 MoU, it was agreed that, when found, two kinds of objects should be retained by the UK: any gold recovered apart from coins considered to have been in private ownership and objects deemed "to be of outstanding significance to the history of the Royal Navy". The 65 objects retained by the UK would seem to belong to this latter category. As for human remains, they are to be treated 'reverently', refraining from disturbing them or bringing them to the surface. The MoU further provides, that "[a]ny human remains that must be removed in order to conduct archaeological work, or that are inadvertently recovered, will be re-interred with proper respect and reverence, and in consultation with Britain". Some of the objects so far retrieved that must be handed over to the UK are still in Canadian labs undergoing a stabilisation and conservation process.

185 Non-public document. On file with the author.

186 See Parks Canada, 'First Artifacts Jointly Owned by Canada and Inuit Recovered from Franklin Wrecks', 26 September 2018 (available at: <https://www.canada.ca/en/parks-canada/news/2018/09/first-artifacts-jointly-owned-by-canada-and-inuit-recovered-from-franklin-wrecks.html>). For later events, see also C. Nardi, 'Trove of artifacts from HMS Erebus help shed light on last days of doomed Franklin expedition', *National Post*, 21 February 2020, at: <https://nationalpost.com/news/trove-of-artifacts-from-hms-erebus-help-shed-light-on-last-days-of-doomed-franklin-expedition>.

187 See Parks Canada, 'Government of Canada and Inuit Heritage Trust Sign Franklin Artifact Memorandum of Understanding', 16 April 2019 (available at: <https://www.canada.ca/en/parks-canada/news/2019/04/government-of-canada-and-inuit-heritage-trust-sign-franklin-artifact-memorandum-of-understanding.html>).

Inuit. Under the terms of the Deed, the British Secretary of State for Defence "irrevocably gifts, assigns, and transfers to Parks Canada the right, title, and interest in and to the Property for Parks Canada's own use absolutely, subject to the terms of this deed" (§ 3.1); and "Parks Canada waives any claim to any award or compensation, in salvage or otherwise, in respect of the Representative Sample of Objects" (§ 5).[188]

Unsurprisingly, even before the transfer of title (and not conditional on it), Canada included the *Erebus* and *Terror* among the arguments in support of its longstanding claim of historical sovereignty over Arctic waters and, in particular, the Northwest Passage. As early as August 2008, when announcing an archaeological mission to find the Royal Navy vessels, then Canadian Environment Minister John Baird remarked, "We certainly think that by establishing our long-standing presence in the Arctic, that can enhance issues of sovereignty", adding that the Northwest Passage was "not far from where this ship is". He concluded noting that "every bit of weight we can put behind our case for sovereignty is important. Adding history to that equation can only enhance that case."[189] When the HMS *Investigator* – the vessel that actually discovered the NWP – was itself (re)discovered in 2010, members of the Canadian government pivoted back to the 'sovereignty' account. Visiting the archaeological site, then Environment Minister Jim Prentice was quoted as saying, "It represent[ed] the convergence of the history of Arctic adventure with the history of Inuit occupation [...] This is a continuous record of our sovereignty."[190] Some years later, on 9 September 2014, when the finding of the HMS *Erebus* was confirmed, then Canadian Prime Minister Stephen Harper said in a statement:

> This is truly a historic moment for Canada. Franklin's ships are an important part of Canadian history given that his expeditions, which took place nearly 200 years ago, laid the foundations of Canada's Arctic sovereignty.[191]

188 This 'Representative Sample of Objects' refers to the 65 objects listed in Annex A of the Deed and retained by the Royal Navy from the outset (see n. 184 above).

189 R. Boswell, 'Finding lost ships will help claim on Arctic: gov't', *Edmonton Journal*, 16 August 2008, at: <https://www.pressreader.com/canada/edmonton-journal/20080816/281500747039104>; and 'Canada launches new Arctic search for Franklin's lost ships', *CBC News*, 15 August 2008, at: <https://www.cbc.ca/news/canada/north/canada-launches-new-arctic-search-for-franklin-s-lost-ships-1.702857>.

190 See P. Gohier, 'Hot on Sir John Franklin's tail', *Macleans*, 29 July 2010, at: <https://www.macleans.ca/news/canada/hot-on-sir-john-franklins-tail/>.

191 'Franklin ship discovery: Stephen Harper's full statement', *CBC News*, 9 September 2014, at: <https://www.cbc.ca/news/politics/franklin-ship-discovery-stephen-harper-s-full-statement-1.2760566>.

A year later, the President of the Canadian Treasury, Tony Clement, reportedly made a similar statement, insisting, "This is part of our history, part of our heritage as a nation and, quite frankly, part of our Arctic sovereignty as well." He added, "I don't think we're going to find a Russian flag on the *Erebus* so I think it underscores our point – in all seriousness – that the British, and of course, we inherited from the British, Canada's Far North."[192]

In the final act of this play (for now), a bitter encounter took place in the May 2019 Arctic Council meeting, when the US Secretary of State labelled Canada's position (as well as others') 'illegitimate'.[193] The Canadian response was, again, firm and unequivocal. "Canada is very clear about the Northwest Passage being Canadian", said Canadian Foreign Minister Chrystia Freeland. "There is both a very strong historic and geographic connection with Canada."[194]

Canada's complex sovereignty rhetoric is built upon legal succession from the UK[195] and the historical presence of indigenous peoples.[196] Straddling both, linking tangible and intangible heritage, the wrecks of the *Erebus* and *Terror* are another building block in that rhetoric, albeit an equally complex

192 'New footage offers look into HMS Erebus wreck', *The Globe and Mail*, 16 April 2015, at: <https://www.theglobeandmail.com/news/national/new-footage-offers-look-into-hms-erebus-wreck/article23993670/>.

193 See L. Cecco, 'Mike Pompeo rejects Canada's claims to Northwest Passage as "illegitimate"', *The Guardian*, 7 May 2019, at: <https://www.theguardian.com/us-news/2019/may/07/mike-pompeo-canada-northwest-passage-illegitimate>.

194 See US Department of State, 'Remarks With Canadian Foreign Minister Chrystia Freeland Before Their Meeting', 7 May 2019 (meeting with US Secretary of State Mike Pompeo) (available at: <https://2017-2021.state.gov/remarks-with-canadian-foreign-minister-chrystia-freeland-before-their-meeting-3/index.html>). The conversation continued: "Having said that," Freeland said, "we collaborate closely with all of the members of the Arctic Council. One country is our neighbor, our neighbor to north and to the south, and we have a very close, very fruitful collaboration. And actually, as we see the conditions of the Northwest Passage changing with our changing climate, I think that's actually grounds for closer collaboration with the United States." Secretary Pompeo concluded saying, "The challenges in the Arctic aren't between the United States and Canada, let me assure you. There are others that threaten to use it in ways that are not consistent with the rule of law. And so we'll continue to have great conversations on these issues with our close friends, the Canadians."

195 Still part of the British Commonwealth, Canada's full independence was achieved in three acts: in 1897, as the Dominion of Canada, in 1931, with the Statute of Westminster, and in 1982, with the adoption of Canada's Constitution.

196 In a press release on 8 May 2019, the Inuit Circumpolar Council – an indigenous peoples' organisation – asserted, "Canada's sovereignty is based on treaties and constructive agreements which recognize both Inuit sovereignty and Canadian sovereignty over the Arctic, including the Northwest Passage." Available at: <https://www.inuitcircumpolar.com/press-releases/inuit-and-canada-share-northwest-passage-sovereignty-icc-canada-president/>.

one. With the 1997 MoU, Canada received from the UK only the 'custody and control' of (but not the title to) the wrecks and their contents. Under the NLCA, in 1999, areas of archaeological, historical, or cultural importance – including those where the wrecks were supposed to be – were transferred to the Inuit. Finally, in 2018, after both vessels had been found, title to the wrecks and to any possible remains recovered thereafter (but not the 65 items recovered from the *Erebus* as of that date) was 'gifted' by the UK to Canada. The use of the sunken (still) British vessels by Canadian leaders as evidence of sovereignty was thus limited and perhaps misused for political reasons even before the wrecks were actually found. Arguably, if the country is willing to build its case on its historical presence in the Arctic – closely linked to the indigenous argument – it could have legitimately used the Thule Inuit period archaeological site found (and excavated) close to the location of the *Investigator* wreck as proof of that historical indigenous presence in these Arctic lands and waterways.[197] However, as is often the case where indigenous peoples are concerned, their historical presence was neglected and their right to their ancestral lands forgotten. "Britain's original claim to what is now Arctic Canada", it has been argued, "was based, like all colonial claims, on a denial of the territorial rights of the Indigenous population."[198] Whilst this is generally true around the world, indigenous land claims have been plausibly recognised in Canada, both socially and legally, and their link with cultural heritage, both tangible and intangible, has been reinforced for historical reasons.[199]

---

197 Numerous archaeological expeditions from the eighteenth century onwards have focussed on the Thule presence across the Canadian Arctic, especially in the Labrador Peninsula. See, for example, the report by L. K. Rankin, 'An archaeological view of the Thule/Inuit occupation of Labrador' (2009), at: <http://www.mun.ca/labmetis/pdf/thule_inuit%20 final%20report.pdf>. See also P. Whitridge, 'Classic Thule [Classic Precontact Inuit]', in: T. M. Friesen and O. K. Mason (eds), *The Oxford Handbook of the Prehistoric Arctic* (Oxford: Oxford University Press, 2016), 821–843.

198 Hodgetts (n. 176), at 87. This has occurred with all discoveries, conquests, and occupations throughout modern (and pre-modern) history. The difference, if any, lies in the individual and collective rights recognised for colonised peoples. For the use of the historical presence of Arctic indigenous peoples by other Arctic States, see Byers (n. 152), at 216–244.

199 Inuit self-government may be one of the most politically advanced in the world. It is based on the 1984 Inuvialuit Final Agreement or Western Arctic Claim and the 1993 Nunavut Land Claims agreement, which, as we have seen, led to the creation of Nunavut in 1999. In 2005, the Nunatsiavut regional government was created within the province of Newfoundland and Labrador under the Labrador Inuit Land Claims Agreement. In 2006, the Nunavik Inuit Land Claims Agreement was reached in northern Quebec, and negotiations are ongoing to establish a regional Inuit government like that of Nunatsiavut. In addition, Parks Canada is making an enormous effort with indigenous peoples to study,

In 2015, between the finds of the *Erebus* and the *Terror*, Canada's government changed. The political 'tone' used by previous administrations regarding the importance of both wrecks changed with it, into a truly complex claim spanning vast territories and strategic maritime routes, an historical indigenous presence closely linked to these territories and their archaeological remains, previous navigation rights claimed by Canada's predecessor State, and sovereignty rhetoric that needs to be accommodated to a constantly evolving legal and political landscape. Without relinquishing any of its territorial or maritime claims, Canada – following widely recognised scientific standards under Parks Canada authority – is engaging in outstanding archaeological research in the Arctic, taking into account the secular indigenous presence and its interest in the *Erebus* and *Terror* remains associated with the Inuits' intangible heritage. Although neither the archaeologists nor the Inuit people are to blame for the (mis)use of these activities by people not associated with the technical projects, it could nevertheless impact the sovereignty claim.

3.2.2.2 *China and the South China Sea*

The South China Sea (SCS) – encompassing a marine area of around 3,500,000 km^2 – is a marginal sea in the Western Pacific Ocean that includes the Gulf of Tonkin. It is bounded, clockwise from the north, by the People's Republic of China (China), the Republic of China (Taiwan), the Philippines, Malaysia, Brunei, Indonesia, and Vietnam.[200] The main geographical features include hundreds of sea elevations, including several archipelago clusters and groups of islands – among others, the Paracel (Xisha), Spratly (Nansha), and Pratas (Dongsha) islands (including the Vereker Banks), the Macclesfield Bank (Zhongsha), and the Scarborough Shoal (Huangyan) – most of which are inhabited. The SCS is connected to the East China Sea via the Taiwan Strait, to the Philippine Sea via the Luzon Strait, to the Sulu Sea via the straits around Palawan and the Strait of Singapore, and to the Java Sea via the Karimata and Bangka Straits. The SCS is thus a region of great geostrategic and economic importance, not only because one-third of the world's maritime shipping passes through it but also because of the extensive natural resources it contains, both living (with fisheries that are crucial for the food security in Southeast Asia) and non-living (with gas and oil reserves believed to lie in its subsoil).

---

maintain, and engage in outreach activities with them with regard to their rich tangible and intangible heritage.

200 For the purposes of this book, Singapore, Cambodia, and Thailand could also be considered interested States in the marine area analysed here.

Although treasure hunters mainly seem to be marauding the Caribbean Sea, the SCS has been (and remains) the best place for their activities, using either basic, amateur, and/or traditional techniques or more professional underwater tools to loot thousands of archaeological or memorial sites.[201] Besides the lack of a general recognition of territorial sovereignty to all of the contested islands and rocks in the SCS, the absence of effective legislation and enforcement – international or domestic – may also explain this. As we have already seen, internationally, the LOSC does not offer an efficient system of underwater cultural heritage protection, and the 2001 UNESCO Convention regime does not apply to the SCS.[202] Domestically, Indonesia, Malaysia, and, to some extent, the Philippines allow (and even encourage) commercial salvage of cultural heritage,[203] whilst Chinese, Thai, and Vietnamese legislation all include some mechanisms for a more controlled system of authorisations.[204]

201 See, generally, N. Pearson, 'Protecting and Preserving Underwater Cultural Heritage in Southeast Asia', in: S. Hufnagel and D. Chappell (eds), *The Palgrave Handbook on Art Crime* (Palgrave Macmillan: London, 2019), 685–730. Public opinion was astonished when information emerged regarding the 'vanishing' of several sunken British, Dutch, Japanese, and US warships from World War II from the SCS. See O. Holmes, M. Ulmanu and S. Roberts, 'The world's biggest grave robbery: Asia's disappearing WWII shipwrecks', *The Guardian*, 3 November 2017, at: <https://www.theguardian.com/world/ng-interactive/2017/nov/03/worlds-biggest-grave-robbery-asias-disappearing-ww2-shipwrecks>; J. Ryall, 'Scavengers pillage wartime wrecks in Southeast Asia', *DW*, 29 May 2017, at: <https://www.dw.com/en/scavengers-pillage-wartime-wrecks-in-southeast-asia/a-39027260>; or 'Malaysia firms plunder sunken wrecks for rare steel used to make sensitive medical, scientific equipment', *The Strait Times*, 27 February 2018, at: <https://www.straitstimes.com/asia/se-asia/malaysia-firms-plunder-sunken-wrecks-for-rare-steel-used-to-make-sensitive-medical>. On the various legal implications, see Z. Lin, 'The protection of sunken WWII warships located in Indonesian or Malaysian territorial waters' (2020) 113 *Marine Policy* 103804; K. Browne, '"Ghost Battleships" of the Pacific: Metal Pirates, WWII Heritage, and Environmental Protection' (2019) 14 *Journal of Maritime Archaeology* 1–28; or M. R. Manders, R. W. de Hoop, S. Adhityatama et al., 'Battle of the Java Sea: One Event, Multiple Sites, Values and Views' (2021) 16 *Journal of Maritime Archaeology* 39–56.

202 Although all SCS interested coastal States are parties to the LOSC (except Cambodia), none (except Cambodia) has ratified the 2001 UNESCO Convention.

203 Indonesia has been (and, unfortunately, still is) one of the best places for treasure hunting. See, quite recently, 'Indonesia reverses course, to allow treasure hunting by private investors and foreigners again', 3 March 2021, *Southeast Asian Archaeology* at: <https://www.southeastasianarchaeology.com/2021/03/05/indonesia-reverses-course-to-allow-treasure-hunting-by-private-investors-and-foreigners-again/>.

204 For a survey of Vietnam's and the Philippines' regulation of underwater cultural heritage, see Y. Jing and J. Li, 'Who Owns Underwater Cultural Heritage in the South China Sea' (2019) 47 *Coastal Management* 107–126, at 112–116. On other SCS riparian States, including Taiwan, see N.-T. A. Hu, 'The 2001 UNESCO Underwater Cultural Heritage Convention and Taiwan's Domestic Legal Regime' (2008) 39 *Ocean Development & International Law* 372–394; Y. Nitiruchirot, 'The Challenges of Underwater Cultural Heritage Protection

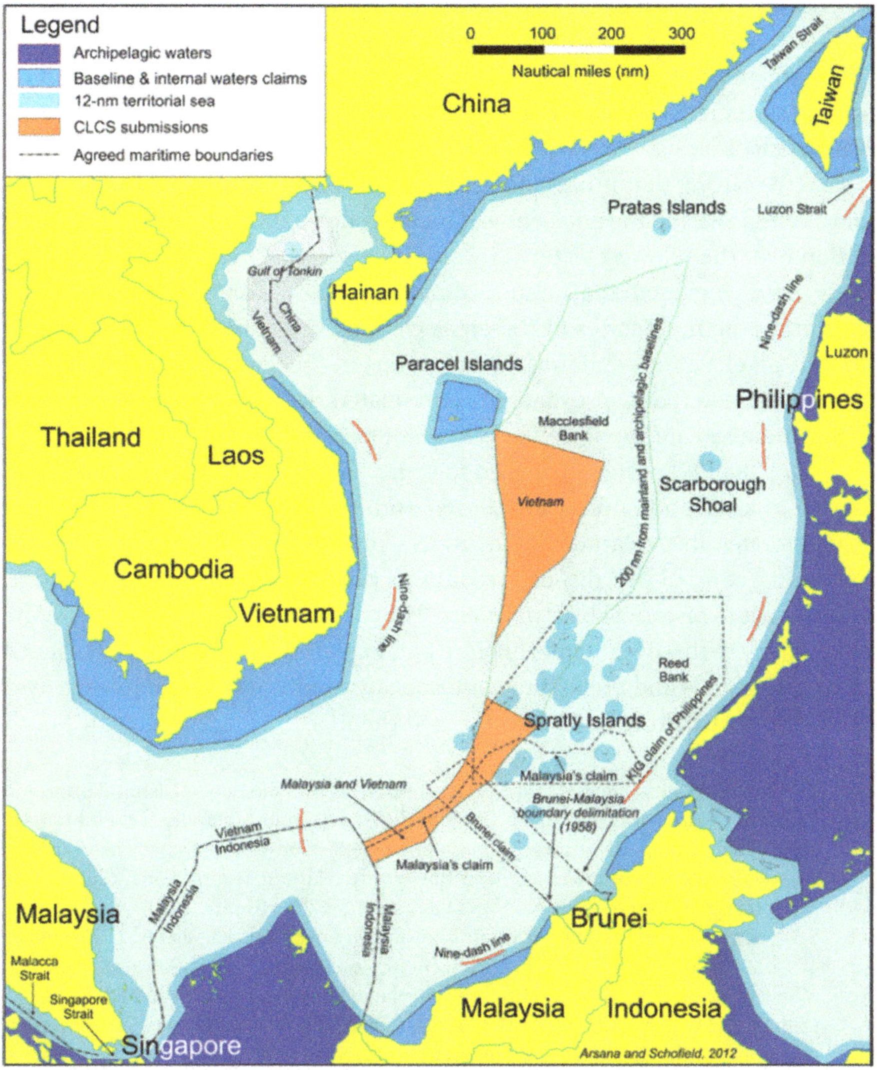

FIGURE 4 Maritime claims in the South China Sea
SOURCE: CLIVE SCHOFIELD, *THE REGIME OF ISLANDS REFRAMED. DEVELOPMENTS IN THE DEFINITION OF ISLANDS UNDER THE INTERNATIONAL LAW OF THE SEA* (BRILL: LEIDEN/BOSTON, 2021), AT 37.

Sovereignty claims and counter-claims are also a common feature of this sea, initially focussed on shores and islands in their own right, but today viewing

in the South China Sea' (2016) 2 *China Oceans Law Review* 244–267; and Z. Hui, 'Legal Protection of Underwater Cultural Heritage in the Taiwan Strait' (2020) 16 *China Oceans Law Review* 68–100.

them as generators of rich marine areas under the law of the sea.[205] Although its public claim dates back to the 1950s, China's current position can be traced to several more recent declarations and diplomatic notes. In 2000, China issued a statement entitled 'Historical Evidence to Support China's Sovereignty over Nansha Islands',[206] and in 2009 it sent the UN Secretary General two *notes verbales* declaring that it has "indisputable sovereignty over the islands in the South China Sea and the adjacent waters, and enjoys sovereign rights and jurisdiction over the relevant waters as well as the seabed and subsoil thereof".[207] These *notes* included the famous 'nine-dash line' – or 'U-shaped' – map, illustrating the boundaries of the areas claimed by China, which encompass virtually all elevations and most of the waters of the South China Sea. In 2011, China reiterated that its "sovereignty and related rights and jurisdiction in the South China Sea are supported by abundant historical and legal evidence".[208]

In 2013, the Philippines proposed to China that they submit their maritime dispute to arbitration under Article 287 and Annex VII LOSC, but China not only reiterated its declaration from 2006 – made when it ratified the LOSC – precluding compulsory dispute resolution procedures under Part XV LOSC with respect to historical bays or titles,[209] but also recalled that "China was the first country to discover, name, explore and exploit the resources of the South China Sea Islands and the first to continuously exercise sovereign powers over them" and that "[i]n 1947, China renamed the maritime features of the South

205 In addition to China, today Vietnam claims sovereignty over the Paracel Islands, Taiwan and Vietnam claim ownership of all the Spratly Islands, and Malaysia, the Philippines, and Brunei claim parts of these islands. Since the Second World War, all the claimants except Brunei have occupied atolls in the Spratlys: Taiwan occupies one, China eight, Malaysia five, the Philippines nine, and Vietnam more than twenty.

206 'Historical Evidence to Support China's Sovereignty over Nansha Islands', 17 November 2000, at: <https://www.fmprc.gov.cn/mfaeng/topics665678/3754666060/t19231.shtml>.

207 *Note Verbale* No. CML/17/2009 from the Permanent Mission of the People's Republic of China to the UN Secretary-General, 7 May 2009, available at: <https://www.un.org/Depts/los/clcsnew/submissionsfiles/mysvnm3309/chn2009remysvnme.pdf>; and *Note Verbale* No. CML/18/2009 from the Permanent Mission of the People's Republic of China to the UN Secretary-General, 7 May 2009, available at: <https://www.un.org/Depts/los/clcsnew/submissionsfiles/vnm3709/chn2009revnm.pdf>. The notes were the initial Chinese reaction to the submissions by Malaysia and Vietnam (jointly and individually in May 2009) of information to the Commission on the Limits of the Continental Shelf under Art. 76(8) LOSC (available at: <http://www.un.org/Depts/los/clcsnew/submissionsfiles/submissionmysvnm332009.htm>).

208 *Note Verbale* No. CML/8/2011 from the Permanent Mission of the People's Republic of China to the UN Secretary-General, 14 April 2011, available at: <https://www.un.org/depts/los/clcsnew/submissionsfiles/mysvnm3309/chn2011rephle.pdf>.

209 See China's Declaration under Art. 298 LOSC (25 August 2006) (source: <https://treaties.un.org/>).

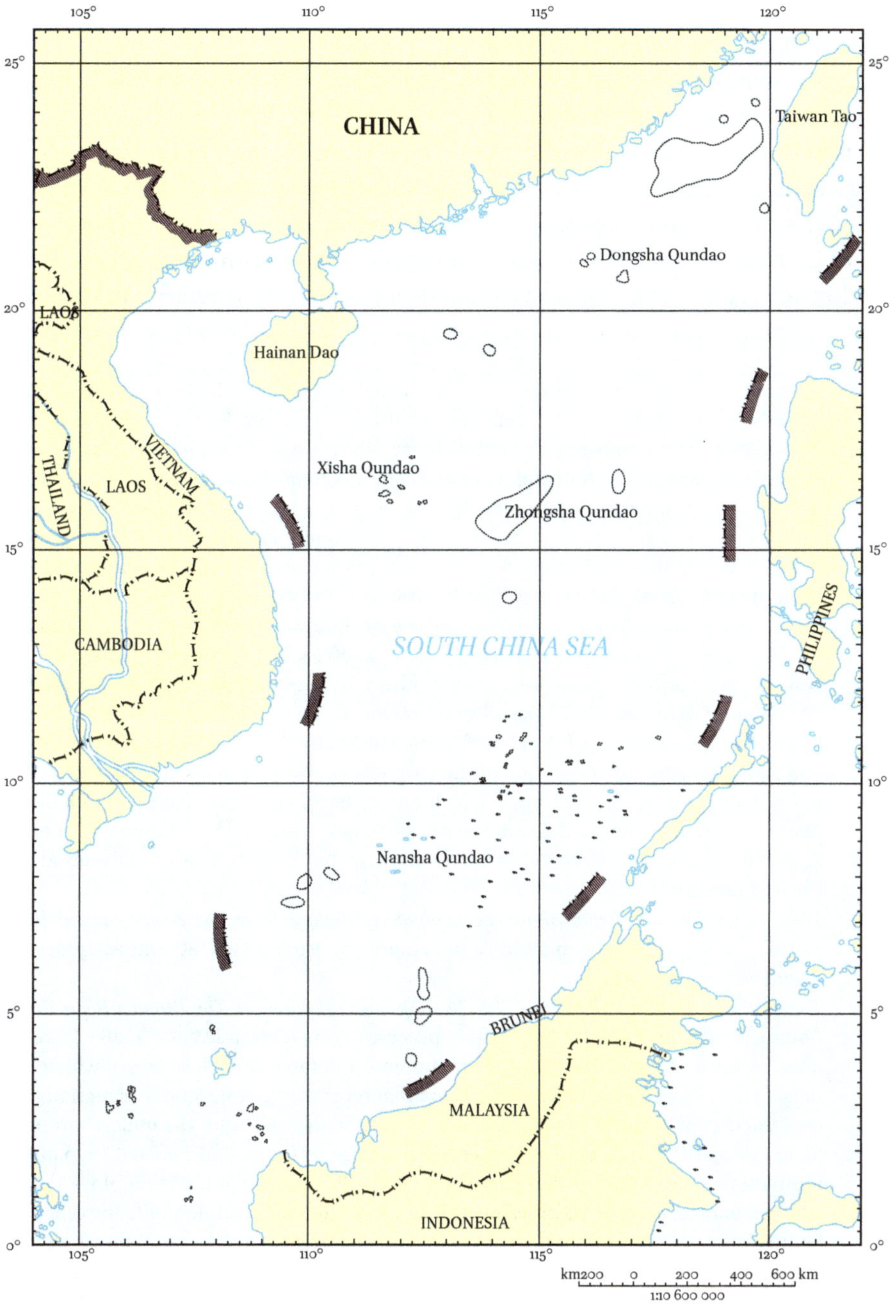

FIGURE 5 The 'Nine-Dash Line' map
SOURCE: MAP ATTACHED TO CHINA'S 7 MAY 2009 NOTE VERBALE FROM THE PERMANENT MISSION OF THE PEOPLE'S REPUBLIC OF CHINA TO THE UNITED NATIONS TO THE SECRETARY-GENERAL OF THE UNITED NATIONS, NO. CML/17/2009 (7 MAY 2009)

China Sea Islands and, in 1948, published an official map which displayed a dotted line in the South China Sea".[210]

As is well known, the arbitration took place, with the arbitral tribunal deciding first on jurisdiction and admissibility[211] and, later, that it had further jurisdiction to consider several submissions made by the Philippines regarding the alleged historical rights and legal value of the Chinese 'nine-dash line' map, the status of the disputed marine features in the area, and the lawfulness of Chinese actions in these features, including the environmental harm done and other aggravating acts and conduct performed by China.[212] Voluntarily

210 'Position Paper of the Government of the People's Republic of China on the Matter of Jurisdiction in the South China Sea Arbitration Initiated by the Republic of the Philippines', 7 December 2014, available at: <http://www.fmprc.gov.cn/mfaeng/zxxx 662805/t1217147.shtml>. A complete assessment of China's position regarding the arbitration can be found in Chinese Society of International Law, 'The South China Sea Arbitration Awards: A Critical Study' (2018) 17 *Chinese Journal of International Law* 206–748 (hereinafter, '*Critical Study*'). See also S. Talmon and B. B. Ja, *The South China Sea Arbitration: A Chinese Perspective* (Hart Publishing: London, 2014); and National Institute for South China Sea Studies, 'A Legal Critique of the Award of the Arbitral Tribunal in the Matter of the South China Sea Arbitration' (2018) 24 *Asian Yearbook of International Law* 151–293. For other views, see, among others, L. Buszynski and C. B. Roberts (eds), *The South China Sea Maritime Dispute: Political, Legal and Regional Perspectives* (Routledge: Oxford, 2014); T. J. Schoenbaum, 'The South China Sea Arbitration Decision and a Plan for Peaceful Resolution of the Disputes' (2016) 47(4) *Journal of Maritime Law & Commerce* 451–77; S. Jayakumar, T. Koh and R. Beckman (eds), *The South China Sea Disputes and Law of the Sea* (Edward Elgar: Cheltenham, 2014); and S. Jayakumar, T. Koh and R. Beckman (eds), *The South China Sea Arbitration: The Legal Dimension* (Edward Elgar: Cheltenham, 2018).

211 *The South China Sea Arbitration* (*The Republic of Philippines* v. *The People's Republic of China*), Award on Jurisdiction and Admissibility, 29 October 2015, at: <https://pcacases.com/web/sendAttach/2579>.

212 *The South China Sea Arbitration* (*The Republic of Philippines* v. *The People's Republic of China*), Award, 12 July 2016, at: <https://pcacases.com/web/sendAttach/2086> (hereinafter, *2016 SCS Award*). Avoiding any comment on enforcement measures – which fall outside its jurisdiction – the Tribunal found that recent large-scale land reclamation and construction of artificial islands by China were incompatible with the obligations on a State during dispute resolution proceedings, insofar as China had inflicted irreparable harm on the marine environment, built a large artificial island in the Philippines' exclusive economic zone, and destroyed evidence of the natural condition of features in the South China Sea that formed part of the Parties' dispute. On the international regime governing islands, including a critical appraisal of this Award, see the recent book in this collection by C. Schofield, *The Regime of Islands Reframed: Developments in the Definition of Islands under the International Law of the Sea*, Brill Research Perspectives in the Law of the Sea (Brill: Leiden/Boston, 2021). See also S. Talmon, 'The South China Sea Arbitration and the Finality of "Final" Awards' (2017) 8(2) *Journal of International Dispute Settlement* 388–401; H. Dipla, 'La sentence arbitrale sur la mer de Chine méridionale et le statut des formations insulaires en droit international' (2018) 23 *Annuaire du droit de la mer* 117–154;

absent from the arbitration,[213] China has nevertheless asserted its 'historic rights' – the core argument of its position[214] – over most of the SCS, although they might be summed up as a continuous interplay of historical weakness, geographical vagueness, and legal inconsistency. Regarding its historical rights, China apparently maintains that its:

> sovereignty and maritime rights and interests in the South China Sea are established and have been consolidated in the long course of history. The Chinese people have since ancient times lived and engaged in production activities in Nanhai Zhudao and relevant waters. China is the first to have discovered, named, and explored and exploited Nanhai Zhudao and relevant waters, and the first to have continuously, peacefully and effectively exercised sovereignty and jurisdiction over them, thus establishing its sovereignty over Nanhai Zhudao and relevant rights and interests in the South China Sea.[215]

However, this historical Chinese presence in the SCS is founded mainly – if not exclusively – on Chinese sources, most of them journalistic rather than scientific, based on unreliable documents, statements, and factual accounts most often shaped by biased nationalistic rhetoric, which are created, re-discovered, and constantly quoting each other.[216] It is also linked to the geographical vagueness, in general, of its historical land frontiers[217] and, in particular, regarding

---

and G. Guillaume, 'Rocks in the Law of the Sea: Some comments on the South China Sea Arbitration Award', *EJIL Talk!*, 25 February 2021, at: <https://www.ejiltalk.org/ricks-in-the-law-of-the-sea-some-comments-on-the-south-china-sea-arbitration-award/>.

213 See M. S. Gau, 'The Sino-Philippine Arbitration of the South China Sea Nine-Dash Dispute: Applying the Rule of Law on Default of Appearance' (2014) 28 *Ocean Yearbook* 81–133.

214 See, among others, Z. Keyuan, 'Historic Rights in International Law and in China's Practice' (2001) 32 *Ocean Development & International Law* 149–168; and F. Dupuy and P.-M. Dupuy, 'A Legal Analysis of China's Historic Rights Claim in the South China Sea' (2013) 107 *American Journal of International Law* 124–141.

215 *Critical Study* (n. 210), at 455.

216 See, among others, L. von Falkenhausen, 'The Regionalist Paradigm in Chinese Archaeology', in: P. L. Kohl and C. Fawcett (eds), *Nationalism, Politics, and the Practice of Archaeology* (Cambridge University Press: Cambridge, 1995), 198–217; M. Flecker, 'The ethics, politics, and realities of maritime archaeology in Southeast Asia' (2002) 31 *International Journal of Nautical Archaeology* 12–24; M. Mohan, 'Historical Fiction: China's South China Sea Claims' (2013) 176 *World Affairs* 83–90; or B. Hayton, *The South China Sea: The Struggle for Power in Asia* (Yale University Press: New Haven, 2014).

217 As is well-known by historians, China's relationship with its weaker neighbouring peoples – Mongols, Tibetans, Manchus, or Hans (with their allegedly less developed culture) – was based on China's superiority and others' suzerainty. Frontiers were not clearly delimited; in a time when 'all under Heaven' meant that all these territories were Chinese, border zones were more acceptable. Land delimitation, apart from the sinuous Great

the SCS and the shape and extent of its maritime claim there.[218] Finally, the legal inconsistency can be seen in China's failure to assert its maritime claims when and how expected: once the law of the sea had been codified by the

Wall, was not clear until the 19th century, when China accepted the 'Westphalian system'. See T. Wang, 'International Law in China: Historical and Comparative Perspectives' (1990) 221 *Recueil des Cours* 195–369; or C.-H. Tang, 'China-Europe', in: B. Fassbender and A. Peters (eds), *The Oxford Handbook of the History of International Law* (Oxford University Press: Oxford, 2012), 701–723.

218 Since 1933, China apparently had in private collections several maps – with 9-, 11-, or 13-dash lines, depending on the map, and based on a previous map from 1904 – which were not invoked until 1948 or 1953 (sources are unclear). For China, however, "[i]n the Qing Dynasty, the Chinese Government marked the Nansha Islands on the authoritative maps and exercised administrative jurisdiction over these islands. The Nansha Islands were marked as Chinese territory in many maps drawn in the Qing Dynasty such as A Map of Administrative Divisions of the Whole China of the 1724 Map of Provinces of the Qing Dynasty, A Map of Administrative Divisions of the Whole China of the 1755 Map of Provinces of the Imperial Qing Dynasty, the 1767 Map of Unified China of the Great Qing for Ten Thousand Years, the 1810 Topographical Map of Unified China of the Great Qing for Ten Thousand Years and the 1817 Map of Unified China of the Great Qing for Ten Thousand Years." Quoted from 'Historical Evidence to Support China's Sovereignty over Nansha Islands', 17 November 2000, at: <http://www.fmprc.gov.cn/mfa_eng/topics_665678/3754_666060/t19231.shtml>. China has also held that "[e]arly in 1948, the dotted line was mapped on China's official map. It was a confirmation of China's rights in the South China Sea formed throughout the history, instead of [a] creation of new claims. For a long time, no State questioned the legitimacy of the dotted line and it also appeared on the official maps of many States." 'Briefing by Xu Hong, Director-General of the Department of Treaty and Law on the South China Sea Arbitration Initiated by the Philippines', 12 May 2016, available at: <http://www.fmprc.gov.cn/mfa_eng/wjdt_665385/zyjh_665391/t1364804.shtml>. It has also been argued in the Chinese literature that although "ancient maps lack precision due to limitations on map drawing techniques, they do establish that China not only considered the South China Sea Islands her territory by action and words, but also illustrated her sovereignty over these areas through visual devices". J. Shen, 'China's Sovereignty over the China Sea Islands: A Historical Perspective' (2002) 1 *Chinese Journal of International Law* 126–130, at 128. See also T.-K. Chang, 'China's Claim of Sovereignty over Spratly and Paracel Islands: A Historical and Legal Perspective' (1991) 23 *Case Western Reserve Journal of International Law* 399–420, at: <https://scholarlycommons.law.case.edu/jil/vol23/iss3/1>; Z. Gao and B. B. Jia, 'The Nine-Dash Line in the South China Sea: History, Status, and Implications' (2013) 107 *American Journal of International Law* 98–124; and E. Franckx and M. Benatar, 'Dots and Lines in the South China Sea: Insights from the Law of Map Evidence' (2012) 2 *Asian Journal of International Law* 89–118.

It is worth recalling that from 1565 to 1898 the Philippines were part of the Spanish Crown. Spain ruled this large archipelago as a Captaincy General depending of the Viceroyalty of New Spain in Mexico (*Nueva España*), including the Scarborough Shoal (*Bajos de Panatog*), which was clearly mapped in the 1734 chart *Carta Hydrographica y Chorographica de las Yslas Filipinas*. Drawn by the Jesuit Pedro Murillo y Velarde, the chart clearly shows those marine features as part of the Spanish Empire. See C. Villoria Prieto,

LOSC,[219] China decided to ratify it. Previously, in 1992, China had declared a 12 nm territorial sea and a 24 nm contiguous zone for the mainland and its offshore islands, Taiwan, and the various affiliated islands "including Diaoyu Island, Penghu Islands, Dongsha Islands, Xisha Islands, Nansha Islands and other islands that belong to the People's Republic of China".[220] But in 1996, when submitting its instrument of LOSC ratification, China had the opportunity to declare – legitimately or otherwise – a wider EEZ and continental shelf encompassing its SCS claim in keeping with the 'nine-dash line' map, as it eventually did in 2009. Yet it remained silent,[221] just as it did when promulgating its *Exclusive Economic Zone and Continental Shelf Act*, whose delimitations again strictly followed the LOSC rules, although in that case it did include an obscure disclaimer to the effect that "[t]he provisions in this Law shall not affect the rights that the People's Republic of China has been enjoying ever since the days of the past".[222]

This legal inconsistency is also at play in its claiming of the vast new zone depicted in the 'nine-dash line' map. What is China claiming with this map: sovereignty over the enclosed features or over the water enclosed within these lines?[223] As noted in the 2016 Arbitral Award,

---

'La producción cartográfica del jesuita Pedro Murillo Velarde (1696–1753)', in: *El Siglo de las Luces, XVI Jornadas de Historia en Llerena* (Sociedad Extremeña de Historia: Llerena, 2015), 129–146. A copy of the chart can be found at: <https://www.wdl.org/es/item/10089/view/1/1/>. On the fate of the chart, see C. Green, 'How a map unearthed under a Newcastle housing estate may hold crucial evidence to land dispute between China and the Philippines', *The Independent*, 13 June 2015, at: <https://www.independent.co.uk/news/uk/home-news/china-and-philippines-diplomatic-row-ignited-after-old-map-found-washed-under-newcastle-housing-estate-10317024.html>.

219 There is no record of China's claim when the four 1958 Geneva Conventions were adopted.

220 Art. 2 of the *Law on the Territorial Sea and the Contiguous Zone of the People's Republic of China*, 25 February 1992, (1992) 21 *Law of the Sea Bulletin* 24–27.

221 China's declaration was as follows: "In accordance with the provisions of the United Nations Convention on the Law of the Sea, the People's Republic of China shall enjoy sovereign rights and jurisdiction over an exclusive economic zone of 200 nautical miles and the continental shelf [...] The People's Republic of China reaffirms its sovereignty over all its archipelagoes and islands as listed in article 2 of the Law of the People's Republic of China on the Territorial Sea and Contiguous Zone which was promulgated on 25 February 1992" (paras. 1 and 3) (source: <https://treaties.un.org/>, also including the Philippines' and Vietnam's protests).

222 Art. 14 of the *Exclusive Economic Zone and Continental Shelf Act*, 26 June 1998, (1998) 38 *Law of the Sea Bulletin* 28–31.

223 Intriguingly enough, China's claim over this vast maritime zone drew on rights recognised by the LOSC to coastal States within their territorial sea (such as policy and enforcement measures, sovereignty over natural resources, or the designation of exploitation blocks) whilst at the same time declaring freedom of navigation. For the Arbitral

> the most insightful formulation by China of its claims in the South China Sea, beyond its claim to sovereignty over islands and their adjacent waters, is as a claim to 'relevant rights in the South China Sea, formed in the long historical course.' In the absence of a more specific indication from China itself, it necessarily falls to the Tribunal to ascertain, on the basis of conduct, whether China's claim amounts to 'historic title'.[224]

There are thus three overlapping claims: a claim to sovereignty over maritime features (including islands), a claim to the maritime waters generated by these features, and a claim to other waters enclosed within the dash lines of the map. The legal dispute over titles to and acquisition of land and islands exceeds the scope of this book. Suffice it to say that:

- With respect to land (including islands), the international law doctrine of title and *effectivités* is clear and has been applied by international courts and tribunals (particularly the ICJ), including the need for evidence of a peaceful and continuous display of authority,[225] which China – in absence of clear title – argues is based on historical presence;
- With respect to the maritime zones generated by marine features, the LOSC rules are clear, and China has consistently claimed that they apply to these

Tribunal, "China does not claim historic title to the waters of South China Sea, but rather a constellation of historic rights short of title" to exploit the natural resources of the waters within the 'nine-dash line' map (*2016 SCS Award*, para. 229). China has also planned to cover most of the SCS with its new Air Defence Identification Zone (ADIZ). See M. Chan, 'Beijing's plans for South China Sea air defence identification zones cover Pratas, Paracel and Spratly islands, PLA Source says', *South China Morning Post*, 31 May 2020, at: <https://www.scmp.com/news/china/military/article/3086679/beijings-plans-south-china-sea-air-defence-identification-zone>.

224 *2016 SCS Award*, para. 209. See S. Kopela, 'Historic Titles and Historic Rights in the Law of the Sea in the Light of the South China Sea Arbitration' (2017) 48 *Ocean Development & International Law* 181–207.

225 *Effectivités* understood as acts of exercise of State authority (*à titre de souverain*, in its French classical expression), thus requiring an intentional act attributable to a State. See, among other *Legal Status of Eastern Greenland* (*Denmark v. Norway*), Judgment, PCIJ 1933 (Ser A/B, No. 53), 46; *Dubai-Sharjah Border Arbitration* (*Dubai/Sharjah*), Award, 19 October 1982, 91 ILM 543; or *Territorial and Maritime Dispute between Nicaragua and Honduras in the Caribbean Sea* (*Nicaragua v. Honduras*), Judgment, *ICJ Reports* 2007, 659, 713–722, paras. 176–208. See further M. G. Kohen, 'Titles and *effectivités* in territorial disputes', in: M. G. Kohen and M. Hébié, *Research Handbook on Territorial Disputes in International Law* (Edward Elgar: Cheltenham, 2018), 145–168. As summarised by Marcelo Kohen, the *effectivités* must be weighed depending on "the nature of the territory, the existence of a holder of title different from those performing the *effectivités*, the existing evidence in this regard and the weight to be attributed to opposite *effectivités* displayed by another entity in the same territory" (ibid., at 157).

features, irrespective of the legal classification thereof[226] and despite their contested title;[227] and

– With respect to the large marine areas depicted on the 'nine-dash line' map and not linked to any land feature, China also bases its claim on its long-standing historical presence, including navigational and other uses.

The first and third aspects (and the second by implication) are thus coloured by historical discourses, making room for Chinese allegations of archaeological evidence, especially that disclosed by underwater archaeology in the SCS. Unfortunately, practice so far shows that China is trying to misuse underwater cultural heritage to support its claim.[228] To this end, for the last three decades, China has adopted a multi-layered policy on underwater cultural heritage that includes well-planned legislative, administrative, enforcement, and political decisions.

---

226 The Arbitral Tribunal said, "As a matter of law, human modification cannot change the seabed into a low-tide elevation or a low-tide elevation into an island. A low-tide elevation will remain a low-tide elevation under the Convention, regardless of the scale of the island or installation built atop it." *2016 SCS Award*, para. 305.

227 As we have already seen, China's title claim is not peaceful since its SCS neighbours also claim sovereignty over the same maritime features.

228 See, in general, E. Pérez-Álvaro and C. Forrest, 'Maritime Archaeology and Underwater Cultural Heritage in the Disputed South China Sea' (2018) 25 *International Journal of Cultural Property* 375–401. See also K.-C. Fu, 'China (including Taiwan)', in: S. Dromgoole (ed.), *The Protection of the Underwater Cultural Heritage: National Perspectives in Light of the UNESCO Convention 2001* (Brill/Nijhoff: The Hague, 2006), 17–41; J. Adams, 'The Role of Underwater Archaeology in Framing and Facilitating the Chinese National Strategic Agenda', in: T. Blumenfield and H. Silverman (eds), *Cultural Heritage Politics in China* (Springer: New York, 2013), 261–82; and M. Flecker, 'Early Chinese Voyaging in the South China Sea: Implications on Territorial Claims' (2017) 1 *Journal of Maritime Studies and National Integration* 1–21. For a Chinese perspective see, among others, H. Zhu and H. Ren, 'Protection of Underwater Cultural Heritage in the South China Sea and Regional Cooperation', in M. H. Nordquist, J. Norton Moore and K.-C. Fu (eds), *Recent Developments in the Law of the Sea and China* (Martinus Nijhoff: Leiden, 2006) 483–490; X. Li and Y.-C. Chang, 'Legal mechanism for the Sino-Foreign cooperative exploitation of the underwater cultural heritage in the South China Sea' (2009) 175 *Ocean & Coastal Management* 144–151; Q. Jinliang, 'Protecting China's maritime heritage: Current conditions and national policy' (2012) 1 *Journal of Marine and Islands Cultures* 46–50; J. Huang, 'Chasing provenance: Legal dilemmas for protecting states with a verifiable link to underwater culture heritage' (2013) 84 *Ocean & Coastal Management* 220–225; B. Lu and S. Zhou, 'China's state-led working model on protection of underwater cultural heritage: Practice, challenges, and possible solutions' (2016) 65 *Marine Policy* 39–47; Y. Jing, 'Protection of underwater cultural heritage in China: new developments' (2019) 29 *International Journal of Cultural Policy* 756–764; Jing and Li (n. 204); or Z. Hui, 'Underwater cultural heritage and the disputed South China Sea' (2020) 34 *China Information* 361–382.

China's bolstering of this policy can be traced back to the 1980s, after the looting and complete destruction in 1985 of the *Geldermalsen* – a Dutch vessel sunk in an SCS reef in 1752 – with an impressive cargo of porcelain auctioned at Christie's Amsterdam in 1986 as 'The Nanking Cargo'.[229] Once China *decided* that the porcelain aboard the *Geldermalsen* was of Chinese origin (and even looted from Chinese territory),[230] its authorities suddenly realised that there was no effective domestic legislation to sanction such activities or to recover illegally exported Chinese heritage. The immediate reaction was the promulgation of the *1989 Regulations Concerning the Management and Protection of Underwater Cultural Relics*.[231] These Regulations cover the basic governance of the underwater cultural heritage. The most interesting issue – addressed in Articles 2 and 3 – relates to ownership of underwater cultural relics,[232] vesting in the State ownership of all cultural relics of Chinese origin, or of unidentified origin, or of foreign origin that remain in Chinese inland waters or territorial waters or under Chinese jurisdiction according to Chinese law. China also reserves the right to identify the owners of cultural relics of Chinese origin that remain in sea areas outside the territorial waters of any foreign country but

---

229 See C. J. A. Jörg, *The Geldermalsen: History and Porcelain* (Kemper Publisher: Groningen, 1986); and G. L. Miller, 'The Second Destruction of the Geldermalsen' (1992) 26 *Historical Archaeology* 124–31. As an example of lots sold at Christie's, see <https://www.christies.com/en/lot/lot-1981011>. Other pieces are currently available on eBay.

230 Once the commercially valuable items had been recovered, the remaining objects and the wreck itself were dynamited by the English treasure hunter Michael Hatcher, already known for previous lootings in the area. There are thus doubts as to the exact location of the *Geldermalsen*. According to some accounts – see for example Garabello and Scovazzi (n. 17), at 23–24, following Hatcher's own account – the looting occurred on Admiral Stellingwerf Reef, off Bintan Island, near Singapore. This was confirmed by one of the controversial purchasers at Christie's, namely, the British Museum, as can be seen on the webpage for the collection at: <https://www.britishmuseum.org/collection/term/x21663>.

231 20 October 1989 (available at: <http://www.china.org.cn/english/zhuanti/3represents/76269.htm>), based on the *1982 Law of the People's Republic of China on the Protection of Cultural Relics*, 19 November 1982 (available at: <http://www.china.org.cn/english/environment/34304.htm>). On China's legislation, see in particular Jing (n. 228) and R. Chai and H. Li, 'A Study on Legislation for Protection of Cultural Relics in China: Origin, Content and Model' (2019) 8 *Chinese Studies* 132–147.

232 Defined in the Regulations as human cultural heritage of historic, artistic, and scientific value, but excluding objects that have remained underwater since 1911 and have nothing to do with important historical events, revolutionary movements, or renowned personages. The Xinhai Revolution in 1911 – which ended the Qing Dynasty – marked the beginning of China's republican era.

under the jurisdiction of a certain country, or in the high seas.[233] Therefore, all underwater cultural heritage located in waters under China's sovereignty or jurisdiction belong to the State, which shall exercise jurisdiction over them.[234] This somewhat exorbitant approach is not unusual: as already discussed, other States – including SCS riparian States[235] – also try to protect their underwater cultural heritage beyond the outer limits of their sovereign waters. But China seems to accept it both ways. As has been noted elsewhere:

> It may seem that the [1989] Regulations have been drafted toward protecting Chinese underwater cultural heritage in every possible zone even if under those premises it relinquishes ownership or jurisdiction over foreign vessels located in China's contiguous zone, continental shelf, and EEZ. China prefers to protect its own cultural heritage than claim jurisdiction over others. This approach follows China's current nationalistic approach to the preservation of cultural heritage.[236]

The 1989 Regulations also provide for the establishment of protective zones and the prevention of threatening activities directed at underwater cultural

233 This may create not only an impossible task – even for a powerful State such as China – but also a complex legal situation. A vast amount of Chinese porcelain, for example, was legally sold or bartered a long time ago and loaded, among others, onto Spanish Manila Galleon trading vessels (some of which sunk in international or third-State waters, such as the *San Felipe* in Japan in 1596, the *Santo Cristo* in the US in 1653, or the *San Cristóbal* in the Philippines in 1798), Portuguese eastern trading-route vessels (e.g. the *Espadarte*, lost in Mozambican waters in 1558), or vessels sailing for the various European commercial East companies (such as the *Mauritius*, sunk off the shore of Gabon in 1609, the *Götheborg*, sunk in Swedish waters in 1745, the *Prince de Conty*, wrecked in French waters in 1746, or the *Griffin*, lost in Philippine waters in 1761, among many others). For some authors, this Chinese heritage "outside the Chinese territory was not preserved under the national UCH protection system". L. Liu and S. Liu, 'From difference to convergence: A comparative analysis of the development of the legal protection of the underwater cultural heritage in China and the 2001 Convention' (2013) 52(167) *Poredbeno pomorsko pravo* 149–165, at 153 (available at: <https://hrcak.srce.hr/file/172531>).

234 "Under the Chinese regime, any archaeological exploration or excavation in waters under Chinese jurisdiction has to be authorized. China has, using its significant maritime forces, enforce[d] these laws within these zones. As such, all excavations, other than official Chinese investigations, are 'unauthorized' and 'illegal'". E. Pérez-Álvaro, *Underwater Cultural Heritage: Ethical Concepts and Practical Challenges* (Routledge: London/New York, 2019), at 205.

235 See Nitiruchirot (n. 204), at 261–263.

236 Pérez-Álvaro and Forrest (n. 228), at 393. For these authors, this Chinese-only protective system is detrimental for other underwater cultural heritage found in waters under China's sovereignty or jurisdiction, including some SCS waters (ibid.).

heritage (Article 5); establish a reporting system for finds (Article 6); try to harmonise other maritime activities with the preservation of underwater cultural heritage, for instance, by means of salvage law (Article 9);[237] and establish a system of rewards and penalties (Article 10).

Despite centralising the competent authority for underwater cultural heritage management in the State Administration of Cultural Heritage (SACH), Article 4 also tasks the cultural heritage departments at various local levels in their respective administrative regions to, "in conjunction with the archaeological and research institutions for cultural relics, be in charge of the work to identify and assess the value of underwater cultural relics. With respect to underwater cultural relics in sea waters, the State Administration of Cultural Heritage may designate local administrative departments of cultural heritage to take charge of the management and protection of underwater cultural relics."[238]

Other legislation aims to round out the 1989 Regulations – considered rather incomplete by some Chinese commentators[239] – such as the *Measures for the administration of foreign-related archaeology activities*, revised in 2016, which regulate archaeological investigation, exploration, and excavation (including underwater) and related studies, scientific and technological protection, and other activities conducted by the relevant Chinese units in collaboration with foreign or international organisations and establish that any foreign or

237 It is worth mentioning that, in accordance with the provisions of Art. 30(1)(d) of the 1989 Salvage Convention, China reserved the right not to apply the provisions of the Convention to the "maritime cultural property of prehistoric, archaeological or historic interest and situated on the sea-bed" (source: <https://www.imo.org/>). In accordance with its *1984 Marine Traffic Safety Law*, China indirectly subjects the issuance of any salvage or removal permit to the competent authorities (Art. 41), which implicitly positions this responsibility with the State Administration of Cultural Heritage, creating a competing jurisdiction with the Harbour Administration, among other authorities (see Jing (n. 228), at 760).

238 Since the enactment of the 1989 Regulations, several provinces have promulgated or revised local regulations to adapt them to the protection of underwater cultural heritage in their territories. In 2006, Zhejiang Province enacted its *Measures of Cultural Relics Protection*, including underwater cultural heritage in Art. 29. In 2009, Fujian Province revised its former *Protection and Administration of Cultural Relics Regulations*, adding a new chapter on underwater cultural heritage. The same year, Guangdong Province enacted the Guangdong provincial measure for implementation of the 1989 Regulations, Art. 26 of which provides for the establishment of new "underwater cultural relics reserves" along its coastline. See Jing (n. 228), at 760–761; and Liu and Liu (n. 233), at 151.

239 Liu and Liu (n. 233), at 154; and Jing (n. 228), at 758. Quite significantly, in February 2018, the SACH released a draft amendment to the Protection Law to replace the previous Regulations in order to align them with the 2001 UNESCO Convention.

international organisation intending to conduct any of those activities must undertake it in collaboration with China (Article 3).[240]

These pieces of legislation are accompanied by administrative and enforcement measures. Under the former, several initiatives, activities, and structural improvements have been implemented.[241] In the 1980s, China began to reshape its underwater cultural heritage infrastructure. In 1987, the Centre for Underwater Archaeology was established within the National Museum of China at Beijing, and in 1989 the first underwater cultural heritage survey was conducted. It was followed by successive prospections and excavations, resulting in the recovery of a large number of cultural objects that have fuelled the construction of new museums since 2007.[242] That same year, excavations were conducted in the Paracel Islands. In 2009, the SACH established the National Conservation Centre for Underwater Cultural Heritage, which has been the administrative body of the National Conciliation Commission for Underwater Cultural Heritage Conservation and the core coordination and implementation department for national underwater cultural heritage conservation work ever since. In 2010, China became one of five States (together with the US, Russia, Japan, and France) to register a manned submersible capable of descending 1,000 m; in 2012, it added another (the *Jiaolong-01*), capable of descending to 7,000 m; in 2014, it launched the 950-tonne, 56-meter-long *Kaougu-01*, its first archaeological vessel; and the 11th Five-Year Plan for National Cultural Relics (2006–2010) included "the establishment of a conservation and research centre for underwater cultural heritage in the South China Sea, and the establishment of a forum for underwater archaeology on the Xisha [Paracel] Islands".[243] With this extensive apparatus, China has performed numerous underwater archaeological prospections and excavations in continental, coastal, and maritime

240 Jing (n. 228), at 759.

241 Sources detailing these developments are mostly in Chinese. This work must thus rely on the secondary sources cited in this section and its footnotes. See also A. S. Erickson and K. Bond, 'Archaeology and the South China Sea: A new maritime archaeology vessel is another component in China's strategy for the South China Sea', 20 July 2015, *The Diplomat* at: <https://thediplomat.com/2015/07/archaeology-and-the-south-china-sea/>.

242 In 2009, two new museums were opened: the Maritime Silk Road Museum in Guangdong (source: <https://www.msrmuseum.com/Home/Enindex>) and the White Crane (*Baiheliang*) Underwater Museum in Chong Qing, under the waters of the Yangtze River (source: <http://www.unesco.org/new/en/culture/themes/underwater-cultural-heritage/about-the-heritage/underwater-museums/the-baiheliang-underwater-museum/>).

243 Jing (n. 228), at 761. These are supposed to be the National Underwater Cultural Heritage Protection South China Sea Base, likely to be located in Hainan, and the Work Station on Yongxing (Woody) Island. Some information from SACH can be found at: <http://english.cach.org.cn/col/col1581/index.html>.

waters, including those of the SCS, such as those of the *Nanhai-I*, found in 1989, or the *Nan'ao-I*, during the 2009–2012 archaeological campaign. Thousands of objects – all allegedly of Chinese origin – have thus been recovered under the last three consecutive Five-Year Plans for National Cultural Relics (2006–2020), especially in the campaigns off the Spratly and Paracel Islands[244] and through the launch of the 'Maritime Silk Road Initiative' as another building block for the 'Silk Road Economic Belt'.[245]

These administrative initiatives have been accompanied by China's growing assertiveness, embodied in different enforcement actions[246] and public declarations.[247] In addition to other non-archaeological activities in disputed

---

244 As stated by the Institute of Archaeology of the Chinese Academy of Social Sciences in relation to new discoveries, in 2014, in the Paracel Islands, the Chinese archaeological teams "will continue to safeguard the relics from damage and theft. China is planning to step up efforts to safeguard its coastline, from the Bohai Sea in the North, to seas around the Xisha and Nansha Islands in the South" (source: <http://www.kaogu.cn/en/News/New_discoveries/2013/1026/43034.html>).

245 See R. Guo, 'China's Maritime Silk Road Initiative and the Protection of Underwater Cultural Heritage' (2017) 32 *The International Journal of Marine and Coastal Law* 510–543; and Y.-C. Chang, 'The "21st Century Maritime Silk Road Initiative" and naval diplomacy in China' (2018) 153 *Ocean & Coastal Management* 148–156. On 'Belt and Road' initiative in general, see M. A. Carrai, J. C. Defraigne and J. Wouters (eds), *The Belt and Road Initiative and Global Governance* (Edward Elgar: Cheltenham, 2020). This initiative has been accompanied by cooperative surveys with interested States such as Kenya in 2010 (Liu and Liu (n. 233), at 154) and the signing of bilateral agreements, for example, with Vietnam in 2013 (Zhong (n. 228), at 373) or Saudi Arabia in 2016, to carry out underwater cultural heritage projects (Zhong (n. 204), at 92).

246 For a low-profile use of force – that of the so-called 'Chinese Maritime Militia' – raising interesting legal questions under the law of international responsibility of States (particularly the question of the attribution of wrongful acts), see J. Kraska and M. Monti, 'The Law of Naval Warfare and China's Maritime Militia' (2015) 91 *International Law Studies* 451–467; J. Chock, 'China's Non-Military Maritime Assets as a Force Multiplier for Security' (2015) 322 *Asia Pacific Bulletin* (at: <https://www.eastwestcenter.org/publications/china's-non-military-maritime-assets-force-multiplier-security>); and, more recently, N. C. Manullang, A. G. Siswandi and C. T. I. Dewi, 'The Status of Maritime Militia in the South China Sea Under International Law Perspective' (2020) 27 *JH Ius Quia Iustum* 23–44 (at: <https://journal.uii.ac.id/IUSTUM/article/view/14958>); and K. Sato, 'China's Maritime Militia: A Legal Point of View', *Maritime Issues*, 12 March 2020 (at: <http://www.maritimeissues.com/politics/maritime-militia-in-east-and-south-china-seas.html>). Quite recently, Chinese assertiveness with these kinds of fishing 'flotillas' in the Spratly Islands was denounced by the Philippine government. See 'Philippines asks Chinese flotilla to leave disputed reef', *DW*, 21 March 2021, at: <https://www.dw.com/en/philippines-asks-chinese-flotilla-to-leave-disputed-reef/a-56943127>.

247 This notwithstanding the confidence-building process initiated between China and the ASEAN members, which eventually led to the signing of the 'Declaration on the Conduct of Parties in the South China Sea', 4 November 2002 (available at: <https://asean.org/?static_post=declaration-on-the-conduct-of-parties-in-the-south-china-sea-2>).

SCS waters,[248] the former include an incident in the Scarborough Shoal – off the coast of the Philippines but claimed by China – that occurred in 2013 when a French-Philippine archaeological team was expelled from the area by force. According to the accounts,[249] Shuguang Liu, head of China's Centre for Underwater Cultural Heritage, said that the foreign team intended "[t]o drag away this shipwreck [...] Because this was material evidence that Chinese people first found the Scarborough Shoal, they wanted to destroy evidence that was beneficial to China."[250]

When first announcing the finding of the *Nan'ao-I* wreck in June 2011, Mr Liu said, "We want to find more evidence that can prove Chinese people went there and lived there, historical evidence that can help prove China is the sovereign owner of the South China Sea."[251] In September 2012, whilst examining porcelain retrieved from a wreck off the Paracels, Chinese Vice Minister of Culture Li Xiaojie was quoted as saying that "[m]arine archaeology is an exercise that demonstrates national sovereignty".[252] If the latter is debatably true, could China prove the former?

248 See, for example, A. Panda, 'China's HD-981 Oil Rig Returns, Near Disputed South China Sea Waters', *The Diplomat*, 27 June 2015, at: <https://thediplomat.com/2015/06/chinas-hd-981-oil-rig-returns-to-disputed-south-china-sea-waters/>.

249 J. Page, 'Chinese Territorial Strife Hits Archaeology', *The Wall Street Journal*, 2 December 2013, at: <https://www.wsj.com/articles/SB10001424052702304470504579164873258159410>. It is worth mentioning that previously, on 8 April 2012, eight Chinese fishing vessels were apprehended by the Philippine authorities in the Scarborough Shoal (source: <http://www.chinadaily.com.cn/world/huangyan/index.html>).

250 In an article he wrote with a highly regarded Chinese academic, this idea was repeated in relation to another disputed scenario: "In April 2011 the Chinese authorities investigated UCH in the Paracel Islands and reported that 26 UCH sites (more than 50% of the UCH sites in the Paracel Islands) had been illegally destroyed and excavated. What is worse, there is a reasonable suspicion that some neighboring countries deliberately damaged Chinese UCH in the South China Sea. For instance, a Ming-dynasty shipwreck located near Huangyan (Scarborough Shoal) was commercially excavated and destroyed by two 2000 ton foreign vessels" (Liu and Liu (n. 233), at 153).

251 Quoted by Zhong (n. 228), at 369. For this author, however, "the presence of a Chinese sunken vessel does not justify China's maritime or territorial claims [but] other claimant states may still be concerned by China's actions in maritime archaeology" (ibid.).

252 'Interview with Li Xiaojie: Underwater Archaeology in the South China Sea can demonstrate sovereignty', *Ifeng*, 22 June 2015, at: <http://finance.ifeng.com/a/20150606/13759861_0.shtml>. See also Page (n. 249) and P. B. Campbell, 'Could Shipwrecks Lead the World to War?', *The New York Times*, 18 December 2015, at: <https://www.nytimes.com/2015/12/19/opinion/could-shipwrecks-lead-the-world-to-war.html>. However, one Chinese academic, has played down the political and legal relevance of these statements (Zhong (n. 228), at 369–370).

As a matter of *fact*, most sinologists and maritime historians agree that China's limited presence in the SCS does not evidence a continuous display of sovereignty over the disputed waters and some of their maritime features.[253] Up to the Song dynasty (960–1279), most naval activities were coastal and aimed at repressing piracy. Maritime trade was essentially left in the hands (and aboard the *dhows*) of Arab, Indian, and Persian merchants. Only after 1090, with the liberalisation of Chinese shipping, was the emergence of a large class of 'ethnic' Chinese merchants possible.[254] Sailors initially preferred to hug the shores, and did not undertake sea expeditions – including the Mongol attempts to attack Japan, Korea, or the Kurile Islands – until the 12th–15th centuries. However, during these periods, a trade ban (*haijin*) was also imposed for several decades.[255] Southern China developed more intensively than northern areas, which were constantly threatened by enemies and politically unstable, and new coastal areas and city ports, such as Yangzhou, Quanzhou, Mingzhou, or Guangdong, flourished. Technological innovations – to some extent a by-product of the Chinese *renaissance*, which predated Europe's – affecting not only river, but also sea navigation, such as the use of compasses and new naval engineering,[256] also fuelled China's new approach

253 See, in general, H. R. Clark, 'Frontier Discourse and China's Maritime Frontier: China's Frontiers and the Encounter with the Sea through Early Imperial History' (2009) 20 *Journal of World History* 1–33; J. Lo, *China as a Sea Power, 1127–1368: A Preliminary Survey of the Maritime Expansion and Naval Exploits of the Chinese People During the Southern Song and Yuan Periods*, ed. by B. A. Elleman (National University of Singapore Press: Singapore, 2011); A. Schottenhammer, 'China's Rise and Retreat as a Maritime Power', in: R. Antony and A. Schottenhammer (eds), *New Discourses on China's Role in East Asian Maritime History* (Otto Harrassowitz: Wiesbaden, 2017), 189–211; and D. Abulafia, *The Boundless Sea: A Human History of the Oceans* (Penguin/Allen Lane: London, 2019), 235–271. See also *Critical Study* (n. 210), at 455–461, paras. 514–516.

254 Here the term 'native Chinese' should be understood in a broad sense. Abulafia (n. 253), at 242. Previously, in 971, under the early Song Dynasty, the Maritime Trade Office in Canton was established.

255 See also Abulafia (n. 253), at 257. These trade-ban periods produced and largely expanded illegal maritime commerce, i.e. "what officials treated as piracy or smuggling". Schottenhammer (n. 253), at 202.

256 "The Song dynasty made technological advances in printing and paper-making, in ceramics and silk-weaving, in the use of the magnetic compass in navigation and gunpowder and firearms in war, in geographical and astronomical lore, in mathematics and engineering, in the building of ships and the building of canals, in botany and agriculture. The Song court encouraged technological developments by giving rewards to inventors of weapons and designers of ships, cash for commoners and gifts and promotions for officials." Lo (n. 253), at 84–85. See also C. A. Ronan, *The Shorter Science and Civilization in China*, vol. 3 (Cambridge University Press: Cambridge, 1986), part of the abridged version of Joseph Needham's monumental work on science and civilisation in China.

to the sea aboard big junks but also smaller sampans and supply and lighter boats. However, Confucian ideas blended with Mongol ones to shape China's maritime activities: trade was considered a second-class activity,[257] albeit one that brought to the mainland both luxury products for the Court and more popular commodities, all subject to a lucrative taxation system supervised by the rulers:

> Maritime trade not only supplied the social and ruling élites with fine and rare luxury articles that were otherwise unavailable in China, but also served as a source of income to fill the state coffers. By *political* decision, maritime space became more and more important primarily for *commercial* purposes.[258]

The system operated on a tribute-for-gift system, based on the 'Mandate from Heaven' imposing a sort of long-distance suzerainty on the neighbouring 'barbaric' peoples.[259] But, crucially for this book's purposes, this claim of 'superiority' was a display of non-territorial authority. This was particularly important in the period of China's strongest presence at sea during the Ming Dynasty (1368–1644), when it became a self-confident, self-sufficient, and self-contained political and commercial power.

The fifteenth century witnessed the fabulous rise, maturation, and decline of the Emperor Yong-le's and his admiral Zheng He's plan for Chinese maritime presence.[260] The latter, a eunuch of Muslim origin in the Ming Court, was more an organiser than a sailor, but he was able to send out and command

---

257 In contrast with Buddhism, which even promoted trade, Chinese court officials "who were influenced by Confucian teachings did not pay much attention to commerce or rather considered it an immoral pursuit of private enrichment". Schottenhammer (n. 253), at 190. However, that did not impede the rise – initiated during the Song dynasty – of a merchant class: "The growing interest of the scholars and officials in practical affairs such as economics and technology, the reliance of the government upon merchants for funds and services, and the development of money and banking, manufacture, and trade, all contributed to the elevation of merchants in China." Lo (n. 253), at 97–98.

258 Schottenhammer (n. 253), at 195.

259 See further W. Yuan-kang, 'Managing Regional Hegemony in Historical Asia: The Case of Early Ming China' (2012) 5 *The Chinese Journal of International Politics* 129–153. For the previous period, see, for example, D. Heng, *Sino–Malay Trade and Diplomacy from the Tenth through the Fourteenth Century* (Ohio University Press: Athens, 2009).

260 "Although much of the information that we encounter in the sources may be exaggerated (definite archaeological evidence is lacking until today), it is clear that never before both the China Seas and the Indian Ocean had seen any naval manoeuvre of similar scope and dimensions. During these few decades in the early fifteenth century, as stated earlier, China was *the* unchallenged maritime power in the world." Schottenhammer (n. 253), at 203.

eight fleets between 1405 and 1433.[261] This has been regarded as the splendour of Chinese naval power and maritime presence, which could provide proof of some of its maritime claims, including those in the SCS. However, neither spatially (the *where*) nor politically (the *why*) do Zheng He's fantastic fleets' voyages support this current politicised view. Where did the fleets mainly sail to or visit? Melaka and Calicut in the first voyage; Java and Siam in the second; Ceylon in the third; again to Melaka, the south of India, and Hormuz and the Persian/Arab Gulf in the fourth; Yemen, Somalia, and Kenya in the fifth; Aden and Calicut in the sixth; Palembang in the seventh, following a loss of interest in these voyages at court; and Java, Sumatra, Melaka, and Bengal in the eighth and final voyage, before Emperor Hong-xi abolished these expeditions. It was an impressive set of routes, until China once again "looked away from the sea".[262] No significant records exist, in the chronicles of Marco Polo or Ibn Battuta, of such visits to the SCS.[263] All the Chinese fleets were headed to the 'Western Ocean' – i.e. the Indian Ocean – with legs of the journeys north to the Persian/Arab Gulf and south to the East African coast down to Madagascar and Zanzibar.

The reasons for this naval effort are still disputed.[264] But as one specialist on Chinese maritime history has warned:

> it is incorrect to consider these expeditions as *colonialist* undertakings in the sense of European colonialism. The politico-economic quality behind these expeditions – as violent as they were at times – was decisively different from what we know as colonialism. Very different from the imperialist European powers, the Ming court did not consider the

261 See, among others, L. Levathes, *When China Ruled the Seas: The Treasure Fleet of the Dragon Throne, 1405–33*, (Oxford University Press: New York, 1994); Y. Liu, C. Zhongping and G. Blue (eds), *Zheng He's Maritime Voyages (1405–1433) and China's Relations with the Indian Ocean World: A Multilingual Bibliography* (Brill: Leiden, 2014); and S. Ward, 'Chinese Whispers: Zheng He's Treasure Ships in the Context of Chinese Maritime Policy in the Ming Dynasty (1368–1644)', in: A. Tripathi (ed.), *Maritime Heritage of Indian Ocean: Proceedings of the International Seminar on Maritime Archaeology 2007* (Sharada Publishing House: Delhi, 2013), 215–229. See also Abulafia (n. 253), at 260–267.

262 Abulafia (n. 253), at 270.

263 Although it was often peacefully sailed for other purposes by Chinese, as well as Korean, Vietnamese, Philippine, and Japanese vessels.

264 See Abulafia (n. 253), at 256–260, and, for the early origins, Lo (n. 253), at 93–126. In general terms, it has been plausibly argued that China's presence at and retreat from the sea "cannot be satisfactorily understood (1) without simultaneously considering both her continental and maritime development and her 'world-historical' integration; and (2) without carefully analysing the specific relationships between politics (including military) and commerce, as well as official and private aspects." Schottenhammer (n. 253), at 192.

> exploitation of foreign wealth as a means of national enrichment, seeking to establish politico-economic circumstances and relations in foreign countries that through *exclusive* exploitation, through the removal of natural or human resources would transfer these into their own domestic value production, as was the case with European colonialist and imperialist countries. The politico-economic motivation and contents of Ming China's violent expansions [were] decisively different in quality from [those] of the European colonialists.[265]

Interestingly enough, as David Abulafia notes, this position does not seem to be held solely by Western (or non-Chinese) academics:

> Modern Chinese historians like to insist that there was a great difference between Zheng He's voyages and those of the Portuguese and Spaniards (which were just beginning in the 1420s and 1430s, in the case of Portugal): the Iberian voyages aimed to conquer territory, if need be by force, and to impose trade networks under their exclusive control, whereas the Ming voyages were by and large peaceful – allowing for the eradication of pirates – and aimed to show the flag rather than to create colonies.[266]

After the mid-fifteenth century, China was absent – other than in coastal zones – from today's disputed waters. European conquests (Spain in the Philippines or Taiwan, Portugal in Indian ports) and trade expansions (by the various commercial companies) closed certain maritime routes to China, leading to its disappearance from those waters.[267] Although by 1759 China had expanded to include more territory than ever before, its presence at sea had all but vanished, and nothing indicates that it continued – or even sought – to exert jurisdictional powers over the neighbouring seas. However, as with its presence, China withdrew of its own volition, not forced by external imposition (at least until the protectorate and opium war eras of the nineteenth century).[268] In the wake of the Second World War, China was considered a great power with a reserved seat on the UN Security Council, and the Maoist

265 Schottenhammer (n. 253), at 204.

266 Abulafia (n. 253), at 270.

267 The various bans on shipyards for building vessels with more than two masts (*haijin* edicts in the 1550s) and the limits on external trade and 'evacuations' of populations from the coasts to inland areas during the 1660s must also be taken into account.

268 This does not translate to a denial of China's fishing presence in the South China Sea, irrespective of its probatory force as an *effectivité*. As the Arbitral Tribunal plainly said, "Chinese fisherman have long made use of the waters of the South China Sea, including in areas beyond the territorial sea of any feature." *2016 SCS Award*, para. 257.

revolution reaffirmed its policy, but only since the 1980s, China has clearly reversed its weak maritime position and vigorously returned to the sea.[269]

As a matter of *law*, we have already seen how current international law – as interpreted and applied by international courts, especially the ICJ – does not give much importance to archaeological activities and the resulting finds as evidence of *effectivités*.[270] To be considered "as constituting a relevant display of authority" the finds would have to "leave no doubt as to their specific reference to the islands in dispute as such".[271] Hence, both relevance and certainty are needed to transform shipwrecks and their cargo into evidence of a continued display of authority over the disputed SCS islands. And if history is not particularly helpful to China in support of its maritime claims, neither are other legal arguments. As the 2016 *South China Sea Award* said, when China ratified the LOSC it relinquished any previous historical rights it might have had, except for those expressly provided for in the 1982 Convention. According to the arbitrators,

> Accession to the Convention reflects a commitment to bring incompatible claims into alignment with its provisions, and its continued operation necessarily calls for compromise by those States with prior claims in excess of the Convention's limits.[272]

Granted, the *Award* only refers to the living and non-living resources within the 'nine-dash line' map[273] and underwater cultural heritage cannot be considered a 'resource' under LOSC.[274] Yet China's archaeological evidence cannot be legally asserted under other international legal regimes either, for example, that of

---

269 For a brief overview see, for example, W. Xiaoyan, 'China's "Sea Power Nation" Strategy', Institute for Security and Development Policy (2014) (available at: <https://isdp.eu/content/uploads/images/stories/isdp-main-pdf/2014-wu-chinas-sea-power-nation-strategy.pdf>). See also Z. Wei and S. Ahmed, 'A General Review of the History of China's Sea-Power Theory Development' (2015) 68 *Naval War College Review* 80–93 (available at: <https://digital-commons.usnwc.edu/nwc-review/vol68/iss4/8>); or E. S. Y. Chan, 'Rethinking uniqueness of China's sea power development' (2020) 12 *Australian Journal of Maritime & Ocean Affairs* 269–275.

270 On *effectivités*, see n. 225 above and accompanying text.

271 *Sovereignty over Pulau Ligitan and Pulau Sipadan (Indonesia/Malaysia)*, Judgment, *ICJ Reports* 2002, 625, at 683, para. 136. In this case, the ICJ was unmoved by many of the examples of naval activities as proof of claims of sovereignty.

272 *2016 SCS Award*, at 111, para. 262.

273 This point is criticised in the Chinese *Critical Study*: "As a matter of fact, China's historic rights in the South China Sea have a scope much greater than those to the living and non-living resources, and the bases for China's historic rights include much more than navigation and fishing activities." *Critical Study*, at 455, para. 512.

274 See above, n. 22.

the 1972 World Heritage Convention. In 2014, the 'Silk Road' was designated a World Heritage Site by UNESCO.[275] Adding the maritime routes to this World Heritage Site would undoubtedly help to provide a more complete picture of this fascinating trade network; however, it would also include disputed waters and islands in the SCS. Should the inscription be submitted, Article 11(3) of the World Heritage Convention expressly warns: "The inclusion of a property situated in a territory, sovereignty or jurisdiction over which is claimed by more than one State shall in no way prejudice the rights of the parties to the dispute." Finally, if China decides to ratify the 2001 UNESCO Convention,[276] its neutral approach to jurisdiction would not help its maritime claims based on underwater archaeological activities and the resulting finds. As already noted, under Article 2(11) of the Convention, "[n]o act or activity undertaken on the basis of this Convention shall constitute grounds for claiming, contending or disputing any claim to national sovereignty or jurisdiction"; whilst Article 10(6) affirms that any decision taken by the coordinating State – as China could be – for activities in the EEZ or on the continental shelf in accordance with the Convention "shall not in itself constitute a basis for the assertion of any preferential or jurisdictional rights not provided for in international law, including the United Nations Convention on the Law of the Sea". Meanwhile, given that China voted in favour of the Convention when it was adopted at UNESCO in 2001 and has not expressed an intention not to become a party to the Convention, it could be argued that China be abide by the interim obligation to refrain from acts that would defeat its object and purpose (Article 18 VCLT).[277] To use underwater archaeological activities as grounds for maritime claims or to impede cooperation with other interested States in activities directed at that heritage and its long-term preservation could be seen as an infringement of that *mild* obligation.

As a matter of *provisional conclusion*, China's claims in the SCS may be as legitimate as those of its neighbours. However, for now, the historical evidence advanced to support them is not enough to sustain an international legal claim. If China contends that underwater cultural heritage located in the disputed waters – wrecks, porcelain, copper, ceramic jars, and other cargoes – is of undisputedly Chinese origin, it must be corroborated by peer-reviewed scientific assessment, preferably through a collaborative regional or international approach and joint archaeological activities, as provided for and encouraged

---

275 'Silk Roads: the Routes Network of Chang'an-Tianshan Corridor', submitted by China, Kazakhstan, and Kyrgyzstan (source: <http://whc.unesco.org/en/list/1442>).

276 Most, if not all, Chinese commentators quoted in this chapter agree on the advisability of ratifying the Convention to reinforce China's policy on the international protection of underwater cultural heritage, particularly with regard to the possibility of regional cooperation in the SCS.

277 See above n. 149.

under the 2001 UNESCO Convention. China may decide to opt in and cooperate with its neighbouring States in the SCS under the Convention system. This would depoliticise any archaeological activities in the disputed waters, increase the certainty of any archaeological finds, and enable joint training of specialists from China and elsewhere. But it would also curtail the possible use of underwater cultural heritage activities to claim, contend, or dispute any entitlement to national sovereignty or jurisdiction in the SCS.

3.2.2.3 *Russia and Crimea*

Unlike in the previous two cases, in which underwater cultural heritage is used to support the basis for a maritime claim, in the case of Crimea, the problem is the alleged destruction of such heritage to support the Russian territorial claim. The case also differs in how these activities are performed: peacefully in the Canadian case; with limited (albeit not negligible) enforcement measures in the case of China; and with the use of force and the illegal occupation of a territory in the case of Russia, an occupation that persists today.[278] That makes this case particularly sensitive and legally complex since other corpuses of international law also apply (namely, human rights law[279] and the law of armed conflicts[280]), in addition to the law of the sea, the law of cultural

278 An account of these facts and legal consequences is provided in W. Czapliński, S. Dębski, R. Tarnogórski and K. Wierczyńska (eds), *The Case of Crimea's Annexation under International Law* (Scholar Publishing House and Centre for Polish-Russian Dialogue and Understanding: Warsaw, 2017); S. Sayapin and E. Tsybulenko, *The Use of Force against Ukraine and International Law: Jus Ad Bellum, Jus In Bello, Jus Post Bellum* (T.M.C. Asser Press: The Hague, 2018); O. Corten, 'The Russian intervention in the Ukrainian crisis: was *jus contra bellum* "confirmed rather than weakened"?' (2015) 2(1) *Journal on the Use of Force and International Law* 17–41; or T. Christakis, 'Les conflits de la sécession en Crimée et dans l'est de l'Ukraine et le droit international' (2014) 141(3) *Journal du droit international* 733–764.

279 Quite recently, in the *Ukraine v. Russia* (*re Crimea*) case, the Grand Chamber of the European Court of Human Rights (ECHR) did not enter into the question of sovereignty but, applying its *Loizidou* doctrine *mutatis mutandis*, determined that the territory of Crimea was under the effective control of Russia, even before the occupation (Judgment on Admissibility, 16 December 2020, Applications nos. 20958/14 and 38334/18, paras. 237–244 and 348–349). See L. A. Sicilianos, 'L'Articulation entre droit international humanitaire et droits de l'homme dans la jurisprudence de la Cour européenne des droits de l'homme' (2017) 27(1) *Swiss Review of International and European Law* 3–17.

280 The International Criminal Court (ICC) Prosecutor has concluded "that there is a reasonable basis at this time to believe that a broad range of conduct constituting war crimes and crimes against humanity within the jurisdiction of the Court have been committed in the context of the situation in Ukraine". (Source: <https://www.icc-cpi.int/Pages/item.aspx?name=201211-otp-statement-ukraine>). See also the ICC 'Report on Preliminary Examination Activities 2020', 14 December 2020 (at: <https://www.icc-cpi.int/itemsDocuments/2020-PE/2020-pe-report-eng.pdf>).

heritage, and general international rules on the acquisition of territory. A territory – Crimea – it is worth noting, with its own set of historical, political, and sociological complexities.

At a crossroads (land and maritime) between the 'classical world' and Asia, between the northern Slavic and Muslim worlds, Crimea was united in a 'Khanate' from the 15th to the 18th century. As a result of the Russo-Turkish War (1768–1774), Crimea was annexed by the Russian Empire in 1783. An autonomous republic within the USSR after the Russian revolution, Crimea became an 'Oblast' during the Second World War but, in its aftermath, most of its Tatar population was deported to central Asia (allegedly because of its support for Nazi Germany) and the territory was ultimately transferred to the Ukrainian SSR from the Russian SSR in 1954.

Ukraine became an independent State in 1991, following the collapse of the Soviet Union, and Crimea was recognised as an Autonomous Republic within the new State. Russia maintained different lease rights on the naval facilities at the port of Sevastopol.[281] In 2003, Russia and Ukraine signed a cooperation agreement on the use of the Sea of Azov and the Strait of Kerch,[282] accompanied by a Joint Statement claiming that "historically the Sea of Azov and the Strait of Kerch are internal waters of Ukraine and Russia".[283]

281 Granted by the 1997 Partition Treaties on the Status and Conditions of the Black Sea Fleet (three treaties signed on 28 May 1997, no official English translation text available) and the 2010 Agreement between Ukraine and Russia on the Black Sea Fleet in Ukraine ('Kharkiv Pact', signed 21 April 2010, no official English translation text available). None of the agreements appears to have been registered in accordance with Art. 102 of the UN Charter. Russia terminated these treaties on 31 March 2014. For more information, see: <https://www.loc.gov/law/foreign-news/article/russia-ukraine-legislature-adopts-law-on-dissolution-of-black-sea-fleet-treaties/>.

282 'Agreement between the Russian Federation and the Ukraine on cooperation in the use of the sea of Azov and the strait of Kerch', 24 December 2003, no UNTS registration. See A. Skaridov, 'The Sea of Azov and the Kerch Straits', in: D. D. Caron and N. Oral (eds), *Navigating Straits: Challenges for International Law* (Brill/Nijhoff: *The Hague*, 2014), 220–237; V. J. Schatz and D. Koval, 'Russia's Annexation of Crimea and the Passage of Ships Through Kerch Strait: A Law of the Sea Perspective' (2019) 50 *Ocean Development & International Law* 275–297; and N. Oral, '*Ukraine* v. *The Russian Federation*: Navigating Conflict over Sovereignty under UNCLOS' (2021) 97 *International Law Studies* 478–508. See also the blog Schatz and Koval keep on the whole case at *Völkerrechtsblog*, and the three detailed posts devoted to 'Ukraine v. Russia: Passage through Kerch Strait and the Sea of Azov' (source: <https://voelkerrechtsblog.org/symposium/russian-perspectives-on-international-law/>).

283 'Joint Statement by the President of Ukraine and the President of the Russian Federation on the Sea of Azov and the Strait of Kerch of 24 December 2003', (2004) 54 *Law of the Sea Bulletin*, at 131.

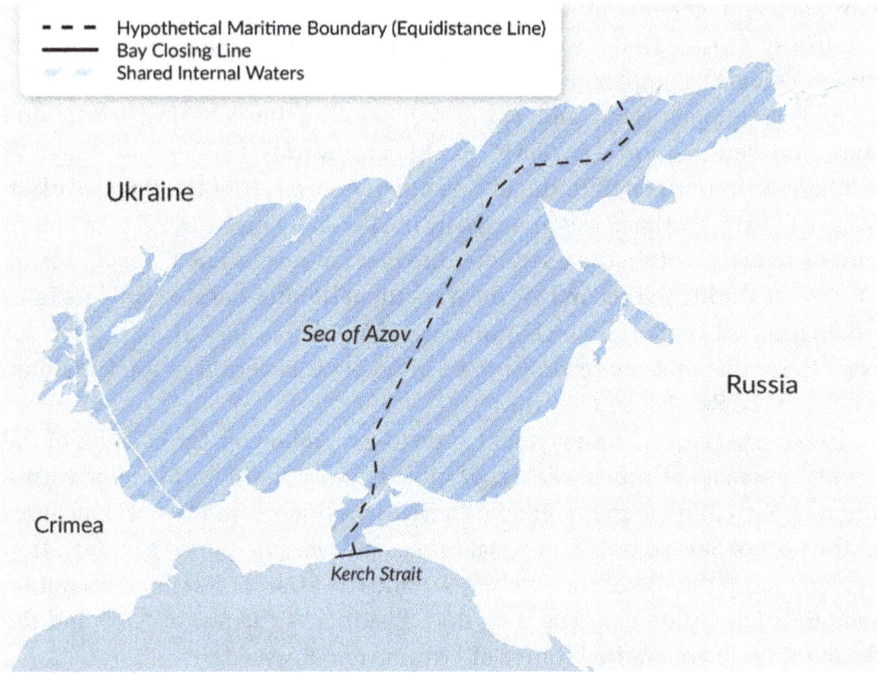

FIGURE 6 Sea of Azov (shared regime)
SOURCE: V. J. SCHATZ & D. KOVAL, 'RUSSIA'S ANNEXATION OF CRIMEA AND THE PASSAGE OF SHIPS THROUGH KERCH STRAIT: A LAW OF THE SEA PERSPECTIVE' (2019) 50 *OCEAN DEVELOPMENT & INTERNATIONAL LAW* 275–297, AT 281

However, in 2014, in the wake of the 'Euromaidan Revolution', Russia annexed Crimea by force after a contested referendum,[284] officially declaring it a federal unit on 18 March 2014. Since then, the government of Ukraine has denounced several decisions taken by the Russian authorities, including navigation incidents resulting in the detention of three Ukrainian vessels (involving two

284 Declared non-valid by UNGA Resolution 68/262, 27 March 2014, which also called upon States and other bodies not to recognise any alteration of the previous territorial status. The EU and the US, along with a clear majority of States, have not recognised Russian annexation. For the last EU declaration on the status of Crimea, see 'Declaration by the High Representative Josep Borrell Fontelles, on behalf of the European Union, on the Autonomous Republic of Crimea and the city of Sevastopol', Council of the EU Press release, 16 March 2020 (available at: <https://www.consilium.europa.eu/en/press/press-releases/2020/03/16/declaration-by-the-high-representative-josep-borrell-fontelles-on-behalf-of-the-european-union-on-the-autonomous-republic-of-crimea-and-the-city-of-sevastopol/>).

warships and their crews) in the Black Sea on 25 November 2018.[285] But the most important case began on 16 September 2016, when Ukraine served on the Russian Federation a Notification and Statement of Claim under Annex VII of the LOSC referring to a dispute concerning coastal State rights in the Black Sea, Sea of Azov, and Kerch Strait, which included arguments related to the preservation of the underwater cultural heritage located in disputed waters.[286] As of July 2021, the Arbitral Tribunal has only decided on jurisdictional issues, since Russia raised several preliminary objections, some upheld and others rejected, with still others being reserved for consideration and decision in the proceedings on the merits.[287] Russia's main objections were to sovereignty claims,[288] which the Court upheld "to the extent that a ruling of the Arbitral Tribunal on the merits of Ukraine's claims necessarily requires it to decide, directly or implicitly, on the sovereignty of either Party over Crimea."[289] As Ukraine's Memorial, submitted on 19 February 2018, has not been made public, a complete assessment of the claims is not possible. The Arbitral Tribunal decided that Ukraine will have "to file a revised version of its Memorial, which shall take full account of the scope of, and limits to, the Arbitral Tribunal's jurisdiction […]".[290] This deprived commentators of Ukraine's original arguments from its first Memorial,[291] although the various written statements by both parties and the text of the *Preliminary Award* made available by the PCA on its website shed some light on how underwater cultural heritage is used in the dispute.

In its Notification, Ukraine asked that:

285 This case was submitted by Ukraine to the ITLOS in April 2019, and the Tribunal ordered the immediate release of the vessels and crews in its Order of 25 May 2019 as a provisional measure. *Case concerning the detention of three Ukrainian naval vessels* (*Ukraine v. Russian Federation*), *Provisional Measures*, Order of 25 May 2019 *ITLOS Reports* 2019.

286 See Permanent Court of Arbitration (PCA), *Dispute concerning coastal state rights in the Black Sea, Sea of Azov, and Kerch Strait* (all cited documents available at: <https://pca-cpa.org/en/cases/149/>).

287 *Dispute Concerning Coastal State Rights in the Black Sea, Sea of Azov, and Kerch Strait* (*Ukraine/Russia*), Preliminary Objections, Award of 21 February 2020 (available at: <https://pcacases.com/web/sendAttach/9272>) (hereinafter, *Preliminary Award*).

288 For Russia, "the dispute with respect to sovereignty over land territory is central, is the real dispute, is where the relative weight of the dispute lies (and overwhelmingly so), and the determination of that dispute is the unavoidable prerequisite to addressing the specific claims". Preliminary Objections of the Russian Federation (vol. I), para. 42.

289 *Preliminary Award*, para. 492.

290 Ibid.

291 Hereinafter, *Ukr. Mem*; likewise, the Notification and Statement of Claim by Ukraine shall hereinafter be cited as *Ukr. Not.*

> The Russian Federation may not without Ukraine's consent and cooperation remove from the seabed or otherwise disrupt or disturb archaeological, historical, or cultural objects or heritage found in Ukraine's territorial sea and contiguous zone, including the sunken Byzantine ship located in the Black Sea near Sevastopol and any artifacts associated with it; any such activities engaged in or authorized by the Russian Federation in those areas are not compatible with [the LOSC] and constitute internationally wrongful acts for which the Russian Federation bears international responsibility.[292]

In its Memorial, Ukraine contended that Russia had breached several LOSC provisos, including Articles 2, 303, and 297, "by interfering with Ukraine's attempts to protect archaeological and historical objects in its territorial sea and by usurping Ukraine's right to regulate with regard to such archaeological and historical objects"; "by unlawfully interfering with Ukraine's exercise of jurisdiction in its contiguous zone and preventing the removal of archaeological and historical objects from the seabed of its contiguous zone"; "by failing to cooperate with Ukraine concerning archaeological and historical objects found at sea"; and by aggravating and extending the dispute between the parties since the arbitration had begun "by continuing to disturb and remove archaeological artifacts found in Ukraine's territorial sea and contiguous zone".[293] Ukraine thus asked the Tribunal to order Russia to:

> Share with Ukraine information on the location of all objects of an archaeological and historical nature that the Russian Federation or its licensees have discovered or surveyed in the seas within 24 nautical miles of Ukraine's declared baselines around the Crimean coast; restore to Ukraine all archaeological objects that it has removed from Ukraine's territorial sea and contiguous zone; and refrain from any future disturbance of, or licensing of third parties to disturb, any such objects found in Ukraine's territorial sea and contiguous zone.[294]

Russia replied to this point in relation to one of Ukraine's 'specific claims', arguing:

> Ukraine's starting point regarding its claim with respect to underwater cultural heritage (Memorial, paras. 218–239) is that "[the LOSC] accords

292 *Preliminary Award*, para. 9(j).
293 *Preliminary Award*, para. 17 (q)(r)(s) and (t).
294 Ibid., para. 18(d).

> Ukraine, *as coastal State*, specific rights with regard to UCH located in *its coastal waters* around Crimea, as well as imposing corresponding duties on the Russian Federation." [*Ukr. Mem.*, para. 219] Ukraine casts its claim with reference to Article 2 ("the sovereignty of a *coastal state*") [*Ukr. Mem.*, para. 265(q)] and also Article 303 (referring to the position of the *coastal State* with respect to controlling traffic in objects of an archaeological and historical nature found at sea). [*Ukr. Mem.*, para. 265 (r),(s)][295]

For Ukraine, "the real dispute before the Tribunal is at the heart of the Convention: the nullification of Ukraine's rights under the Convention, including in its territorial sea, exclusive economic zone, and continental shelf".[296] Russian conduct thus entailed breaches of the LOSC with "profound consequence for Ukraine", affecting, among other things, "the underwater cultural heritage of mankind".[297] In addition, when discussing the Arbitral Tribunal's jurisdiction, Ukraine recalled that:

> No one disputes that Ukraine wants Russia to cease its aggression against Ukraine and its illegal occupation of Ukrainian territory. But the only point in discussion before the Tribunal is that Ukraine also wants Russia, inter alia, to stop stealing its living and non-living maritime resources, to

295 Preliminary Objections of the Russian Federation (vol. 1), para. 42(d). In the original paragraph from the Russian objection, the original footnotes – with the emphasis added by Russia – were included in square brackets. For Russia, "In essence, the Tribunal would have to identify and resolve the overlapping entitlements by delimiting the maritime zones belonging to each Party in order then to rule on Ukraine's claims as to its rights relating to hydrocarbons, fisheries, and other natural resources, protection of the marine environment, and preservation of maritime archaeological objects and sites [...] Such rights are inextricably linked to delimitation: on the one hand, delimitation rules are rooted in maritime rights (in particular, rights over resources have played a crucial role in the development of the modern law of the sea); on the other hand, sea boundary delimitations determine both the respective maritime areas of the Parties and their rights deriving from them." Preliminary Objections of the Russian Federation (vol. 1), para. 168. See also ibid., para. 174.

Russian Federation further contended (ibid., para. 47(d)) – and Ukraine contested – that, because they were made (or escorted) by navy vessels, underwater archaeology activities were of a military nature (and thus outside the Arbitral Tribunal's jurisdiction). See Rejoinder of Ukraine on Jurisdiction, para. 116. This was rejected by the Tribunal: "The Arbitral Tribunal considers that the undertaking of archaeological expeditions by the Russian Federation's military (at least in some instances in cooperation with civilians) does not allow the Arbitral Tribunal to find that the dispute between the Parties regarding underwater cultural heritage concerns military activities." *Preliminary Award*, para. 340 (footnotes omitted).

296 Written Observations and Submissions of Ukraine on Jurisdiction, para. 4.

297 Ibid.

> stop disturbing its underwater cultural heritage, and to end its harassment of vessels *en route* to Ukrainian ports.[298]

The argument thus advanced by Ukraine was, basically, that Russia was disturbing, when not outright destroying, cultural heritage in which Ukraine has a legal interest if not a preferential right.[299] For Ukraine, this was one of the 'nullification' actions performed by Russia to erase any historical Ukrainian presence in Crimea and its surrounding waters, an action denounced by Ukrainian and independent media,[300] echoed by academics[301] and civil society,[302] and voiced by Ukraine before international institutions, particularly UNESCO.

Hence, on 3 April 2014, Ukraine sent a report to UNESCO warning that "[t]he ever growing presence of Russian military forces is having a negative impact on Crimean cultural heritage" (including sites on the World Heritage List – i.e., the Ancient City of Tauric Chersonese and its chora, inscribed in 2013 – and the

---

298 Ibid., para. 56. See further para. 176. In its rejoinder, Ukraine again recalled that "[t]he tangible and fundamental interests at stake – relating, among other things, to living and non-living resources, free navigation, and irreplaceable underwater archaeological sites – are precisely those the Convention was developed to safeguard" (Rejoinder of Ukraine on Jurisdiction, para. 48).

299 It should be recalled that whilst Ukraine is a party to the 2001 UNESCO Convention, Russia is not and, indeed, has firmly opposed it (see n. 30 above and accompanying text).

300 See, among others, 'Russian archaeologists appropriate over a million Crimean artifacts', 30 May 2019, *Ukrinform* at: <https://www.ukrinform.net/rubric-society/2711132-russian-archaeologists-appropriate-over-a-million-crimean-artifacts.html>; H. Coynash (Human Rights Protection Group), 'Crimea: Destroying Built Heritage, Erasing the Past', 13 March 2019, *Habitat International Coalition* at: <http://www.hlrn.org/activitydetails.php?id=pmtmZg==#.YDDpFS0rxfF>; A. Shandra, 'Crimea's occupied cultural heritage', 10 September 2019, *Euromaidan Press* at: <http://euromaidanpress.com/2016/09/10/crimeas-occupied-cultural-heritage/>; 'Ukraine moves to fight Russia's destruction of cultural heritage in occupied Crimea', 22 May 2020, *The Ukrainian Weekly* at: <http://www.ukrweekly.com/uwwp/ukraine-moves-to-fight-russias-destruction-of-cultural-heritage-in-occupied-crimea/>; or 'Halya Coynash: Ukraine fights destruction of cultural heritage in Crimea', 4 May 2020, *Kyiv Post* at: <https://www.kyivpost.com/article/opinion/op-ed/halya-coynash-ukraine-takes-vital-move-to-fight-destruction-of-cultural-heritage-in-crimea.html>.

301 See, for example, A. Charron, 'Russia's Recolonization of Crimea' (2020) 119 *Current History* 275–281.

302 See, among others, Chatham House, 'Crimea's Occupation Exemplifies the Threat of Attacks on Cultural Heritage', 4 February 2020 (available at: <https://www.chathamhouse.org/2020/02/crimeas-occupation-exemplifies-threat-attacks-cultural-heritage>); 'Facelift Or Farce? "Restoration" Of Palace Shocks Crimean Tatars', *Radio Free Europe/Radio Liberty*, 18 February 2018, at: <https://www.rferl.org/a/crimea-khan-s-palace-restoration-bakhchisary-shock-tatars-persecution-unesco/29046866.html>.

tentative list); that "[t]he reported massive transfer of priceless cultural objects from Crimean museums to the Russian capital is alarming"; that Russia should honour "its obligations under international law related to cultural property"; and that Russia had blocked or stopped in Crimea expert work within the framework of the 2001 UNESCO Convention and activities of the Centre of Oceanology of the Ukrainian National Academy of Sciences, an active participant for decades in the Intergovernmental Oceanographic Commission.[303] The UNESCO Executive Council adopted its Decision 194 EX/32, expressing its "deep concern that the growing presence of Russian military forces [...] places Crimea's cultural heritage in danger".[304]

The Russian answer was not long in coming. Not only did it ignore the accusations regarding the negative impact on heritage sites, it also stated, "Allegations concerning a massive transfer of certain cultural values from Crimea to other Russian cities are absolutely unfounded. This information is not confirmed, at least in presentations by Ukrainian opponents who appear to mean 'looting' by 'transfer'."[305] Interestingly, it went on to note, in language as plain as it was subtle:

> In March 2014, Russia took the responsibility for Crimea, including the protection of its cultural heritage. Among numerous civilizations that have left their rich heritage here, the Russian Crimea is not least [...] This being so, there is no reason to talk about risks of devastation or to assume that Russia would tolerate a 'massive transfer' of objects of cultural heritage from Crimea.[306]

And with regard to the blocking of activities directed at underwater cultural heritage, Russia recalled:

> So far, the Russian Federation has not become a party to the 2001 UNESCO Convention on the Protection of the Underwater Cultural Heritage. However, after the reunification of Crimea with Russia, the latter has committed itself to preserve the Crimean cultural heritage and has paid close attention to the preservation of underwater cultural heritage sites

303 UNESCO Doc. 194 EX/32, 4 April 2014. For an updated version as of July 2020, see UNESCO Doc. 210 EX/5.I.C, 9 October 2020.

304 UNESCO Decision 194 EX/32, 15 May 2014, para. 5.

305 UNESCO Doc. 195 EX/5.INF.5, 21 October 2014, at 6. See also 'Information on the situation in the Republic of Crimea (the Russian Federation) within the scope of UNESCO competence. As of April 8, 2015' (available at: <http://russianunesco.ru/rus/article/2070>).

306 Ibid., at 7.

located in this region, including five underwater cultural heritage sites that were earlier inscribed by Ukraine in the state register in the framework of the 2001 Convention.[307]

From a legal point of view, this creates a highly complex scenario: since Crimea is not under Russian sovereignty but rather is occupied by Russia,[308] as noted earlier, the law of armed conflict applies. Under that law, especially the 1907 Hague Regulations, the 1949 Fourth Geneva Convention, and the 1954 Hague Convention,[309] ratified by both parties:

- the domestic legislation of the occupied State continues to apply in occupied territories;
- the occupying power must facilitate the safeguarding efforts of the national authorities in occupied territories;
- both parties must prevent any vandalism or misappropriation of cultural property; and,
- according to the first protocol of the 1954 Convention, the occupying power is required to prevent any export of artefacts from the occupied territory.

This would leave Russia with no excuse for non-compliance with Ukraine's cultural property laws,[310] meaning it should implement its own rules only when absolutely necessary. However, as Russia has argued, in keeping with its logic of sovereignty (as opposed to occupation), the law applicable in Crimea is that enacted by the Russian Federation or by the 'Republic of Crimea'.[311] On

307 Ibid., at 13.

308 See, *mutatis mutandis, Legal Consequences of the Construction of a Wall in the Occupied Palestinian Territory*, Advisory Opinion, *ICJ Reports* 2004, 136, at 167, para. 78.

309 Regulations Respecting the Laws and Customs of War on Land annexed to the Fourth Hague Convention, adopted 18 October 1907, entered into force 26 January 1910 (available at: <https://ihl-databases.icrc.org/ihl/INTRO/195>); Geneva Convention relative to the Protection of Civilian Persons in Time of War, adopted 12 August 1949, entered into force 21 October 1950, 75 UNTS 287; and Convention for the Protection of Cultural Property in the Event of Armed Conflict, adopted 14 May 1954, entered into force 7 August 1956, 249 UNTS 215 (for its 1st Protocol, 249 UNTS 358).

310 For a general overview of the Ukraine's system of cultural heritage protection, see the 'Heritage Assessment Report' Ukraine submitted in 2016 to the Council of Europe (available at: <https://rm.coe.int/ukraine-comus-heritage-assessment-report-english-version/168071bcb0>). The main Ukrainian law was the 'Law of Ukraine on Protection of Cultural Heritage' of 8 June 2000 (as amended in 2007) (available in the UNESCO International Heritage Laws Database at: <https://en.unesco.org/sites/default/files/ua_law_protection_cultural_heritage_engtof.pdf>).

311 For a non-authoritative translation into English of the legislative texts, as well as for other documents on Crimea's occupation, one possible source (used in the following footnotes except where otherwise stated) is: <https://cis-legislation.com/index.fwx>.

18 March 2014, a document having the form of a treaty was signed between Russia and the self-proclaimed leaders of the 'Republic of Crimea' and of the city of Sevastopol.[312] Article 23 of that document establishes that the laws and regulations of the Russian Federation will be applicable in the Republic of Crimea and the city of Sevastopol from the time of their accession to the Russian Federation. It follows that the laws and regulations of Crimea and Sevastopol will remain in force until the end of the transition period or until the adoption of the relevant new laws by the Russian Federation. This implies the full legislative subordination of the new 'Republic' to Russian lawmakers, who, since then, have enacted various laws governing archaeological activities and the underwater cultural heritage in Crimea.

On 12 February 2015, *Federal Law No. 9-FZ* 'On basic principles of legal regulation of relations in the field of culture and tourism in connection with the accession of the Republic of Crimea to the Russian Federation and establishment of new constituent entities within the Russian Federation – the Republic of Crimea and the city of federal importance Sevastopol'[313] was promulgated. Additionally, a State Committee for the Protection of the Cultural Heritage of 'the Republic of Crimea'[314] has been established, and various agreements have been signed between the Russian and Crimean authorities on different aspects of the 'new' State's control and supervision of the "preservation, use, promotion and state protection of cultural heritage sites [and] definition of the boundaries of historical and cultural reserves of federal importance on the territory".[315] Furthermore, according to reports, Russia is planning to enact a new law on underwater cultural heritage, which will apply in Crimean waters.[316]

---

312 *The Treaty between the Russian Federation and the Republic of Crimea on the Accession of the Republic of Crimea to the Russian Federation and on Forming New Constituent Entities within the Russian Federation*, 18 March 2014, effective as of 1 March 2014. Another non-authoritative English translation text can be found at: <https://en.wikisource.org/wiki/Treaty_on_the_Accession_of_the_Republic_of_Crimea_to_Russia>.

313 Making applicable in Crimea too *Law No. 73-FZ*, of 25 June 2002, 'About objects of cultural heritage (historical and cultural monuments) of the people of the Russian Federation' (as amended on 29 December 2020).

314 Its website (in Russian only) can be found at: <http://gkokn.rk.gov.ru/>, retrieved from the US Library of Congress website (available at: <https://www.loc.gov/item/lcwaN0022837/>).

315 UNESCO Doc. 195 EX/5.INF.5, 21 October 2014, at 7.

316 'A new law to protect underwater cultural heritage', 28 March 2017, *Russkiy Mir Foundation* at: <https://russkiymir.ru/en/news/222350/>. By July 2021, no new legislation has been enacted by Russia. See L. D. Bashirova, M. O. Ulyanova, A. A. Kovalev *et al.*, 'On the Legal Status of Maritime Cultural Heritage and Its Management in the Russian Sectors of the Baltic Sea' (2021) 16 *Journal of Maritime Archaeology*, 111–132, at 113–117.

In short, to this author's knowledge,[317] research (and the competence of researchers), authorisations and permits, the conducting of archaeological activities, and the submission and evaluation of reports from sites and activities, among other things, are under the complete supervision of the Russian authorities in Crimea, with the Centre for Underwater Archaeological Heritage of the Institute of Archaeology at the Russian Academy of Sciences having a central role in the evaluation of the prospective research. Archaeological work is only possible if officially attached to a Russian or 'Crimean' research group. Archaeologists from Ukraine and Russia had had common projects and close contact with each other until 2014.[318] Their education system, technology, experience, and infrastructure for underwater archaeology were also very similar until then. However, this smooth cooperation seems to have disappeared. In any case, the Russian position is that "[t]he underwater heritage sector established in 2011 continues to operate within the State Committee for the Protection of Cultural Heritage of the Republic of Crimea. Republic authorities pursue their work in this field."[319]

Previous Ukrainian maritime and oceanographic institutions in Crimea, located at Sevastopol, and part of the Intergovernmental Oceanographic Commission's International Oceanographic Data and Information Exchange Programme have been closed by the new occupying authorities, including, for example, the O. O. Kovalevsky Institute of Biology of the Southern Seas and the Marine Hydrophysical Institute of the Ukrainian National Academy of Sciences.[320] Likewise, the Black Sea Centre for Underwater Research, one of the most important Ukrainian centres implementing the 2001 UNESCO

317 Some of the information that follows has been disclosed to me, as both an academic and a member of the ICOMOS International Committee on the Underwater Cultural Heritage (ICUCH), by Ukrainian, Russian, and third-country archaeologists and oceanographers with experience in Black Sea marine activities, including those related to underwater cultural heritage in disputed areas in and around Crimea. Of course, the opinions that follow do not reflect the position of ICUCH-ICOMOS or any of these sources, some of whom prefer to remain anonymous due to the sensitive nature of the situation in Ukraine and Crimea.

318 Russia maintained, however, that "Crimean agencies and institutes employ specialists who deal with underwater cultural heritage. Russian and Ukrainian experts and scientists have an extensive experience of working together in this area. Long-term contacts among them are not only professional but also friendly." See 'Follow-up of the situation in the Autonomous Republic of Crimea (Ukraine)', UNESCO Doc. 195 EX/5.INF.5, 21 October 2014, at 13.

319 Ibid.

320 Ibid., at 2.

Convention, was evacuated outside Crimea to the city of Mykolaiv, where it remained until its disappearance.[321]

According to various sources, the occupying authorities in Crimea were allegedly abusing the practice of international cultural exchanges (maintaining these with Russian museums and institutions only),[322] including scientific and cultural events dedicated to archaeology, and, in keeping with their sovereignty logic, presenting Crimean archaeological monuments as heritage belonging to the Russian Federation. Whether this was an attempt to legitimise the peninsula's annexation by the Russian Federation is still up for debate and further proof is needed, although some high-ranking officials' attitudes do point in that direction. As President Putin explained *in extenso* in the wake of the annexation:

> [...] Crimea is where our people live, and the peninsula is of strategic importance for Russia as the spiritual source of the development of a multifaceted but solid Russian nation and a centralised Russian state. It was in Crimea, in the ancient city of Chersonesus or Korsun, as ancient Russian chroniclers called it, that Grand Prince Vladimir was baptised before bringing Christianity to Rus.
>
> In addition to ethnic similarity, a common language, common elements of their material culture, a common territory, even though its borders were not marked then, and a nascent common economy and government, Christianity was a powerful spiritual unifying force that helped involve various tribes and tribal unions of the vast Eastern Slavic world in the creation of a Russian nation and Russian state. It was thanks to this spiritual unity that our forefathers for the first time and forevermore saw themselves as a united nation. All of this allows us to say that Crimea, the ancient Korsun or Chersonesus, and Sevastopol have invaluable civilisational and even sacral importance for Russia, like the Temple Mount in Jerusalem for the followers of Islam and Judaism.
>
> And this is how we will always consider it.[323]

---

321 See 'Follow-up of the situation in the Autonomous Republic of Crimea (Ukraine)', UNESCO Doc. 207 EX/5.I.C, 13 September 2019, at 18.

322 See, for example, 'The expedition of experts to study the historical and cultural monuments of the south coast of the Crimea has finished', 8 May 2018, *The Hermitage News* at: <https://www.hermitagemuseum.org/wps/portal/hermitage/news/news-item/news/2018/news_106_18/?lng=>, which reports that the south coast of Crimea "is not only full of monuments of material culture, but also has an entirely special significance in Russia's cultural code".

323 Presidential Address to the Federal Assembly, 4 December 2014 (available at: <http://en.kremlin.ru/events/president/news/47173>).

Before the UNESCO, Ukraine has warned:

> Given the total absence of international control over the archaeological activities on the occupied peninsula and taking into consideration that Russia bears no obligations under the 2001 UNESCO Convention on the Protection of the Underwater Cultural Heritage, the situation in this sphere is non-transparent and causes great concerns as to potential looting of the underwater heritage and its illegal trafficking of the goods of the sunken cultural property.[324]

To some extent, the International Council on Monuments and Sites (ICOMOS) – the most important NGO advising UNESCO on cultural and archaeological matters – shares these concerns about the lack of reliable information on the current state of cultural heritage in Crimea under Russian occupation and administration. In meticulously diplomatic language, it has noted that:

> considering the complex and sensitive situation, ICOMOS can only continue to insist on the need for an independent and neutral assessment informed by in-situ missions, under a UNESCO mandate, to the sites concerned, both the World Heritage and non-World Heritage sites, covering all heritage categories that may be concerned.[325]

As in any other war, *truth is the first victim*. The Ukrainian figures are likely overstated, but Russia's attitude does not help clarify the actual situation or its intentions. Without an effective monitoring system, there is virtually no control of any reported activity directed at or incidentally affecting the underwater cultural heritage. Several cultural conventions contraventions have already

---

324 UNESCO Doc. 210 EX/5.I.C, 9 October 2020, at 23. However, as of March 2018, following an Ukrainian enquiry about the application of a monitoring mechanism under the 2001 UNESCO Convention – which does not actually exist – during the 6th Meeting of States Parties (30–31 May 2017), the Secretariat of the Convention had not received any information concerning possible violations of the Convention's provisions. 'Follow-up of the situation in the Autonomous Republic of Crimea (Ukraine)' UNESCO Doc. 204 EX/5, Part I.D, 9 March 2018, at 3.

325 UNESCO Doc. 210 EX/5.I.C, 9 October 2020, at 35. As a State party to the 2001 UNESCO Convention, Ukraine could perfectly well ask the Conference of State Parties to request its Scientific Technical and Advisory Body (STAB) to send an assistance mission to the zone, as has occurred in other cases, when requested by Haiti, Madagascar, Panama, Bulgaria, or Guatemala (source: <http://www.unesco.org/new/en/culture/themes/underwater-cultural-heritage/2001-convention/advisory-body/missions/>). The problem would be whether the mission to Crimea would be accepted.

been alleged by Ukraine before different national[326] and international courts and tribunals, i.e. the ECHR, the ICJ, and an arbitral tribunal; and the ICC's Office of the Prosecutor keeps the 'Crimean file' open under several possible accusations.[327] Although the 2001 UNESCO Convention cannot be invoked before these international adjudicative bodies against Russia since the latter has not ratified it, nor can any monitoring or assistance mission under the Convention's STAB be used, the principles embodied in it might be alleged by inference – as protection of a particular portion of the cultural heritage – without a direct reference to the 2001 UNESCO Convention.[328]

Contrary to other conventions (especially the 1949 and 1954 conventions and the 1972 WHC), the 2001 UNESCO Convention lacks any monitoring system beyond State-to-State surveillance. Under Article 8 of the UNESCO Constitution, because the 2001 Convention was adopted *by* the UNESCO General Conference, each of the organisation's Member States – irrespective of its participation in it, i.e. including Russia – agrees to submit reports to the UNESCO on the laws, regulations, and statistics relating to its educational, scientific, and cultural institutions and activities, as well as on the actions taken under such conventions.[329] However, neither this *sur pièce* monitoring system

326 Such as the case on the restitution of 'Crimean gold' before the Dutch courts. See E. Campfens, 'Whose Cultural Heritage? Crimean Treasures at the Crossroads of Politics, Law and Ethics' (2017) 22 *Art Antiquity & Law* 193–212.

327 Of course, as the ICC has already said in the *Al Mahdi* case, the destruction of cultural heritage is a war crime. See *The Prosecutor v. Ahmad Al Faqi Al Mahdi*, Case No. ICC-01/12-01/15, Trial Chamber VIII Judgment, 27 September 2016. Moreover, depending on the accumulated behaviours, deliberate, widespread, and serious destruction of cultural heritage could be tantamount to a crime of genocide. See International Criminal Tribunal for the Former Yugoslavia, *Prosecutor v. Radislav Krstić*, Case No.: IT-98-33-T, Trial Chamber Judgment, 2 August 2001, para. 580, quoted and endorsed by the ICJ in the *Genocide* case: "simultaneous attacks on the cultural and religious property and symbols of the targeted group [...] may legitimately be considered as evidence of an intent to physically destroy the group". *Application of the Convention on the Prevention and Punishment of the Crime of Genocide* (*Bosnia and Herzegovina* v. *Serbia and Montenegro*), Judgment, *ICJ Reports* 2007, 43, at 186, para. 344).

328 For example, in the case of an alleged Russian violation of the 1972 WHC or the 1954 Convention and its protocol, these treaties would spatially apply to the territory of the signatories and would thus include the territorial sea around Crimea and the UCH located therein.

329 Art. 8, Constitution of the United Nations Educational, Scientific and Cultural Organization (adopted 16 November 1945, entered into force 4 November 1946, 4 UNTS 275). These reports are to be submitted, at such times and in such manner as is determined by the General Conference, to the Committee of Conventions and Recommendations of the UNESCO Executive Council, which will analyse their contents. Initially also applicable to the 1970 Convention on the Means of Prohibiting and Preventing the Illicit Import,

nor any other has yet been established for the 2001 UNESCO Convention.[330] Furthermore, realistically, it seems to be a rather poorly developed monitoring mechanism although it might, at least, be the only one that could oblige Russia to submit a public report on its conduct regarding underwater cultural heritage in Crimea (if Russia considers it a territory under its sovereignty).

Crimean waters are *de lege* but not *de facto* covered by the 2001 Convention. Unlike Russia, Ukraine is a State Party to the Convention, Article 14 of which requires States Parties to "take measures to prevent the entry into their territory, the dealing in, or the possession of, underwater cultural heritage illicitly exported and/or recovered, where recovery was contrary to this Convention". Article 18(1) further provides that each State Party must "take measures providing for the seizure of underwater cultural heritage in its territory that has been recovered in a manner not in conformity with this Convention". As already noted, under the logic of international law governing occupation, the domestic legislation of the occupied State continues to apply in occupied territories, including the implementation of ratified international conventions. Thus, Russia should have to comply with these rules. However, this seems unlikely to happen in the immediate future.

In any case, what all these claims and counterclaims mean for underwater cultural heritage and for maritime delimitation in the Black Sea is undeniable:[331] the legal status of the Azov Sea, as well as the extent of the Ukrainian EEZ and the projection of its continental shelf into the Black Sea, are significant maritime concerns strongly affected by the ultimate legal status of Crimea.

Export and Transfer of Ownership of Cultural Property (until 2012), today it only applies to the 1960 Convention against Discrimination in Education, the 1989 Convention on Technical and Vocational Education, and 15 UNESCO recommendations on education, culture, and science. On this monitoring system, see UNESCO, *The Committee on Conventions and Recommendations* (2020) (available at: <http://portal.unesco.org/en/ev.php-URL_ID=32176&URL_DO=DO_TOPIC&URL_SECTION=201.html>).

330 A monitoring system for the Convention is today under discussion. See 'Evaluation of UNESCO's standard-setting work of the Culture Sector, part VI – 2001 Convention on the Protection of Underwater Cultural Heritage', UNESCO Doc. IOS/EVS/PI/174 REV, at 23–24 (available at: <https://unesdoc.unesco.org/ark:/48223/pf0000368446?posInSet=2&queryId=N-99620a76-e942-40ee-b421-74cb017adfb5>).

331 It should be recalled that the Black Sea is considered one of the world's finest underwater laboratories due to its anoxic (un-oxygenated) layer, which preserves artefacts better than any other marine environment. For more information about this extraordinary underwater archaeological landscape, see the 'Maritime Archaeology Project at the Black Sea' (MAP), source: <http://blackseamap.com>.

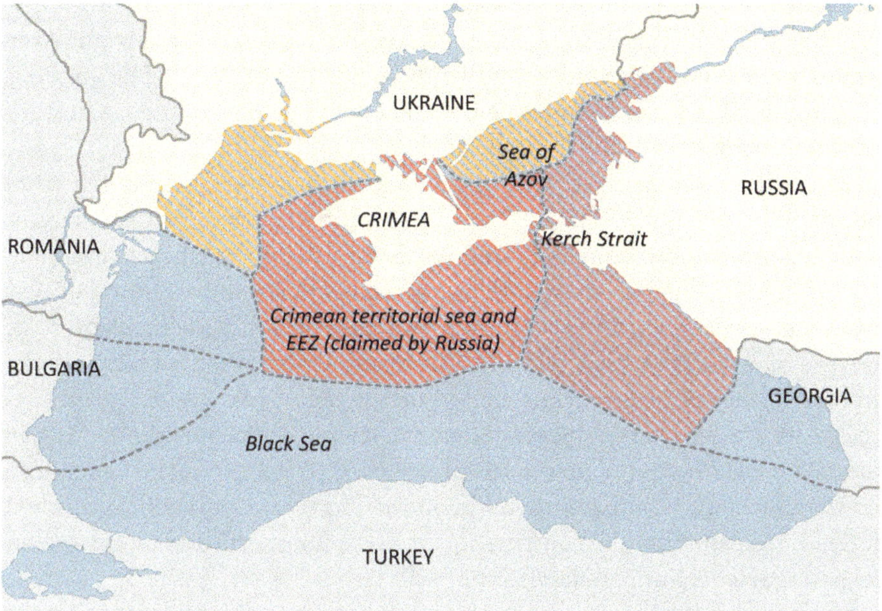

FIGURE 7 Potential impact of the sovereignty dispute over Crimea on the Black Sea
SOURCE: V. J. SCHATZ AND D. KOVAL, "UKRAINE V. RUSSIA: PASSAGE THROUGH KERCH STRAIT AND THE SEA OF AZOV (PART I)", *VÖLKERRECHTSBLOG*, 10 JANUARY 2018

Considered in perspective, the Azov Sea seems like a 'return to the future': in 1985, when the Soviet Union claimed straight baselines off its mainland coasts and islands in the Arctic Ocean and off its coasts in the Baltic and Black Seas,[332] one of the segments enclosed some waters that lead to the Sea of Azov.[333] At the time, the Azov Sea was surrounded by a single State – the USSR – and claimed as a 'historic bay', somewhat contradicting what had been codified by Article 10(6) LOSC three years earlier and also established under Article 7(6) of the 1958 Geneva Convention on the Territorial Sea and the Contiguous

332 Source: <https://www.un.org/Depts/los/LEGISLATIONANDTREATIES/PDFFILES/RUS_1985_Declaration.pdf>.

333 For the US, despite acknowledging that "[s]egment 35–36 closes a body of water that leads to the Sea of Azov" and perhaps knowing that these baselines are among those "not meeting the appropriate standards [, they] generally have minimal effect on the outer limit of the territorial sea." US Department of State, *Limits in the Seas No. 109. Continental Shelf boundary: Turkey-USSR and Straight Baselines: USSR* (*Black Sea*), at 9 (available at: <https://www.state.gov/wp-content/uploads/2019/12/LIS-109.pdf>). This apparently follows a longstanding US position: for Philip Jessup, writing in 1927, the Soviet claim "seem[ed] reasonable and [...] would not be contested". P. C. Jessup, *The Law of Territorial Waters and Maritime Jurisdiction* (G. A. Jennings: New York, 1927), at 383.

Zone.[334] However, following the USSR's collapse in 1991 and Ukraine's emergence as an independent State, the LOSC conditions ceased to apply: the Azov Sea was suddenly surrounded by two different littoral States. But, in 2003, Ukraine and Russia concluded an Agreement defining the Azov Sea as "historically internal waters of the Russian Federation and Ukraine" (Article 1).[335] The treaty further establishes a particular navigation regime for the Kerch Strait between the two littoral States[336] and refers other maritime matters (such as shipping, navigation, search-and-rescue, fishing, pollution, and environmental questions) either to already existing agreements or the conclusion of new ones, again between the two parties.[337] In case of a disagreement over the treaty's interpretation or application, the dispute is to be settled bilaterally or "through other peaceful means chosen by the Sides" (Article 4). This makes the treaty a (purportedly objective) bilateral regime, which no other nation, in particular, no other naval power, has protested.[338] But it cannot be denounced by Ukraine since it "apparently relies on the [2003] Cooperation Agreement for both its claim that the construction of Kerch Strait Bridge is illegal and for its passage rights through Kerch Strait".[339]

334 For one commentator, "some 'claims' categorised as being 'historic' today – such as the Sea of Azov – were probably misnamed or at least loosely entitled as 'historic', because they were – even at the time of the inception of the 'claim' – in any case internal waters in the light of then-existent international law or at least constituted 'ancient rights'." C. Symmons, *Historic Waters in the Law of the Sea: A Modern Re-Appraisal* (Brill/Nijhoff: Leiden/Boston, 2008), at 299.

335 Under this same proviso, the "Sea of Azov shall be delimited along the line of the state border by agreement between the two sides". Similarly, "issues related to the waters of the Kerch Strait shall be settled by agreement between the sides". There is no reference to national sectors in connection with the border in the Azov Sea, and no mention of a border in the Kerch Strait (Art. 1).

336 Under Art. 2, commercial vessels and warships under either the Russian flag or the Ukrainian flag shall enjoy freedom of movement in the Azov Sea and Kerch Strait. Commercial vessels flying other flags, headed for Russian or Ukrainian ports or returning from them, "may access the Azov Sea and pass through the Kerch Strait". Whereas "warships and other non-commercial ships" belonging to third States, headed for Russian or Ukrainian ports, "may access the Azov Sea and pass through Kerch Strait by invitation or permission from one of the Sides agreed upon with the other Side".

337 Art. 3 of the 2003 Agreement.

338 For two commentators, "the claim of shared internal waters seems to have met with little opposition, which may, however, also be the result of the Sea of Azov's remoteness and little importance for strategic purposes". Schatz and Koval, *Russia's Annexation ...* (n. 282), at 281.

339 Ibid. The basis for jurisdiction before the PCA in the aforementioned case is Art. 287 and Annex VII (Art. 1) LOSC, which would seem to follow what Art. 4 of the 2003 Agreement says on resolving disputes bilaterally, "as well as through other peaceful means chosen by

Since occupying Crimea in 2014, Russia has upheld the principle whereby the annexation affords rights not only to the territory of the peninsula itself, but also to the sea waters around it, including Kerch Strait, which is fully and exclusively controlled by the Russian fleet in the Black Sea.[340] Ukraine's Azov coast thus remains isolated and the treaty rules for the Strait – now *de facto* dividing a single State, i.e. Russia – are in legal limbo awaiting the arbitral award on the merits. As for activities in the Strait, such as bridge construction or navigation control, any activity directed at or incidentally affecting underwater cultural heritage thus remains outside of any possible Ukrainian surveillance.[341]

Finally, Russia has not made public its position regarding the EEZ and the continental shelf projected from the Crimean coast. Presumably, such a declaration will trigger an avalanche of protests, not only by Ukraine but from third States as well, who will not recognise it as a by-product of the illegal annexation.

Purportedly, Russia may be 'nullifying' Ukrainian heritage – particularly its underwater cultural heritage – in Crimea and its surrounding waters.[342] The rationale behind this decision could be the erasure – through decontextualisation, absorption, merging, and melding – of any distinctive Ukrainian historical or cultural heritage. These alleged Russian activities without any kind of independent scientific control, as well as the irreparable dispersal of underwater heritage objects and collections, could make this nullification process irreversible. The loss of such historical records deprives Ukraine's land (and consequently maritime) claims of one possible (albeit relative) type of evidence of ancient presence. Even worse, not only land and sea may be lost, but also memory.

---

the Sides". However, one might wonder whether the Agreement is still in force or terminated due to a fundamental change of circumstances.

340 Schatz and Koval, *Völkerrechtsblog* ... (n. 282), Part II.

341 Different media have reported that, during the construction of the new bridge over the Kerch Strait, thousands of pieces of underwater cultural heritage – some of invaluable historical significance – have been excavated, recovered, and removed from their original context without any archaeological record. See, for example, 'Stolen Heritage: How Russia is Destroying Crimean Archaeological Sites', *Hromadske International*, 4 January 2018, at: <https://en.hromadske.ua/posts/stolen-heritage-how-russia-is-destroying-crimean-archaeological-sites>; confirmed by the 'Russian side' in 'Ancient Greek artifact unearthed at Crimean bridge construction site', *TASS Russian News Agency*, 22 March 2017, at: <https://tass.com/society/936787>.

342 In any case, the diverse composition and history of Crimea as a separate and distinct entity cannot be ignored when speaking of 'Russian' or 'Ukrainian' cultural heritage.

4 Some Concluding Remarks: On Law, Politics, and Ethics

Ancient remains have undeniably been used by political leaders to identify, create, shape, distinguish, galvanise, neglect, and/or deny the existence of peoples and, later, nations. Sometimes, they have been artificially used to trace boundaries. Historically, buried sovereignty has been found, alleged, and contested by States in their territorial claims. Now, submerged archaeological objects are also being used to support and contest competing maritime claims in different parts of the world. As this book has sought to show, the cases of Canada in the Arctic, China in the South China Sea, and Russia in Crimea are of paramount importance in this regard.

Like archaeology in general, underwater archaeology has had a complex two-way relationship with diplomacy, military endeavours, and technology, particularly during the Cold War. The finding of the *Titanic* and the public announcement thereof are a good example. Dr Ballard was authorised to find the wreck of the White Star liner once the debris field of two US nuclear submarines lost in the Northwest Atlantic (the USS *Thresher* and USS *Scorpion*) had been mapped.[343] The public disclosure of the find was also intended to send a clear political message to the Soviets that the US was capable of finding 'anything' at the bottom of the sea. The interest in the *Titanic* persists today, especially in relation to monitoring how metals behave under high pressure, at low temperatures, and in low light, and with regard to the particular biological environment around the wreck. This monitoring and deep-sea research analysis enrich today's underwater heritage projects, partly because the relationship also works the other way, i.e. from diplomacy to archaeology. During the Cold War, overflights along strategic routes to detect submarine traffic led to the mapping of large parts of the oceans, including the identification of anomalies that remained in place, never moving, thus suggesting the location of wrecks, sometime of historical importance.[344]

In other cases, technology was merged with methodology to send a message to other stakeholders: treasure hunters. This was the case, for example, of the

343 See, for example, J. Roach, 'Titanic Was Found During Secret Cold War Navy Mission', *National Geographic*, 21 November 2017, at: <https://www.nationalgeographic.com/history/article/titanic-nuclear-submarine-scorpion-thresher-ballard>; W. J. Broad, 'Secret Sub to Scan Sea Floor for Roman Wrecks', *The New York Times*, 7 February 1995, at: <https://www.nytimes.com/1995/02/07/science/secret-sub-to-scan-sea-floor-for-roman-wrecks.html>.

344 The flip side of this strategic/archaeological coin is the well-known fact that submarines have historically taken (and continue to take) advantage of electro-magnetic distortions created by shipwrecks embedded in the sea bottom as anti-sonar camouflage.

archaeological missions to Skerki Bank,[345] which included a nuclear-powered deep submergence vessel – the US *NR-1* – that helped map the archaeological site. As two of the scientists aboard the mission said:

> One of the goals of the Skerki projects was to see whether archaeologists could work effectively in the deeper oceans with the new robotic technology. This was 'experimental archaeology': the idea was to test techniques of survey, excavation, and conservation in a previously unexplored environment, in part in response to the challenges of treasure hunters who were claiming that archaeologists were not capable of working in the deep sea. The Skerki projects have shown that careful documentation of the sea floor with robotic technology, using sophisticated, high resolution optical and acoustic remote-sensing, is possible.[346]

Underwater archaeology thus methodologically differs from 'historical salvors' (a.k.a. treasure hunters), who may also use advanced technology, but only to *find* underwater 'treasures' – i.e. valuable cargoes that can be traded as commodities – and retrieve (rather than excavate) as many items as possible in the shortest period of time in order to sell them for private profit. Unfortunately, for decades neither public opinion nor judges or diplomats were aware of the abysmal difference between archaeologists and 'treasure salvors'.

•••

Underwater archaeology was thus not genuinely considered when the law of the sea was codified at UNCLOS III. It was neglected as part of marine scientific research in the drafting of Part XIII of the LOSC. Otherwise, the Convention would have given coastal States a new jurisdiction in their EEZ

345 Skerki Bank is a geographical feature in the Mediterranean located along the route between ancient Carthage (in current Tunisia) and Ostia (in current Italy). It is home to numerous shipwrecks and their cargo, including from the pre-Roman and Roman periods, several medieval wrecks, modern sailing vessels, and the remains of sunken WWII vessels.

346 A. M. McCann and J. P. Oleson, 'Deep-water shipwrecks off Skerki Bank: The 1997 Survey', (2004) *Journal of Roman archaeology. Supplementary series, no. 58*, at 23–24 [footnotes omitted]. See further n. 355 below and accompanying text. Spanish scientists have also recently demonstrated that this deep-sea archaeology is possible, when surveying and properly recovering historical items from the site of the *Mercedes*, at a depth of more than 1,000 m, previously *found* (and looted) by *Odyssey Marine Exploration*, a treasure-hunting company (source: <http://www.unesco.org/new/en/culture/themes/underwater-cultural-heritage/underwater-cultural-heritage/best-practices-of-underwater-cultural-heritage/the-nuestra-senora-de-las-mercedes-project-spain/>).

or on their continental shelves. The drafting and final wording of Article 303 LOSC bears witness to the limited scope ultimately accepted. However, since the LOSC's entry into force (and even before), underwater archaeology – as discussed in the first part of this book – has been recognised as a scientific discipline. The urgent need to go beyond what the LOSC eventually regulated with regard to 'archaeological and historical objects found at sea' was also explained. The international scientific community, with the support of several interested States, insisted on the need to delineate a new legal canvas to adequately preserve underwater cultural heritage for future generations. The principles of international cooperation, *in situ* preservation as the first option, non-commercialisation, the scientific approach, and respect for the marine environment prevailed in the negotiations. They were articulated through the idea of the 'legal interest' of all stakeholders rather than the 'preferential rights' of individual States. The 2001 UNESCO Convention thus sidestepped the inevitably distorting discussion of title and ownership of the underwater cultural heritage. Instead, as the Preamble begins, when adopting the Convention, the UNESCO General Conference acknowledged "the importance of underwater cultural heritage *as an integral part of the cultural heritage of humanity* and a particularly important element in the history of peoples, nations, and their relations with each other concerning their *common heritage*" [emphasis added].

Arguably, this does not mean that coastal States' claim of a sort of archaeological maritime zone to protect underwater cultural heritage is not a plausible policy effort. Its legal translation into a maritime zone overlapping a declared contiguous zone has generally been accepted by State practice, thus changing the content of the rights established in Article 303(2) LOSC. If coastal States have the sovereign and exclusive right to regulate any activity directed at or incidentally affecting the underwater cultural heritage located in their territorial sea, then they also have the jurisdictional right to regulate and authorise these activities in their contiguous zones, where declared. However, extending this jurisdiction beyond the outer limit of the contiguous zone, as several States have done, is not yet supported by generally accepted practice.

In these cases, underwater cultural heritage and underwater archaeology have been pointed to as the rationale for these declarations. The basis of the maritime claim *is* the protection of the underwater cultural heritage, thereby adding a new jurisdiction to the coastal States' existing customs, fiscal, immigration and sanitary jurisdiction in the contiguous zone. The protection refers to *any* underwater cultural heritage located in this zone.[347] Some domestic laws do declare that this heritage (and even that located up to the outer limit of the continental shelf)

347 Here, China's legislation differs since it purportedly only protects underwater cultural heritage of Chinese origin.

is part of the respective national historical or cultural heritage, thereby establishing a title link with the submerged remains. But this assertive ownership is not the basis for the maritime spatial claim. That is the main difference with the sovereignty claims this book has discussed in the cases of Canada in the Arctic, China in the South China Sea, and Russia in Crimea.

In these three cases, underwater cultural heritage has been used in the legal claims, pointing to its location and provenance as evidence of a longstanding presence in the claimed maritime areas, either (*i*) as sovereign waters to oppose free navigation (in the Northwest Passage), (*ii*) as sovereign maritime features affording broader maritime rights (in the South China Sea), or (*iii*) to allege its absence or decontextualisation to deny others' maritime rights (in Crimea and the Kerch Strait). This book's hypothesis is that these assertions are neither legally nor ethically acceptable.

•••

Maritime boundary delimitation is one of the most extensively researched fields in international law. Built on the main principle whereby 'the land dominates the sea',[348] international adjudicative bodies – ICJ, ITLOS, and arbitral tribunals – have generally applied a multiple-stage methodology when delimiting the territorial sea, the EEZ and/or the continental shelf.[349] The existence and location of underwater cultural heritage to be considered a 'special' or a 'relevant' circumstance is yet to be assessed by international adjudicative bodies.

In land adjudication cases, vestiges of cultural heritage have not been considered relevant evidence of *effectivités*, as seen in the discussion of the *Preah Vihear* and *Qatar/Bahrain* cases before the ICJ. And this is logical: too often, archaeological remains provide limited information, and it was not until quite recently that archaeological methodology, techniques, and technology have allowed us to refine the results to the point where we can identify

348 *North Sea Continental Shelf* (*Federal Republic of Germany v Denmark*), Merits, Judgment, *ICJ Reports* 1969, 3, para. 96.

349 Departing from its cases in *Maritime Delimitation and Territorial Questions* (*Qatar v. Bahrain*) and *Maritime Delimitation in the Black Sea* (*Romania v. Ukraine*), a recent application by the ICJ of these methodologies – two-stage for the territorial sea and three-stage for the EEZ and continental shelf – may be seen in *Maritime Delimitation in the Caribbean Sea and the Pacific Ocean* (*Costa Rica v. Nicaragua*) *and Land Boundary in the Northern Part of Isla Portillos* (*Costa Rica v. Nicaragua*), Judgment, *ICJ Reports* 2018, 139. See further D. Vidas, 'The Delimitation of the Territorial Sea, the Continental Shelf, and the EEZ: A Comparative Perspective', in: A. Oude Elferink, T. Henriksen, and S. Busch (eds.), *Maritime Boundary Delimitation: The Case Law; Is It Consistent and Predictable?* (Cambridge University Press: Cambridge, 2018), 33–61.

the anthropological origin of found objects or attribute them to an old social group (whose successors, however, may be scattered across several modern States currently disputing the same territory). In underwater archaeology, this is particularly evident with some ancient remains. Imagine the possible (current) national origin of a Phoenician vessel found off the Spanish coast, a *dhow* embedded off the Indian coast, a Maori *waka* discovered in a remote Polynesian reef, a Mesoamerican boat found in the Fonseca Gulf, a Viking *drakkar* wrecked on a Scottish firth, or a junk discovered in the area of the Mekong Delta.

This cannot be seen as precluding any possibility of alleging the actual existence of an archaeological vestige as proof of sovereignty in a territorial dispute. If clearly and scientifically identified, historically attributed, and territorially well-defined, archaeological remains could constitute proof of a "possession so long continued as to have become accepted by the law as a title".[350] Although an undeniably complex task, land and underwater archaeology, performed with an unbiased methodology, adequate techniques, and state-of-the-art technologies may be truly helpful in providing an accurate explanation of the historical human presence on maritime features such as coasts, reefs, or islands.[351] The importance of past archaeological activities may also help an international court or tribunal determine the best title to any of these features.[352]

Historical arguments could perfectly well include archaeological evidence – today easier to verify thanks to new methodological approaches[353] and

350 *Territorial Sovereignty … (Eritrea and Yemen)* (n. 59), at 239, para. 106.

351 As has been said with regard the South China Sea dispute: "Shipwrecks can have no bearing on historical claims. However, archaeology can. If there is genuine archaeological evidence for prolonged occupation on some of the islands in the Spratlys and Paracels, that could go some way towards justifying a claim. So far, none has been forthcoming, to the author's knowledge. Even if archaeological evidence was produced, it would be viewed with some scepticism internationally. By openly declaring the nationalistic intent of their archaeological programme, and by preventing any form of international participation, Chinese cultural officials do their country a disservice." Flecker (n. 228), at 18.

352 The relevance of other – perhaps analogous – maritime scientific activities (for example, hydrographic historical activities) has not been equally weighed by international adjudicative bodies yet. See, for example, the differences between the ICJ's approach in *Territorial and Maritime Dispute (Nicaragua* v. *Colombia)*, Judgment, *ICJ Reports* 2012, 624, at 644, paras. 35–36, and the Arbitral Tribunal's opinion on the South China Sea in *2016 SCS Award*, paras. 327–332.

353 Archaeology has abandoned the almost exclusively 'white-man approach to white-man history', and current research includes indigenous, slave-trade, and gender studies, among others. See, for example, J. Benjamin, M. O'Leary, J. McDonald et al., 'Aboriginal artefacts on the continental shelf reveal ancient drowned cultural landscapes in northwest Australia' (2020) 15(7) *PLoS ONE* e0233912; J. Webster, 'Slave Ships and Maritime Archaeology: An Overview' (2008) 12/1 *International Journal of Historical Archaeology* 6–19; J. A. Irwin and D. Conlin, 'The maritime archaeology of slave ships: overview, assessment and prospectus'

impressive technological advances, particularly in modern underwater archaeology.[354] The problem is thus not technical. As in other marine disciplines, such as oceanography or cartography, new data-gathering methods along with historical records, novel satellite imagery, or side-scan profiles supplemented with authentic vintage maps, could be of great help to international judges and arbitrators.[355]

However, when politics meets and subverts history, when reliable ancient charts are substituted with wishful mapping, when selective excavations preempt scientific projects, and when biased narratives impede a comprehensive reading of the past, then problems arise. In too many cases, the archaeologists may not share the political goal, despite being instrumental to it. The illiberal nature of the sponsoring or supervising authority imposes limits on the archaeologists' work and on the publication of their results.

A nationalist approach misrepresents the essence of what underwater archaeology should be: a scientific tool to better understand a shared history and the historical remains left beneath the waters. It thus hinders the plain explanation of historical (and pre-historical) events, which are distorted by a biased observer. Such a nationalistic approach to archaeology in general, and to underwater archaeology in particular, is not only counterproductive – since it does not allow a pure scientific method – but also unethical.

•••

In contrast, the main purpose of the 2001 UNESCO Convention is to preserve, enhance, and make visible underwater cultural heritage as part of the cultural

(2016) *Underwater Archaeology Proceedings* 72–74; P. J. Turner, S. Cannon, S. DeLand et al., 'Memorializing the Middle Passage on the Atlantic seabed in Areas Beyond National Jurisdiction' (2020) 122 *Marine Policy* 104254; or J. Ransley, 'Boats are for Boys: Queering Maritime Archaeology' (2005) 37(4) *World Archaeology* 621–629.

354 Marine robotics (manned and unmanned), remote sensing, photogrammetry, 3D visual mapping and imaging, dynamic positioning and tracking systems, or new scuba rebreathers are now being combined with older technologies still used in underwater archaeology. See, for example, R. D. Ballard (ed.), *Archaeological Oceanography* (Princeton University Press: Princeton, 2008); A. Caiti, G. Casalino, G. Conte and S. M. Zanoli, 'Innovative technologies in underwater archaeology: field experience, open problems, and research lines' (2006) 22(1) *Chemistry and Ecology* S383–S396; F. Castro and P. Drap, 'A arqueologia marítima e o futuro' (2017) 11 *VESTÍGIOS – Revista Latino-Americana de Arqueologia Histórica* 41–55; or M. L. Brennan et al., 'Telepresence-Enabled Maritime Archeological Exploration in the Deep' (2018) 13(2) *Journal of Maritime Archaeology* 97–122.

355 As Schofield aptly states, "this has the potential to change in the future as technologies mature, gain wider acceptance and bearing in mind judicial discretion to accept the most convincing evidence in a particular case". Schofield (n. 212), at 92.

heritage of humanity.[356] Ethical standards are founding elements of current underwater archaeology,[357] as evidenced in the 2001 UNESCO Convention, both through its main principles and in the annexed archaeological rules.[358] As its Preamble says, "*cooperation among States*, international organizations, scientific institutions, professional organizations, archaeologists, divers, other interested parties and the public at large is essential for the protection of underwater cultural heritage" [emphasis added]. It further considers that:

> survey, excavation and protection of underwater cultural heritage necessitate the availability and application of *special scientific methods* and the use of suitable techniques and equipment as well as a high degree of professional specialization, all of which indicate a need for uniform governing criteria [emphasis added].

International scientific cooperation is the bold element of today's underwater archaeology projects.[359] To differing degrees, in two of the cases discussed in this book such cooperation has been minimised, if not entirely dispensed with. Arguably, the Canadian case is different since the methodology used, the activities performed, and the published results follow widely accepted archaeological rules, which are not so clearly respected in the South China Sea and Crimean cases. The absence of openly monitored archaeological activities

---

356 This does not mean that underwater cultural heritage had been declared 'common heritage of humankind'. See T. M. Šošić, 'The common heritage of mankind and the protection of the underwater cultural heritage', in: B. Vukas and T. M. Šošić (eds), *International Law: New Actors, New Concepts – Continuing Dilemmas; Liber Amicorum Božidar Bakotić* (Brill/Nijhoff: The Hague/Boston, 2010), 319–350.

357 See T. J. Maarleveld, 'Ethics, Underwater Cultural Heritage, and International Law', in: A. Catsambis, B. Ford and D. L. Hamilton (eds), *The Oxford Handbook of Maritime Archaeology* (Oxford University Press: Oxford/New York, 2001), 917–941; and Pérez-Álvaro (n. 234). As has been argued, "underwater archaeologists should be guided by codes of practice and codes of ethics such as the ICOM *Code of Professional Ethics*, and the Australian Institute for Maritime Archaeology (AIMA) *Code of Ethics*". J. P. Delgado and M. Staniforth, 'Underwater Archaeology', in UNESCO-EOLSS (available at: <https://www.eolss.net/sample-chapters/C04/E6-21-01-10.pdf>). The ICOM *Code of Professional Ethics* (renamed the *Code of Ethics for Museums* in 2001) and the AIMA *Code of Ethics* are available at <https://icom.museum/wp-content/uploads/2018/07/ICOM-code-En-web.pdf> and <https://www.aima-underwater.org.au/files/AIMA_Documents/AIMA_Code_of_Ethics.pdf>, respectively.

358 Again, it is worth recalling that the rules of the Convention's Annex are, basically, those widely accepted and adopted by the international archaeological community in the 1996 ICOMOS Sophia Charter and, further, that these rules are an integral part of the Convention and not a simple set of recommendations.

359 Art. 19 of the 2001 UNESCO Convention is devoted to cooperation and information sharing, and Art. 21 to cooperation in training in underwater archaeology.

and peer-reviewed scientific publications of the results according to internationally accepted standards fosters suspicions of biased actions, which are confirmed if the final goal is not the preservation and enhancement of underwater cultural heritage for the benefit of humankind but claims of sovereignty over disputed waters.

The final and decisive outcome of any land or underwater archaeological activity must be the discovery, study, protection and curation, management in its natural context, enhancement, public education, and dissemination of knowledge about the historical remains *for the benefit of all humankind*, not for a select group of people (whether a local people, an entire nation, a stakeholder group, or a club of *connoisseurs*). The protection and enhancement of heritage for all humankind is one of the building-blocks of current international cultural heritage law.[360] A quick review, for example, of the preambles of the main universal conventions protecting tangible or intangible heritage bears witness to this assumption.[361] The 1954 Hague Convention intimates that "damage to cultural property belonging to any people whatsoever means damage to the cultural heritage of all mankind, since each people makes its contribution to the culture of the world". The WHC considers that "parts of the cultural or natural heritage are of outstanding interest and therefore need to be preserved as part of the world heritage of mankind as a whole". And the 2003 Intangible Heritage Convention recalls "the universal will and the common concern to safeguard the intangible cultural heritage of humanity".[362] Finally, Article 2(3) of the 2001 UNESCO Convention establishes: "States Parties shall preserve underwater cultural heritage for the benefit of humanity in conformity with the provisions of this Convention." International courts have also

360 See, generally, F. Francioni, 'Principi e criteri ispiratori per la protezione internazionale del patrimonio culturale', in F. Francioni, A. del Vecchio and P. de Caterini (eds), *Protezione internazionale del patrimonio culturale: interessi nazionali e difesa del patrimonio comune della cultura* (Giuffrè: Milan, 2000), 11–20. The inter-generational approach to managing common heritage of humankind has also been explored, for example, for the natural resources in the Area. See, among others, A. Jaeckel, K. M. Gjerde and J. A. Ardron, 'Conserving the common heritage of humankind – Options for the deep-seabed mining regime' (2017) 78 *Marine Policy* 150–157.

361 The trend towards a more *universalist* approach (or 'cultural internationalism', in John Merryman's famous dichotomy) can be traced back to the *Roerich Pact* (157 LNTS 290). See E. Clément, 'Le concept de *responsabilité collective* de la communauté internationale pour la protection des biens culturels dans les conventions et recommandations de l'UNESCO' (1993) *Revue Belge du Droit International* 535–551. See, previously, J. H. Merryman, 'Two Ways of Thinking About Cultural Property' (1986) 80 *American Journal of International Law* 831–853.

362 Convention for the Safeguarding of the Intangible Cultural Heritage, adopted 17 October 2003, entered into force 20 April 2006, 2368 UNTS 3.

pointed in this direction. In its judgment on the request for interpretation in the *Temple of Preah Vihear* case, the ICJ stated that:

> the Temple of Preah Vihear is a site of religious and cultural significance for the peoples of the region and is now listed by UNESCO as a world heritage site [...]. In this respect, the Court recalls that under Article 6 of the World Heritage Convention, to which both States are parties, Cambodia and Thailand *must co-operate between themselves and with the international community in the protection of the site as a world heritage.*[363]

The ICC's approach in the *Al Mahdi* case is also worth recalling:

> all the sites but one [under attack in Mali since 2012] were UNESCO World Heritage sites and, as such, their attack appears to be of particular gravity as their destruction does not only affect the direct victims of the crimes, namely the faithful and inhabitants of Timbuktu, but also people throughout Mali *and the international community.*[364]

As expressed in these conventions and judicial decisions, the responsibility to preserve cultural heritage for the benefit of humankind lies with all States. In the case of the 2001 UNESCO Convention, as analysed earlier in this book, this includes activities by the 'coordinating State' in the EEZ and the continental shelf on behalf of the States Parties as a whole and not in its own interest; furthermore, in the Area, these activities shall be performed for the benefit of humanity as a whole, on behalf of all States Parties (Articles 10(6) and 12(6), respectively). The surrounding idea is, again, not to act for the national but rather the general benefit. This is in line with the general principle set out in Article 2(11) of the 2001 Convention, whereby "[n]o act or activity undertaken on the basis of this Convention shall constitute grounds for claiming, contending or disputing any claim to national sovereignty or jurisdiction". This implies a clear limitation among States Parties on using underwater archaeology – though not underwater cultural heritage – in their maritime

363 *Request for Interpretation of the Judgment of 15 June 1962 in the Case concerning the* Temple of Preah Vihear (Cambodia v. Thailand) (*Cambodia v. Thailand*), Judgment, ICJ Reports 2013, 281, at 317, para. 106 [emphasis added]. As Alessandro Chechi aptly underlines, this is, however, another example of the "ICJ's dismaying case-load in cultural heritage". A. Chechi, 'The 2013 judgment of the ICJ in the *Temple of Preah Vihear* case and the protection of world cultural heritage sites in wartime' (2016) 6(2) *Asian Journal of International Law* 353–378, at 373.

364 ICC, *The Prosecutor v. Ahmad Al Faqi Al Mahdi*, Case No. ICC-01/12–01/15, Trial Chamber VIII Judgment, 27 September 2016, at 38, para. 80 [emphasis added].

claims.[365] Article 2(11) refers to "acts or activities" undertaken on the basis of the Convention, that is, either activities "directed at underwater cultural heritage" or "activities incidentally affecting underwater cultural heritage".[366] Those "directed at underwater cultural heritage" include an array of different activities provided for in the Convention, such as general domestic measures of protection (as envisaged in Articles 2(4) and (5), but also others, such as authorisations for responsible, non-intrusive access by the general public to *in situ* underwater cultural heritage (Article 2(10)), the authorisation of salvage activities (Article 4), or all the authorisations and permits issued under Articles 9 and 10 for the EEZ or the continental shelf, or for the Area under Articles 11 and 12. Last but not least, no activity based on the 2001 UNESCO Convention – nor the Convention itself – shall prejudice the rights, jurisdiction, and duties of States under international law, including the LOSC; and the 2001 Convention shall always be interpreted and applied in the context of and in a manner consistent with international law, including the LOSC (Article 3).

•••

When adopting the 2001 UNESCO Convention, Russia voted against the text and publicly stated that it would not ratify the Convention.[367] Conversely, Canada and China voted in favour of its adoption by the UNESCO General Conference on 2 November 2001. Explaining its vote, Canada stated that it "supports fully the adoption of the draft Convention on the Protection of the Underwater Cultural Heritage during the course of this General Conference".[368] China remained silent but, as already seen, most Chinese scholars are in favour of the Convention's ratification.[369] As with any treaty, unless otherwise decided by the negotiating States, the 2001 UNESCO Convention is not binding on a party in relation to any act or fact taking place or any situation ceasing to exist before the date of the treaty's entry into force for that party (Article 28

365 Nor does it contradict the customary acceptance of declared contiguous zones as maritime archaeological zones, as crystallised in Art. 8 of the 2001 UNESCO Convention.

366 The former means "activities having underwater cultural heritage as their primary object and which may, directly or indirectly, physically disturb or otherwise damage underwater cultural heritage" (Art. 1(6)), whilst the latter means "activities which, despite not having underwater cultural heritage as their primary object or one of their objects, may physically disturb or otherwise damage underwater cultural heritage" (Art. 1(7)).

367 UNESCO, *Records of the General Conference, Proceedings of the 31st session*, 2 November 2001, vol. 2, at 562 (available at: <http://unesdoc.unesco.org/images/0012/001289/128966m.pdf>).

368 Reprinted in Garabello and Scovazzi (n. 17), at 242.

369 See above n. 276 and accompanying text.

VCLT). However, its impact on current Canadian and Chinese maritime claims must not be underestimated and future ratification may be adjourned, if not ultimately ruled out.

Among the States Parties to the 2001 UNESCO Convention, at least,[370] underwater archaeological activities cannot be grounds for maritime claims. On the contrary, such activities must be considered scientific and cooperative efforts. International cooperation on underwater archaeology projects seeking to shed light on historical events for the benefit of humankind should not be used as a tool of *hard* diplomacy (including maritime claims). Instead, scientific *soft* diplomacy – as a projection of soft power – has proven to be much more meaningful, fruitful, and useful for States. Hard disputes may be softened through collaboration on less sensitive matters, as the preservation of underwater cultural heritage may be.[371] As this author has personally experienced, this has been (and currently is) the very fertile approach pursued by Spain in its cultural relations with former Spanish territories in America and Asia, especially when it abandons rigid language rife with terms such as title, ownership, sovereignty, or exclusive jurisdiction.

List of Figures

Acknowledgements

This book originated in several lectures given on the subject in recent years. However, the main argument already nested in my computer in late 2019,

370 It could be argued – for the sake of consistency – that States Parties must not use these archaeological activities as grounds for maritime claims even against non-States Parties to the Convention.

371 For other cultural heritage disputes, see A. Chechi, *The Settlement of International Cultural Heritage Disputes* (Oxford University Press: Oxford, 2014).

when various similar maritime claims took form. Then, in early 2020, Davor Vidas kindly invited me to write for Brill's *Law of the Sea* collection.

To some extent, this book echoes and develops some of my own reflections over the past twenty years, during which time I have tried to analyse – successfully or not – the development of the 2001 UNESCO Convention in the general framework of the law of the sea and the law of cultural heritage. If I have thus often quoted my own work, I beg the reader not to view it as an exercise in intellectual vanity, but rather a way of checking the success – or lack thereof – of my engagement with the matter.

Good friends – including Davor – have accompanied me from the outset in this endeavour. Some have shared ideas, given advice, suggested readings or corrected mistakes. Filipe Castro, Jim Delgado, Hakan Oniz, and Chris Underwood are among them. Others have helped me with different chapters. In this regard, the invaluable feedback from Marc-André Bernier, as well as that from Michael Byers, Elena Conde, and Mary Lou Doyle, was of great utility in the discussion of the Canadian claim to Arctic waters; likewise, the suggestions received from David Abulafia and Craig Forrest were quite helpful for the section on China's claim in the South China Sea, as was the assistance of Dragomir Garvov, John Albertson, and other colleagues whose names – unfortunately – cannot be cited now for the Russian-Crimean case.

Special thanks should also be given to the Brill editors and particularly to Don Rothwell, who decisively improved the original text. Thanks as well to Kari Friedenson for her meticulous language revision of the English text, funded by my university. Of course, the views expressed herein are solely those of the author, as are any errors.

This book deals with ethics applied to underwater archaeology. Upon finishing the final draft, I received the terrible news of the passing of Thijs Maarleveld, one of the most respected and highly regarded figures in the world of underwater archaeology, who devoted part of his writings to the ethical aspects. Thijs honoured me with his friendship. The conclusions of this work are in his memory.

Last but not least, thanks must be given to Bárbara, Gonzalo, and Pablo – my beloved family – for allowing me the many hours spent in front of the computer that made this book possible.

UNIVERSITAT JAUME I

Author's Biographical Note

Born in Cádiz, Spain (1965), Dr Mariano J. Aznar has been Professor of Public International Law at the University Jaume I since 2008. He was previously Associate (1998–2008) and Assistant Professor (1994–1998) at the University of Valencia. He has been a visiting scholar at NYU (1995) and a visiting scholar (2000) and visiting fellow (2016) at the Lauterpacht Centre for International Law at the University of Cambridge, and he is a Life Member of Clare Hall College (*Cantab.*). He has also been a visiting professor at the University of Naples 'Parthénope' (2004), University of Paris II – Panthéon Assas (2005), University of Rome 'Tor Vergata' (2007), and University College London Qatar (2020). He is a founding member of the European Society of International Law (ESIL) and a former member of its Board (2004–2012). Editor-in-Chief of the *Spanish Yearbook of International Law* (2013–2021), the author has been a consultant scholar at the Penn Cultural Heritage Center at the University of Pennsylvania since 2012. He is also a member of the International Committee on the Underwater Cultural Heritage (ICUCH/ICOMOS).

Dr Aznar's main research interests are the international responsibility of States, disarmament, maintenance of international peace and security, and the protection of underwater cultural heritage. He has published four monographs and authored numerous scientific articles published in the RGDIP, ICLQ, EJIL, REDI, SYBIL, LJIL, GYBIL, IJMCL, and ODIL among others. He has also contributed to the Commentary to the UN Charter (Cot & Pellet (eds), 2005), the Commentary to the ICJ Statute (Oellers-Frahm, Tomuschat & Zimmermann (eds), 2006, 2012, and 2018), and the Commentary to the Vienna Convention on the Law of Treaties (Corten & Klein (eds), 2006 and 2011), as well as to the *Traité de droit international de la mer* (Thouvenin & Forteau (eds), 2017).

Co-author of the *Green Book for the Protection of the Spanish Underwater Cultural Heritage* (2010), he is a legal expert on the protection of the underwater cultural heritage, acting both for the Spanish Government and for UNESCO. He has also advised Algeria, Ecuador, El Salvador, Nicaragua, and Qatar, among other States, on legal issues related to cultural heritage. An advocate and counsel of the Kingdom of Spain before the International Tribunal for the Law of the Sea and representative of Spain before the Meeting of States Parties of the UNESCO Convention on the Protection of the Underwater Cultural Heritage, he participated in the drafting of the Operational Guidelines of that Convention and the new Spanish Law on Maritime Navigation. Dr Aznar is a Patron of Spain's National Museum of Underwater Archaeology (ARQVA). More information at www.subarq.org.

References

Bibliography

Abulafia, D., *The Boundless Sea. A Human History of the Oceans* (Penguin/Allen Lane: London, 2019).

Adams, J., 'The Role of Underwater Archaeology in Framing and Facilitating the Chinese National Strategic Agenda', in: T. Blumenfield and H. Silverman (eds), *Cultural Heritage Politics in China* (Springer: New York, 2013), 261–82.

Arend, C. A., 'Archaeological and Historical Objects: The International Legal Implications of UNCLOS III' (1982) 22 *Virginia Journal of International Law* 777–803.

Atala, S., 'Indigenous archaeology and decolonizing practice' (2006) 30(3) *American Indian Quarterly* 280–310.

Aznar, M. J., *La protección del patrimonio cultural subacuático* (Tirant: Valencia, 2004).

Aznar, M. J., 'Treasure hunters, sunken State vessels and the 2001 UNESCO Convention on the Protection of Underwater Cultural Heritage' (2010) 25 *The International Journal of Marine and Coastal Law* 209–236 [doi: 10.1163/157180910X12665776638623].

Aznar, M. J., 'The contiguous zone as an archaeological maritime zone' (2014) 29 *The International Journal of Marine and Coastal Law* 1–51 [doi: 10.1163/15718085-12341305].

Aznar, M. J., 'Exporting Environmental Standards to the Protection of Underwater Cultural Heritage in the Area', in: J. Crawford, A. G. Koroma, S. Mahmoudi and A. Pellet (eds), *The International Legal Order: Current Needs and Possible Responses – Essays in Honour Djamchid Momtaz* (Brill: Leiden/Boston, 2017), 255–273.

Aznar, M. J., 'The human factor in territorial disputes', in: M. G. Kohen and M. Hébié, *Research Handbook on Territorial Disputes in International Law* (Edward Elgar: Cheltenham, 2018), 291–342.

Aznar, M. J., '*In situ* preservation of underwater cultural heritage as an international legal principle' (2018) 13 *Journal of Maritime Archaeology* 67–81 [doi: 10.1007/s11457-018-9192-4].

Aznar, M. J., 'La Convention UNESCO pour la protection du patrimoine culturel subaquatique: une évaluation dix ans après son entrée en vigueur' (2018) 23 *Annuaire du droit de la mer* 197–211.

Aznar, M. J., 'The notions of "preferential right" and "interest" of states in the protection of the underwater cultural heritage' (2019) 38 *Revista Electrónica de Estudios Internacionales* 1–37 [doi: 10.17103/reei.38.07].

Ballard, R. D. (ed.) *Archaeological Oceanography* (Princeton University Press: Princeton, 2008).

Banet, C. (ed.), *The Law of the Seabed* (Brill: Leiden/Boston, 2020).

Bashirova, L. D., Ulyanova, M. O., Kovalev, A. A. et al., 'On the Legal Status of Maritime Cultural Heritage and Its Management in the Russian Sectors of the Baltic Sea' (2021) 16 *Journal of Maritime Archaeology*, 111–132 [doi: 10.1007/s11457-020-09288-4].

Bass, G., 'The Development of Maritime Archaeology', in: B. Ford, D. L. Hamilton and A. Catsambis (eds), *The Oxford Handbook of Maritime Archaeology*, at: <https://www.oxfordhandbooks.com/view/10.1093/oxfordhb/9780199336005.001.0001/oxfordhb-9780199336005-e-0?print=pdf> [doi: 10.1093/oxfordhb/9780199336005.013.0000].

Bederman, D., 'The UNESCO draft convention on underwater cultural heritage: a critique and counter-proposal' (1999) 30 *Journal of Maritime Law & Commerce* 331–354.

Bederman, D., 'The Sea' in: B. Fassbender and A. Peters (eds), *The Oxford Handbook of the History of International Law* (Oxford University Press: Oxford, 2012), 359–379.

Benjamin, J., O'Leary, M., McDonald, J. et al., 'Aboriginal artefacts on the continental shelf reveal ancient drowned cultural landscapes in northwest Australia' (2020) 15(7) *PLoS ONE e0233912* [doi: 10.1371/journal.pone.0233912].

Blau, S. and Skinner, M., 'The use of forensic archaeology in the investigation of human rights abuse: Unearthing the past in East Timor' (2005) 9 *The International Journal of Human Rights* 449–463 [doi: 10.1080/13642980500349857].

Boisson de Chazournes, L., La Rosa, A-M and Mbengue, M. M., 'Art. 18 Convention of 1969', in: Corten, O. and Klein, P. (eds), *The Vienna Contention on the Law of Treaties. A Commentary* (Oxford University Press: Oxford, 2011), 369–403.

Bonifácio Ramos, J. L., *O achatamento de bens culturais subaquáticos* (Livraia Petrony: Lisbon, 2008).

Bonnet, F.-X., 'Archeology and Patriotism: Long Term Chinese Strategies in the South China Sea', paper presented at the Southeast Asia Sea conference (Ateneo Law Center, Makati, 27 March 2015), at: <http://www.imoa.ph/archeology-and-patriotism-long-term-chinese-strategies-in-the-south-china-sea/>.

Brennan, M. L. et al., 'Telepresence-Enabled Maritime Archaeological Exploration in the Deep' (2018) 13(2) *Journal of Maritime Archaeology* 97–122.

Broadbent, N. D. and Rose, L., 'Historical Archaeology and the Byrd Legacy: The United States Antarctic Service Expedition, 1939–41' (2002) 110 *The Virginia Magazine of History and Biography* 237–258.

Browne, K., '"Ghost Battleships" of the Pacific: Metal Pirates, WWII Heritage, and Environmental Protection' (2019) 14 *Journal of Maritime Archaeology* 1–28 [DOI: 10.1007/s11457-018-9223-1].

Burke, D. C., *International Disputes and Cultural Ideas in the Canadian Arctic* (Palgrave Macmillan: London, 2018).

Buszynski, L. and Roberts, C. R. (eds), *The South China Sea Maritime Dispute: Political, Legal and Regional Perspectives* (Routledge: Oxford, 2014).

Byers, M. and Lalonde, S., 'Who Controls the Northwest Passage?' (2009) 42 *Vanderbilt Journal of Transnational Law* 1133–1210.

Byers, M. and Lodge, E., 'China and the Northwest Passage' (2019) 18 *Chinese Journal of International Law* 57–90 [doi:10.1093/chinesejil/jmz001].

Byers, M., *Who Owns the Arctic: Understanding Sovereignty Disputes in the North* (Douglas and McIntyre: Vancouver, 2009).

Byers, M., *International Law and the Arctic* (Cambridge University Press: Cambridge, 2013).

Caiti, A., Casalino, D. J., Conte, G. and Zanoli, S. M., 'Innovative technologies in underwater archaeology: field experience, open problems, and research lines' (2006) 22(1) *Chemistry and Ecology* S383–S396 [doi: 10.1080/02757540600572321].

Campfens, E., 'Whose Cultural Heritage? Crimean Treasures at the Crossroads of Politics, Law and Ethics' (2017) 22 *Art Antiquity & Law* 193–212.

Carducci, G., 'New Developments in the Law of the Sea: The UNESCO Convention on the Protection of Underwater Cultural Heritage' (2002) 96(2) *American Journal of International Law* 419–434.

Carrai, M. A., Defraigne, J. C. and Wouters, J. (eds), *The Belt and Road Initiative and Global Governance* (Edward Elgar: Cheltenham, 2020) [doi: 10.4337/9781789906226].

Carty, A., 'The Corfu Channel Case – and the Missing Admiralty Orders' (2004) 3 *The Law and Practice of International Courts and Tribunals* 1–35.

Castro, F. and Drap, P., 'A arqueologia marítima e o futuro' (2017) 11 *VESTÍGIOS – Revista Latino-Americana de Arqueologia Histórica* 41–55 [doi: 10.31239/vtg.v11i1.10550].

Chai, R. and Li, H., 'A Study on Legislation for Protection of Cultural Relics in China: Origin, Content and Model' (2019) 8 *Chinese Studies* 132–147 [doi: 10.4236/chnstd.2019.83011].

Chan, E. S. Y., 'Rethinking uniqueness of China's sea power development' (2020) 12 *Australian Journal of Maritime & Ocean Affairs* 269–275 [doi: 10.1080/18366503.2020.1834061].

Chang, T. K., 'China's Claim of Sovereignty over Spratly and Paracel Islands: A Historical and Legal Perspective' (1991) 23 *Case Western Reserve Journal of International Law* 399–420 (at: <https://scholarlycommons.law.case.edu/jil/vol23/iss3/1>).

Chang, Y.-C., 'The "21st Century Maritime Silk Road Initiative" and naval diplomacy in China' (2018) 153 *Ocean and Coastal Management* 153 148–156 [doi: 10.1016/j.ocecoaman.2017.12.015].

Charron, A., 'Russia's Recolonization of Crimea' (2020) 119 *Current History* 275–281 [doi: 10.1525/curh.2020.119.819.275].

Chechi, A., *The Settlement of International Cultural Heritage Disputes* (Oxford University Press: Oxford, 2014).

Chechi, A., 'The 2013 judgment of the ICJ in the *Temple of Preah Vihear* case and the protection of world cultural heritage sites in wartime' (2016) 6(2) *Asian Journal of International Law* 353–378 [doi: 10.1017/S2044251315000156].

Cheng, A. C., 'All in the same boat?: Indigenous property rights in underwater cultural heritage' (2010) 32 *Houston Journal of International Law* 695–732.

Chinese Society of International Law, 'The South China Sea Arbitration Awards: A Critical Study' (2018) 17 *Chinese Journal of International Law* 206–748.

Chock, J., 'China's Non-Military Maritime Assets as a Force Multiplier for Security' (2015) 322 *Asia Pacific Bulletin* (at: <https://www.eastwestcenter.org/publications/china's-non-military-maritime-assets-force-multiplier-security>).

Christakis, T., 'Les conflits de la sécession en Crimée et dans l'est de l'Ukraine et le droit international' (2014) 141(3) *Journal du droit international* 733–764.

Christie, G., 'Indigeneity and sovereignty in Canada's far north: The Arctic and Inuit sovereignty' (2011) 110 *The South Atlantic Quarterly* 330–346.

Churchill, R. R. and Lowe, A. V., *The Law of the Sea*, 3rd edn (Manchester University Press: Manchester, 1999).

Clark, H. R., 'Frontier Discourse and China's Maritime Frontier: China's Frontiers and the Encounter with the Sea through Early Imperial History' (2009) 20 *Journal of World History* 1–33.

Clément, E., 'Le concept de *responsabilité collective* de la communauté internationale pour la protection des biens culturels dans les conventions et recommandations de l'UNESCO' (1993) *Revue Belge du Droit International* 535–551.

Conde, E. and Scopelliti, M., 'Arctic Region', *Oxford Bibliographies*, available at <https://www.oxfordbibliographies.com/view/document/obo-9780199796953/obo-9780199796953-0090.xml>.

Conde, E., 'El régimen de los espacios polares el espacio ártico', in: F. M. Mariño (ed.), *Instrumentos y regímenes de cooperación internacional*, 2nd edn (Trotta: Madrid, 2017), 407–426.

Czapliński, W., Dębski, S., Tarnogórski, R. and Wierczyńska, K. (eds), *The Case of Crimea's Annexation under International Law* (Scholar Publishing House and Centre for Polish-Russian Dialogue and Understanding: Warsaw, 2017).

Delgado, J. P. (ed.), *Encyclopaedia of Underwater and Maritime Archaeology* (British Museum Press: London, 1997).

Delgado, J. P. and Staniforth, M., 'Underwater Archaeology', in UNESCO-EOLSS (available at: <https://www.eolss.net/sample-chapters/C04/E6-21-01-10.pdf>).

Dörr, O. and Schmalenbach, K., 'Article 18. Obligation not to defeat the object and purpose of a treaty prior to its entry into force'. In: Dörr, O. and Schmalenbach, K. (eds) *Vienna Convention on the Law of Treaties* (Springer: Berlin/Heidelberg, 2012), [doi: 10.1007/978-3-642-19291-3_20].

Dromgoole, S. and Gaskell, N., 'Who has a right to historic wrecks and wreckage?' (1993) 2 *International Journal of Cultural Property* 217–273.

Dromgoole, S., 'Revisiting the relationship between marine scientific research and the underwater cultural heritage' (2010) 25 *The International Journal of Marine and Coastal Law* 33–61.

Dromgoole, S., Reflections on the Position of the Major Maritime Powers with Respect to the UNESCO Convention on the Protection of the Underwater Cultural Heritage 2001' (2013) 38 *Marine Policy* 116–123.

Dromgoole, S., *Underwater Cultural Heritage and International Law* (Cambridge University Press: Cambridge, 2013).

Dupuy, F. and Dupuy, P.-M., 'A Legal Analysis of China's Historic Rights Claim in the South China Sea' (2013) 107 *American Journal of International Law* 124–141.

Elia, R., 'US Protection of Underwater Cultural Heritage Beyond the Territorial Sea: Problems and Prospects' (2000) 29 *The International Journal of Nautical Archaeology* 43–56.

Fassbender, B. and Peters, A. (eds), *The Oxford Handbook of the History of International Law* (Oxford University Press: Oxford, 2012).

Flecker, M., 'The ethics, politics, and realities of maritime archaeology in Southeast Asia' (2002) 31 *International Journal of Nautical Archaeology* 12–24.

Flecker, M., 'Early Chinese Voyaging in the South China Sea: Implications on Territorial Claims' (2017) 1 *Journal of Maritime Studies and National Integration* 1–21. For a more complete version of this article, see Michael Flecker, 'Early Voyaging in the South China Sea: Implications on Territorial Claims' (2015) *Nalanda-Sriwijaya Centre Working Paper No. 19*, at 47 (at: <https://www.iseas.edu.sg/articles-commentaries/nsc-working-papers/early-voyaging-south-china-sea-implications-territorial-claims/>).

Forrest, C., 'A New International Regime for the Protection of Underwater Cultural Heritage' (2002) 51 *International and Comparative Law Quarterly* 511–554 [doi: https://doi.org/10.1093/iclq/51.3.511].

Forrest, C., *Maritime legacies and the law: effective legal governance of WWI wrecks* (Edward Elgar: Cheltenham, 2019).

Forteau, M. and Thouvenin, J.-M. (eds), *Traité de droit international de la mer* (Editions A. Pedone: Paris, 2017).

Francioni, F., 'Principi e criteri ispiratori per la protezione internazionale del patrimonio culturale', in F. Francioni, A. del Vecchio and P. de Caterini (eds), *Protezione internazionale del patrimonio culturale: interessi nazionali e difesa del patrimonio comune della cultura* (Giuffrè Editore: Milan, 2000), 11–20.

Franckx, E., 'The legal regime of navigation in the Russian Arctic' (2009) 18(2) *Journal of Transnational Law & Policy* 327–342.

Franckx, E., and Benatar, M., 'Dots and Lines in the South China Sea: Insights from the Law of Map Evidence' (2012) 2 *Asian Journal of International Law* 89–118.

Freestone, D., Laffoley, D., Douvere, F. and Badman, T., *World Heritage in the High Seas: An Idea Whose Time Has Come* (UNESCO: Paris, 2016), at: <https://whc.unesco.org/en/news/1535/>.

Fu, K.-c., 'A Chinese Perspective on the UNESCO Convention on the Protection of the Underwater Cultural Heritage' (2003) 18 *International Journal of Maritime & Commercial Law* 109–126.

Fu, K.-c., 'China (including Taiwan)', in: S. Dromgoole (ed.), *The Protection of the Underwater Cultural Heritage: National Perspectives in Light of the UNESCO Convention* 2001 (Brill/Nijhoff: The Hague, 2006), 17–41.

Galili, E., Benjamin, J., Eshed, V., Rosen, B., McCarthy, J. and Kolska-Horwitz, L., 'A submerged 7000-year-old village and seawall demonstrate earliest known coastal defence against sea-level rise' (2019) 14 *PLoS ONE* 1–17 [doi: 10.1371/journal.pone.0222560].

Gao, Z. and Jia, B. B., 'The Nine-Dash Line in the South China Sea: History, Status, and Implications' (2013) 107 *American Journal of International Law* 98–124.

Garabello, R. and Scovazzi, T., *The Protection of the Underwater Cultural Heritage: before and after the 2001 UNESCO Convention* (Brill/Nijhoff: Leiden/Boston, 2003).

Garabello, R., *La Convenzione UNESCO sulla protezione del patrimonio culturales subacqueo* (Giuffrè Editore: Milan, 2004).

Gaskell, N. and Forrest, F., *The Law of Wreck* (Routledge: London, 2019).

Gately, I. and Benjamin, J., 'Archaeology Hijacked: Addressing the Historical Misappropriations of Maritime and Underwater Archaeology' (2018) 13(1) *Journal of Maritime Archaeology* 15–35 [doi: 10.1007/s11457-017-9177-8].

González, A., 'Negotiating the Convention on Underwater Cultural Heritage: Myths and Reality', in: R. Garabello and T. Scovazzi, *The Protection of the Underwater Cultural Heritage, before and after the 2001 UNESCO Convention* (Leiden/Boston: Brill/Nijhoff, 2003), 83–88.

Guo, R., 'China's Maritime Silk Road Initiative and the Protection of Underwater Cultural Heritage' (2017) 32 *The International Journal of Marine and Coastal Law* 510–543 [doi. 10.1163/15718085-12323033].

Hafner, A., Öniz, H., Semaan, L. and Underwood, Ch. J., *Heritage at Risk. Threats-Challenges-Solutions* (ICOMOS/ICUCH, 2020), available at: <https://openarchive.icomos.org/id/eprint/2488/>.

Hayton, B., *The South China Sea: The Struggles for Power in Asia* (Yale University Press: New Haven, 2014).

Hayton, B., 'When Good Lawyers Write Bad History: Unreliable Evidence and the South China Sea Territorial Dispute' (2017) 48(1) *Ocean Development & International Law* 17–34.

Heng, D., *Sino–Malay Trade and Diplomacy from the Tenth through the Fourteenth Century* (Ohio University Press: Athens, 2009).

Hodgetts, L. M., 'The rediscovery of HMS *Investigator*: Archaeology, sovereignty and the colonial legacy in Canada's Arctic' (2019) 13(1) *Journal of Social Archaeology* 80–100.

Hu, N.-T. A., 'The 2001 UNESCO Underwater Cultural Heritage Convention and Taiwan's Domestic Legal Regime' (2008) 39 *Ocean Development & International Law* 372–394 [doi: 10.1080/00908320802459151].

Huang, J., 'Chasing provenance: Legal dilemmas for protecting states with a verifiable link to underwater culture heritage' (2013) 84 *Ocean & Coastal Management* 220–225.

Huayou, Z. and Huaifeng, R., 'Protection of Underwater Cultural Heritage in the South China Sea and Regional Cooperation', in: M. H. Nordquist, J. N. Moore and K.-C. Fu (eds), *Recent Developments in the Law of the Sea and China* (Martinus Nijhoff: Leiden, 2006) 483–490.

Institut de Droit International, 'The Legal Regime of Wrecks of Warships and Other State-owned Ships in International Law', Resolution adopted on 29 August 2015, Tallinn Session (at <http://www.justitiaetpace.org/idiE/resolutionsE/2015Tallinn09en.pdf>).

International Law Commission, *Yearbook of the International Law Commission*, vol. II, 1956.

Ioannides, N. A., 'The "Predominant Interest" Concept in Maritime Boundary Delimitation' (2020) 51 *Ocean Development & International Law* 217–240 [doi: 10.1080/00908320.2020.1757215].

Irwin, J. A. and Conlin, D., 'The maritime archaeology of slave ships: overview, assessment and prospectus' (2016) *Underwater Archaeology Proceedings* 72–74.

Jaeckel, A., Gjerde, K. M. and Ardron, J. A., 'Conserving the common heritage of humankind – Options for the deep-seabed mining regime' (2017) 78 *Marine Policy* 150–157 [doi: 10.1016/j.marpol.2017.01.019].

Jayakumar, S., Koh, T. and Beckman, R. (eds), *The South China Sea Disputes and Law of the Sea* (Edward Elgar: Cheltenham, 2014).

Jayakumar, S., Koh, T. and Beckman, R. (eds), *The South China Sea Arbitration: The legal dimension* (Edward Elgar: Cheltenham, 2018).

Jessup, P. C., *The Law of Territorial Waters and Maritime Jurisdiction* (G. A. Jennings: New York, 1927), at 383.

Jing, Y. and Li, J., 'Who Owns Underwater Cultural Heritage in the South China Sea' (2019) 47 *Coastal Management* 107–126 [doi: 10.1080/08920753.2019.1540908].

Jing, Y., 'Protection of underwater cultural heritage in China: new developments' (2019) 29 *International Journal of Cultural Policy* 756–764 [doi: 10.1080/10286632.2017.1372753].

Jinliang, Q., 'Protecting China's maritime heritage: Current conditions and national policy' (2012) 1 *Journal of Marine and Islands Cultures* 46–50.

Jörg, C. J. A., *The Geldermalsen: History and Porcelain* (Kemper Publisher: Groningen, 1986).

Juhl, K., 'The Contribution by (Forensic) Archaeologists to Human Rights Investigations of Mass Graves' (2005) 5 *Am-Profil* (available at: <https://am.uis.no/getfile

.php/13201047/Arkeologisk%20museum/2015/Store%20bilder%20til%20ny%20 nettsider/amprofil-5.pdf>).

Keyuan, Z., 'Historic Rights in International Law and in China's Practice' (2001) 32 *Ocean Development & International Law* 149–168.

Koh, H. H., *The Trump Administration and International Law* (Oxford University Press: Oxford, 2018).

Kohen, M. G., 'Titles and *effectivités* in territorial disputes', in: M. G. Kohen and M. Hébié (eds), *Research Handbook on Territorial Disputes in International Law* (Edward Elgar: Cheltenham, 2018), 145–168.

Kohl, P. L. and Fawcett, C., *Nationalism, Politics and the Practice of Archaeology* (Cambridge University Press: Cambridge, 1996).

Kohl, P. L., Kozelsky, M. and Ben-Yehuda, N. (eds), *Selective Remembrances: Archaeology in the Construction, Commemoration, and Consecration of National Pasts* (University of Chicago Press: Chicago, 2007).

Kopela, S., 'Historic Titles and Historic Rights in the Law of the Sea in the Light of the South China Sea Arbitration' (2017) 48 *Ocean Development & International Law* 181–207.

Kraska, J. and Monti, M., 'The Law of Naval Warfare and China's Maritime Militia' (2015) 91 *International Law Studies* 451–467.

Lalonde, S. and Lasserre, F., 'The Position of the United States on the Northwest Passage: Is the Fear of Creating a Precedent Warranted?' (2013) 44(1) *Ocean Development & International Law* 28–72 [doi: 10.1080/00908320.2012.726832].

Lenihan, D. J., 'Recent Advances in Underwater Archaeology', in: R. A. Williamson and P. R. Nickens (eds), *Science and Technology in Historic Preservation: Advances in Archaeological and Museum Science*, vol. 4 (Springer: Boston, 2000) [doi: 10.1007/978-1-4615-4145-5_6].

Levathes, L., *When China ruled the seas: the Treasure Fleet of the Dragon Throne, 1405–33* (Oxford University Press: New York, 1994).

Li, X. and Chang, Y.-C., 'Legal mechanism for the Sino-Foreign cooperative exploitation of the underwater cultural heritage in the South China Sea' (2009) 175 *Ocean & Coastal Management* 144–151 [doi: 10.1016/j.ocecoaman.2019.04.004].

Lin, Z., 'The protection of sunken WWII warships located in Indonesian or Malaysian territorial waters' (2020) 113 *Marine Policy 103804* [doi: 10.1016/j.marpol.2019.103804].

Liu, L., 'Exploration and analysis on regional cooperation scheme for protection of underwater cultural heritage in South China Sea' (2017) 19 *Journal of Chang'an University (Social Science Edition)*, at: <http://skxb.chd.edu.cn/oa/DArticle.aspx?type=view&id=20170212>.

Liu, L. and Liu, S., 'From difference to convergence: A comparative analysis of the development of the legal protection of the underwater cultural heritage in China and the 2001 Convention' (2013) 52(167) *Poredbeno pomorsko pravo* 149–165, at: <https://hrcak.srce.hr/file/172531>.

Liu, Y., Chen, Z. and Blue, G., (eds), *Zheng He's Maritime Voyages (1405–1433) and China's Relations with the Indian Ocean World: A Multilingual Bibliography* (Brill: Leiden, 2014).

Lo, J.-p., *China as a Sea Power, 1127–1368: A Preliminary Survey of the Maritime Expansion and Naval Exploits of the Chinese People During the Southern Song and Yuan Periods*, ed. by B. A. Elleman (National University of Singapore Press: Singapore, 2011).

Lu, B. and Zhou, S., 'China's state-led working model on protection of underwater cultural heritage: Practice, challenges, and possible solutions' (2016) 65 *Marine Policy* 39–47 [doi: 10.1016/j.marpol.2015.12.003].

Lund, C., 'Protection of the Under-Water Cultural Heritage', in: U. Leanza (ed.), *Il regime giuridico internazionale del Mare Mediterraneo* (Editoriale Scientifica: Naples, 1987), 351–354.

Maarleveld, T. J., 'Ethics, Underwater Cultural Heritage, and International Law' in: A. Catsambis, B. Ford and D. L. Hamilton (eds) *The Oxford Handbook of Maritime Archaeology* (Oxford University Press: Oxford/New York, 2001), 917–941 [doi: 10.1093/oxfordhb/9780199336005.013.0040].

Maarleveld, T. J., 'The Notion of "Verifiable Links" in the 2001 UNESCO Convention on the Protection of the Underwater Cultural Heritage' (2014) 19 *Art Antiquity and Law* 101–119.

Manders, M. R., de Hoop, R. W., Adhityatama, S. et al., 'Battle of the Java Sea: One Event, Multiple Sites, Values and Views' (2021) 16 *Journal of Maritime Archaeology* 39–56 [doi: 10.1007/s11457-020-09287-5].

Manullang, N. C., Siswandi, A. G. and Dewi, C. T. I., 'The Status of Maritime Militia in the South China Sea Under International Law Perspective' (2020) 27 *JH Ius Quia Iustum* 23–44 (at: <https://journal.uii.ac.id/IUSTUM/article/view/14958>).

Martínez Vargas, J. R. and Vega Barbosa, G., *Tratado de Derecho del Mar* (Valencia: Tirant, 2016).

McCann, A. M. and Oleson, J. P., 'Deep-water shipwrecks off Skerki Bank: The 1997 Survey', in: *Journal of Roman archaeology. Supplementary series, no. 58* (2004).

Merryman, J. H., 'Two Ways of Thinking About Cultural Property' (1986) 80 *American Journal of International Law* 831–853 [doi: 10.2307/2202065].

Miller, G. L., 'The Second Destruction of the Geldermalsen' (1992) 26 *Historical Archaeology* 124–31.

Mohan, M., 'Historical Fiction: China's South China Sea Claims' (2013) 176 *World Affairs* 83–90.

Nafziger, J., 'The UNESCO Convention on the Protection of the Underwater Cultural Heritage: Its Growing Influence' (2018) 49 *Journal of Maritime Law and Commerce* 371–400.

Naldi, G., 'The Status of the Disputed Waters Surrounding Gibraltar' (2013) 28 *The International Journal of Marine and Coastal Law* 701–718.

National Institute for South China Sea Studies, 'A Legal Critique of the Award of the Arbitral Tribunal in the Matter of the South China Sea Arbitration' (2018) 24 *Asian Yearbook of International Law* 151–293 [doi: 10.1163/9789004437784_009].

Nitiruchirot, Y., 'The Challenges of Underwater Cultural Heritage Protection in the South China Sea' (2016) 2 *China Oceans Law Review* 244–267.

O. Corten, O., 'The Russian intervention in the Ukrainian crisis: was *jus contra bellum* "confirmed rather than weakened"?' (2015) 2(1) *Journal on the Use of Force and International Law* 17–41.

O'Keefe, P. and Nafziger, J., 'The Draft Convention on Underwater Cultural Heritage' (1994) 25 *Ocean Development & International Law* 391–418 [doi: 10.1080/00908329409546041].

Oral, N., '*Ukraine* v. *The Russian Federation*: Navigating Conflict over Sovereignty under UNCLOS' (2021) 97 *International Law Studies* 478–508.

Oxman, B. H., 'Marine Archaeology and the International Law of the Sea' (1988) 12 *Columbia*-VLA *Journal of Law & the Arts* 353–372.

Pearson, N., 'Protecting and Preserving Underwater Cultural Heritage in Southeast Asia', in: S. Hufnagel and D. Chappell (eds), *The Palgrave Handbook on Art Crime* (Palgrave Macmillan: London, 2019), 685–730 [doi: 10.1057/978-1-137-54405-6_31].

Pérez-Álvaro, E. and Forrest, C., 'Maritime Archaeology and Underwater Cultural Heritage in the Disputed South China Sea' (2018) 25 *International Journal of Cultural Property* 375–401.

Pérez-Álvaro, E., 'Climate change and underwater cultural heritage: Impacts and challenges' (2016) 21 *Journal of Cultural Heritage* 842–848 [doi: /10.1016/j.culher.2016.03.006].

Pérez-Álvaro, E., *Underwater Cultural Heritage: Ethical Concepts and Practical Challenges* (Routledge: London/New York, 2019).

Pharand, D., 'Historic Waters in International Law with Special Reference to the Arctic' (1971) 21(1) *The University of Toronto Law Journal* 1–14.

Pharand, D., 'The Arctic Waters and the Northwest Passage: A Final Revisit' (2007) 38(1–2) *Ocean Development & International Law* 3–69 [doi: 10.1080/00908320601071314].

Potter, R. A., *Finding Franklin: The Untold Story of a 165-Year Search* (McGill-Queen's University Press: Montreal, 2016).

Ra'anan, U., *The Frontiers of a Nation* (Hyperion Press: Westport, CT, 1976).

Ransley, J., 'Boats Are for Boys: Queering Maritime Archaeology' (2005) 37(4) *World Archaeology* 621–629 [doi: 10.1080/00438240500404623].

Rau, M., 'The UNESCO Convention on Underwater Cultural Heritage and the International Law of the Sea' (2002) 6 *Max Planck Yearbook of United Nations Law* 387–472.

Reid, R. S., 'The Canadian Claim to Sovereignty Over the Waters of the Arctic' (1974) 12 *Canadian Yearbook of International Law* 111–136.

Reisman, W. M. and Skinner, C., *Fraudulent Evidence before Public International Tribunals: The Dirty Stories of International Law* (Cambridge University Press: Cambridge, 2014).

Rey da Silva, A., 'Sailing the waters of sustainability: Reflections on the future of maritime cultural heritage protection in the global sea of development' (2020) 10 *European Journal of Postclassical Archaeologies* 107–134.

Roberts, H., 'The British Ratification of the Underwater Heritage Convention: Problems and Prospects' (2018) 67(4) *International and Comparative Law Quarterly* 833–865 [doi: 10.1017/S0020589318000210].

Ronan, C. A., *The Shorter Science and Civilization in China*, by J. Needham, vol. 3 (Cambridge University Press: Cambridge, 1986).

Rothwell, D. R. and Stephens, T., *The International Law of the Sea*, 2nd edn (Hart Publishing: Oxford, 2016).

Rothwell, D. R., 'The Canadian-U.S. Northwest Passage Dispute: A Reassessment' (1993) 26(2) *Cornell International Law Journal* 331–372.

Rothwell, D. R., *Arctic Ocean Shipping: Navigation, Security and Sovereignty in the North American Arctic, Brill Research Perspectives in the Law of the Sea* (Brill: Leiden/Boston, 2018).

Rothwell, D. R., Elferink, A. O., Scott, K. and Stephens, T. (eds), *The Oxford Handbook of the Law of the Sea* (Oxford University Press: Oxford, 2015).

Sarid, E., 'International Underwater Cultural Heritage Governance: Past Doubts and Current Challenges' (2017) 35 *Berkeley Journal of International Law* 219–261 [doi: 10.15779/Z383R0PT20].

Sato, K., 'China's Maritime Militia: A Legal Point of View', *Maritime Issues*, 12 March 2020 (at: <http://www.maritimeissues.com/politics/maritime-militia-in-east-and-south-china-seas.html>).

Sayapin, S. and Tsybulenko, E., *The Use of Force against Ukraine and International Law: Jus Ad Bellum, Jus In Bello, Jus Post Bellum* (T. M. C. Asser Press: The Hague, 2018).

Schatz, V. J. and Koval, D., 'Russia's Annexation of Crimea and the Passage of Ships Through Kerch Strait: A Law of the Sea Perspective' (2019) 50 *Ocean Development & International Law* 275–297 [doi: 10.1080/00908320.2019.1605677].

Schatz, V. J. and Koval, D., 'Ukraine v. Russia: Passage through Kerch Strait and the Sea of Azov', *Völkerrechtsblog* (available at: <https://voelkerrechtsblog.org/symposium/russian-perspectives-on-international-law/>).

Schoenbaum, T. J., *Admiralty and Maritime Law*, 6th edn (West Academic: St Paul, MN, 2018).

Schoenbaum, T. J., 'The South China Sea Arbitration Decision and a Plan for Peaceful Resolution of the Disputes' (2016) 47(4) *Journal of Maritime Law & Commerce* 451–77 [doi: http://dx.doi.org/10.2139/ssrn.2931150].

Schofield, C., *The Regime of Islands Reframed: Developments in the Definition of Islands under the International Law of the Sea, Brill Research Perspectives in the Law of the Sea* (Brill: Leiden/Boston, 2021).

Schottenhammer, A., 'China's Rise and Retreat as a Maritime Power', in: R. Antony and A. Schottenhammer (eds), *New Discourses on China's Role in East Asian Maritime History* (Otto Harrassowitz: Wiesbaden, 2017), 189–211 (available at: <https://biblio.ugent.be/publication/8543927/file/8543932.pdf>).

Schug, D. M., 'International maritime boundaries and indigenous people: The case of the Torres Strait' (1996) 20(3) *Marine Policy* 209–222.

Scovazzi, T., 'A Contradictory and Counterproductive Regime', in: R. Garabello and T. Scovazzi (eds), *The Protection of the Underwater Cultural Heritage: Before and After the 2001 UNESCO Convention* (Brill: Leiden/Boston, 2003), 3–18.

Scovazzi, T., 'Sunken Spanish Ships before American Courts' (2018) 34 *The International Journal of Marine and Coastal Law* 245–290.

Shen, J., 'China's Sovereignty over the China Sea Islands: A Historical Perspective' (2002) 1 *Chinese Journal of International Law* 126–130.

Sheng-ti Gau, M., 'The Sino-Philippine Arbitration of the South China Sea Nine-Dash Dispute: Applying the Rule of Law on Default of Appearance' (2014) 28 *Ocean Yearbook* 81–133.

Sicilianos, L. A., 'L'Articulation entre droit international humanitaire et droits de l'homme dans la jurisprudence de la Cour européenne des droits de l'homme' (2017) 27/1 *Swiss Review of International and European Law* 3–17.

Silberman, N. A., 'If I forget thee, O Jerusalem: archaeology, religious commemoration and nationalism in a disputed city, 1801–2001' (2001) 7(4) *Nations and Nationalism* 487–504.

Skaridov, A., 'The Sea of Azov and the Kerch Straits', in: D. D. Caron and N. Oral (eds), *Navigating Straits: Challenges for International Law* (Brill/Nijhoff: The Hague, 2014), 220–237 [doi: 10.1163/9789004266377012].

Smith, G. W., 'The Transfer of Arctic territories from Great Britain to Canada in 1880, and some related matters, as seen in official correspondence' (1961) 14 *Arctic* 53–73 [doi: 10.14430/arctic3660].

Smith, G. W., 'Sovereign in the North: The Canadian Aspect of an International Problem,' in R. S. J. MacDonald (ed.), *The Arctic Frontier* (University of Toronto Press: Toronto, 1966), 195–211.

Smith, L. C. and Stephenson, S. R., 'New Trans-Artic shipping routes navigable by mid-century' (2013) 110(13) PNAS *E1191–1195* [doi: 10.1073/pnas.1214212110] (available at <https://www.pnas.org/content/pnas/110/13/E1191.full.pdf>).

Soons, S., *Marine Scientific Research and the Law of the Sea* (TMC Asser Instituut: The Hague, 1982).

Šošić, T. M., 'The common heritage of mankind and the protection of the underwater cultural heritage', in: B. Vukas and T. M. Šošić (eds), *International Law: New Actors, New Concepts – Continuing Dilemmas. Liber Amicorum Božidar Bakotić* (Brill/Nijhoff: The Hague/Boston, 2010), 319–350 [doi: 10.1163/ej.9789004181823.i-614.100].

Stenton, D., Fratpietro, S., Keenleyside, A., & Park, R., 'DNA identification of a sailor from the 1845 Franklin northwest passage expedition' (2021) 57 *Polar Record* E14 [doi: 10.1017/S0032247421000061].

Strati, A., 'Protection of the Underwater Cultural Heritage: from the Shortcomings of the UN Convention on the Law of the Sea to the Compromises of the UNESCO Convention', in: A. Strati (ed.), *Unresolved Issues and the New Challenges to the Law of the Sea* (Brill: Leiden/Boston, 2006), 21–62.

Symmons, C., *Historic Waters in the Law of the Sea: A Modern Re-Appraisal* (Brill/Nijhoff: Leiden/Boston, 2008).

Talmon, S., 'The South China Sea Arbitration and the Finality of "Final" Awards' (2017) 8(2) *Journal of International Dispute Settlement* 388–401 [doi: 10.1093/jnlids/idw027].

Talmon, T., and Jia, B. B., *The South China Sea Arbitration: A Chinese Perspective* (Hart Publishing: London, 2014).

Tang, C.-H., 'China-Europe', in: B. Fassbender and A. Peters (eds), *The Oxford Handbook of the History of International Law* (Oxford University Press: Oxford, 2012), 701–723.

Têtu, P.-L., Lasserre, F., Pelletier, S. and Dawson, J., '"Sovereignty" over submerged cultural heritage in the Canadian Arctic waters: case study from the Franklin expedition wrecks (1845–48)' (2019) 42(2) *Polar Geography* 71–88 [doi: 10.1080/1088937X.2019.1578288].

They, M., *La protection internationale du patrimoine culturel de la mer. Les compétences de l'État sur les biens culturels submergés* (Brill/Martinus Nijhoff: Leiden/Dordrecht, 2018).

Todorov, A. A., 'The Russia-USA legal dispute over the straits of the Northern Sea Route and similar case of the Northwest Passage' (2017) 29 *Arctic and North* 63–75.

Trinidad, J., 'The Disputed Waters around Gibraltar' (2016) 86 *British Yearbook of International Law* 101–154.

Turner, P. J., Cannon, S., DeLand, S. et al., 'Memorializing the Middle Passage on the Atlantic seabed in Areas Beyond National Jurisdiction' (2020) 122 *Marine Policy* 104254 [doi: 10.1016/j.marpol.2020.104254].

UNESCO, *The Committee on Conventions and Recommendations* (2020) (source: <http://portal.unesco.org/en/ev.php-URL_ID=32176&URL_DO=DO_TOPIC&URL_SECTION=201.html>).

Vadi, V., 'Investing in culture: underwater cultural heritage and international investment law' (2009) 42 *Vanderbilt Journal of Transnational Law* 853–904.

Van der Zwaag, D. L., 'Canada and the Governance of the Northwest Passage: Rough Waters, Cooperative Currents, Sea of Challenges', in: D. D. Caron and N. Oral (eds),

Navigating Straits: Challenges for International Law (Brill/Nijhoff: Leiden/Boston, 2013), 87–121 [doi: 10.1163/9789004266377006].

Varmer, O., 'Closing the Gaps in the Law Protecting Underwater Cultural Heritage on the Outer Continental Shelf' (2014) 33(2) *Stanford Environmental Law Journal* 251–286.

Varmer, O. and Blanco, C. M., 'The case for using the law of salvage to preserve underwater cultural heritage: The integrated marriage of the law of salvage and historic preservation' (2018) 49 *Journal of Maritime Law & Commerce* 401–424.

Varmer, O., Gray, J. and Alberg, D., 'United States: Responses to the 2001 UNESCO Convention on the Protection of the Underwater Cultural Heritage' (2010) 5 *Journal of Maritime Archaeology* 129–141.

Verdú Baeza, J., 'El patrimonio cultural subacuático y el Estrecho de Gibraltar. El caso de la Bahía de Algeciras/Gibraltar' (2016–2017) 2 *Cuadernos de Gibraltar – Gibraltar Reports* 123–146 [doi: 10.25267/CuadGibraltar.2017.i2.07].

Vidas, D., 'The Delimitation of the Territorial Sea, the Continental Shelf, and the EEZ: A Comparative Perspective', in: A. Oude Elferink, T. Henriksen, and S. Busch (dds.), *Maritime Boundary Delimitation: The Case Law: Is It Consistent and Predictable?* (Cambridge University Press: Cambridge, 2018), 33–61 [doi: 10.1017/9781108344302.003].

Vidas, D., Freestone, D. and McAdam, J. (eds), *International Law and Sea Level Rise: Report of the International Law Association Committee on International Law and Sea Level Rise, Brill Research Perspectives in the Law of the Sea* (Brill: Leiden/Boston, 2019).

Villoria Prieto, C., 'La producción cartográfica del jesuita Pedro Murillo Velarde (1696–1753)', in: *El Siglo de las Luces, XVI Jornadas de Historia en Llerena* (Sociedad Extremeña de Historia: Llerena, 2015), 129–146.

von Falkenhausen, L., 'The Regionalist Paradigm in Chinese Archaeology', in: P. L. Kohl and C. Fawcett (eds), *Nationalism, Politics, and the Practice of Archaeology* (Cambridge University Press: Cambridge, 1995), 198–217.

Wang, T., 'International Law in China: Historical and Comparative Perspectives' (1990) 221 *Recueil des Cours* 195–369.

Ward, S., 'Chinese Whispers: Zheng He's Treasure Ships in the Context of Chinese Maritime Policy in the Ming Dynasty (1368–1644)', in: A. Tripathi (ed.), *Maritime Heritage of Indian Ocean: Proceedings of the International Seminar on Maritime Archaeology* 2007 (Sharada Publishing House: Delhi, 2013), 215–229 (at: <https://www.academia.edu/45121719/Chinese_Whispers_Zheng_Hes_Treasure_Ships_in_the_Context_of_Chinese_Maritime_Policy_in_the_Ming_Dynasty_1368_1644_?auto=download&email_work_card=download-paper>).

Webster, J., 'Slave Ships and Maritime Archaeology: An Overview' (2008) 12(1) *International Journal of Historical Archaeology* 6–19 [doi: 10.1007/s10761-007-0040-8].

Wei, Z. and Ahmed, S., 'A General Review of the History of China's Sea-Power Theory Development' (2015) 68 *Naval War College Review* 80–93 (available at: <https://digital-commons.usnwc.edu/nwc-review/vol68/iss4/8).

Whitridge, P., 'Classic Thule [Classic Precontact Inuit]', in: T. M. Friesen and O. K. Mason (eds), *The Oxford Handbook of the Prehistoric Arctic* (Oxford University Press: Oxford, 2016), 821–843.

Yuan-kang, W., 'Managing Regional Hegemony in Historical Asia: The Case of Early Ming China' (2012) 5 *The Chinese Journal of International Politics* 129–153.

Zhong, H., 'Legal Protection of Underwater Cultural Heritage in the Taiwan Strait' (2020) 16 *China Oceans Law Review* 68–100.

Zhong, H., 'Underwater cultural heritage and the disputed South China Sea' (2020) 34 *China Information* 361–382 [doi: 10.1177/0920203X20905302].

Treaties and Other International Agreements

1945 Constitution of the United Nations Educational, Scientific and Cultural Organization, adopted 16 November 1945, entered into force 4 November 1946, 4 UNTS 275.

1954 Convention for the Protection of Cultural Property in the Event of Armed Conflict, adopted 14 May 1954, entered into force 7 August 1956, 249 UNTS 215.

1969 Vienna Convention on the Law of Treaties, adopted 23 May 1969, entered into force 27 January 1980, 1155 UNTS 331.

1970 Convention on the Means of Prohibiting and Preventing the Illicit Import, Export and Transfer of Ownership of Cultural Property, adopted 14 November 1970, entered into force 24 April 1972, 823 UNTS 231.

1972 Convention concerning the Protection of the World Cultural and Natural Heritage, adopted 16 November 1972, entered into force 17 December 1975, 1037 UNTS 151.

1978 Treaty between Australia and the Independent State of Papua New Guinea concerning sovereignty and maritime boundaries in the area between the two countries, including the area known as Torres Strait, and related matters, adopted 18 December 1978, entered into force 15 February 1985, 1429 UNTS 207.

1982 United Nation Convention on the Law of the Sea, adopted 10 December 1982, entered into force 16 November 1994, 1833 UNTS 3.

1988 Agreement Between the Government of Canada and the Government of the United States of America on Arctic Cooperation, signed 11 January 1988, entered into force 11 January 1988, 1852 UNTS 59.

1989 International Convention on Salvage, adopted 28 April 1989, entered into force 14 July 1996, 1953 UNTS 165.

1992 Agreement between the Government of the United States of America and the Government of the French Republic concerning the Wreck of the CSS Alabama, (1992) 20 *Law of the Sea Bulletin* 26–27.

1997 Memorandum of Understanding Between the Governments of Great Britain and Canada Pertaining to the Shipwrecks of the HMS *Erebus* and HMS *Terror*, 5 August 1997 (available at: <https://assets.publishing.service.gov.uk/government/uploads/system/uploads/attachmentdata/file/458500/MOUFOI0286-15.pdf>).

1997 Partition Treaties on the Status and Conditions of the Black Sea Fleet (three treaties signed 28 May 1997, no official English translation text available).

2001 Convention on the Protection of the Underwater Cultural Heritage, adopted 2 November 2001, entered into force 2 January 2009, 2562 UNTS 1.

2003 Agreement between the Government of the French Republic and the Government of the United States of America Regarding the Wreck of "La Belle", adopted 31 March 2003, entered into force 31 March 2003, 2238 UNTS 413.

2003 Convention for the Safeguarding of the Intangible Cultural Heritage, adopted 17 October 2003, entered into force 20 April 2006, 2368 UNTS 3.

2003 Agreement between the Russian Federation and Ukraine on Cooperation in the Use of the Sea of Azov and the Kerch Strait, 24 December 2003, no UNTS registration, no official English translation text available.

2007 International Convention on the Removal of Wrecks, adopted 18 May 2007, entered into force 14 April 2015, 46 ILM 694.

2010 Agreement between Ukraine and Russia on the Black Sea Fleet in Ukraine ('Kharkiv Pact'), signed 21 April 2010, no official English translation text available.

2014 Treaty between the Russian Federation and the Republic of Crimea on the Accession of the Republic of Crimea to the Russian Federation and on Forming New Constituent Entities within the Russian Federation, 18 March 2014, effective as of 1 March 2014, no official English translation text available.

National Legislation and Official Documents, and International Institutional Documents

Algeria

Presidential Decree No. 04-344, establishing a Zone Contiguous to the Territorial Sea, 6 November 2004.

Association of Southeast Asian Nations

Declaration on the Conduct of Parties in the South China Sea, 4 November 2002.

Barbados

Marine Boundaries and Jurisdiction Act of 1978, 25 February 1978.

Coastal Zone Management Act (1 May 2000).

Bermuda

Historic Wrecks Act 2001 (as amended 2004), 27 December 2001.

Brazil

Law No. 7.542 (as amended by Law No. 10.166 of 2000), 26 September 1986.

Canada

Order Respecting Geographical Coordinates of Points from which Baselines May Be Determined (Territorial Sea Geographical Coordinates (Area 7) Order), 10 September 1985.

Canada National Marine Conservation Areas Act 2002, 13 June 2002.

Canada's Arctic and Northern Policy Framework, 10 September 2019.

Historic Sites and Monuments Act (R.S.C., 1985, c. H-4).

Nunavut Act (S.C. 1993, c. 28).

Canada National Parks Act (S.C. 2000, c. 32).

Parks Canada, News Release, 26 September 2018.

Parks Canada, 'Government of Canada and Inuit Heritage Trust Sign Franklin Artifact Memorandum of Understanding', 16 April 2019.

Cape Verde

Law No. 60/IV/92, 21 December 1992.

China

Law on the Territorial Sea and the Contiguous Zone of the People's Republic of China, 25 February 1992, (1992) 21 *Law of the Sea Bulletin* 24–27.

Exclusive Economic Zone and Continental Shelf Act, 26 June 1998, (1998) 38 *Law of the Sea Bulletin* 28–31.

Law of the People's Republic of China on the Protection of Cultural Relics, 19 November 1982.

Regulations Concerning the Management and Protection of Underwater Cultural Relics, 20 October 1989 (as amended in 2002).

'Historical Evidence To Support China's Sovereignty over Nansha Islands', 17 November 2000.

Note Verbale No. CML/17/2009 from the Permanent Mission of the People's Republic of China to the UN Secretary-General, 7 May 2009.

Note Verbale No. CML/18/2009 from the Permanent Mission of the People's Republic of China to the UN Secretary-General, 7 May 2009.

Note Verbale No. CML/8/2011 from the Permanent Mission of the People's Republic of China to the UN Secretary-General, 14 April 2011.

'Position Paper of the Government of the People's Republic of China on the Matter of Jurisdiction in the South China Sea Arbitration Initiated by the Republic of the Philippines', 7 December 2014.

'Briefing by Xu Hong, Director-General of the Department of Treaty and Law on the South China Sea Arbitration Initiated by the Philippines', 12 May 2016.

'China's Arctic Policy', White Paper published on 26 January 2018.

Colombia

Ley nº 26 Normas sobre antigüedades y valores náufragas, 24 January 1986.

Ley 1675 por medio de la cual se reglamentan los artículos 63, 70 y 72 de la Constitución Política de Colombia en lo relativo al Patrimonio Cultural Sumergido, 30 July 2013.

Cyprus

A Law to Provide for the Proclamation of the Contiguous Zone by the Republic of Cyprus, 2 April 2004.

Cuba

Legislative Decree No. 158, Contiguous Zone, 12 April 1995.

Denmark

Act No. 749 of 2007, Act on Nature Conservation, 21 June 2007.

Dominican Republic

Act 66–77, 22 May 2007.

European Union

'Declaration by the High Representative Josep Borrell Fontelles, on behalf of the European Union, on the Autonomous Republic of Crimea and the city of Sevastopol', Council of the EU press release, 16 March 2020 (available at: <https://www.consilium.europa.eu/en/press/press-releases/2020/03/16/declaration-by-the-high-representative-josep-borrell-fontelles-on-behalf-of-the-european-union-on-the-autonomous-republic-of-crimea-and-the-city-of-sevastopol/>).

Greece

Law 3028/2002 on the Protection of Antiquities and the Cultural Heritage in General, 28 June 2002.

Guyana

Maritime Boundaries Act 1977 (30 June 1977).

Iceland

Territorial Waters and Maritime Zones Act 1976, 22 December 1976.

Law No. 41 concerning the Territorial Sea, the Economic Zone and the Continental Shelf (1 June 1979), Art. 4.

International Criminal Court

Report on Preliminary Examination Activities 2020, 14 December 2020.

Ireland

National Monuments (Amendment) Act, 1987, 22 July 1987.

Italy

Law 61 on the Establishment of an Ecological Protection Zone Beyond the Outer Limit of the Territorial Sea, 8 February 2006.

Korea (DPR)

Decree by the Central People's Committee establishing the Economic Zone of the People's Democratic Republic of Korea, 21 June 1977.

Korea (Republic of)

Territorial Sea and Contiguous Zone Act (as amended 21 March 2017).

Madagascar

Loi N° 99-028, portant refonte du Code Maritime, 3 February 2000.

Mauritius

Maritime Zones Act No. 2 of 2005, 1 April 2005.

Mexico

Ley Federal de Monumentos y Zonas Arqueológicos, Artísticos e Históricos, 6 May 1972 (as amended 2018).

Mozambique

Lei nº 4/96, 4 January 1996.

Netherlands

Kingdom Act of 28 April 2005 (Contiguous Zone (Establishment) Act).

Decree of 14 June 2006 (Contiguous Zone (Outer Limits) Decree).

Norway

Act No. 57 relating to Norway's territorial waters and contiguous zone, 27 June 2003.

Organisation of the United Nations

UNGA Resolution 68/262, 27 March 2014.

UNGA Resolution 72/249, 24 December 2017.

UNSC Resolution 22 (1947), 9 April 1947.

Philippines

Presidential Decree No. 1599 of 11 June 1978 establishing an Exclusive Economic Zone and for other purposes, 11 June 1978.

Russia

Law No. 73-FZ, 25 June 2002, 'About objects of cultural heritage (historical and cultural monuments) of the people of the Russian Federation' (as amended on 29 December 2020).

South Africa

Maritime Zones Act No. 15 1994, 11 November 1994.

National Heritage Resources Act No. 25 1999, 28 April 1999.

Spain

Law 16/1985, of 25 June, on the Spanish Historical Heritage.

Note by the Spanish Ministry of Foreign Affairs and Cooperation of 23 March 2007.

Suriname

Maritime Zones Act (7 Abril 2017).

Taiwan

Law on the Territorial Sea and Contiguous Zone of the Republic of China, 21 January 1998.

Tanzania

Territorial Sea and Exclusive Economic Zone Act, 1989 (no date).

Ukraine-Russia

Joint Statement by the President of Ukraine and the President of the Russian Federation on the Sea of Azov and the Strait of Kerch of 24 December 2003, (2004) 54 *Law of the Sea Bulletin* 131.

Ukraine

Law of Ukraine on Protection of Cultural Heritage, 8 June 2000 (as amended in 2007).

'Heritage Assessment Report' submitted by Ukraine in 2016 to the Council of Europe.

United Kingdom

Imperial Order in Council (31 July 1880), in C. O. 42, Vol. 764.

British High Commission Note No. 90/86, 9 July 1986.

Hansard, House of Commons, Written Answers for 24 January 2005, Col. 46W.

United States

Contiguous Zone of the United States – Proclamation by the President of the United States of America, 2 September 1999.

National Marine Sanctuaries Act (NMSA) (2000), 16 USC s.1431 *et seq.*

Sunken Military Craft Act (SMCA) (2004), 10 U.S.C. 113.

US Department of State, *Limits in the Seas No. 109. Continental Shelf boundary: Turkey-USSR and Straight Baselines: USSR (Black Sea)*, 29 September 1988.

US Department of State, *Limits in the Seas No. 112: US Responses to Excessive National Maritime Claims*, 9 March 1992.

US Department of State: 'Remarks With Canadian Foreign Minister Chrystia Freeland Before Their Meeting', 7 May 2019 (meeting with US Secretary of State Mike Pompeo).

Vanuatu

Maritime Zones Act No 6 of 2010, 18 June 2010.

Venezuela

Aquatic Areas Organic Act (17 November 2014).

Vietnam

Decree No 92/2002/ND-CP, on detailed regulations to implement some articles of the Law on Cultural Heritage, 11 November 2002.

Yugoslavia (Former)

Act concerning the Coastal Sea and the Continental Shelf, 23 July 1987.

Cases

1928 *Isla de Palmas*, UNRIAA, vol. 2, 1928, 829.

1933 *Legal Status of Eastern Greenland (Denmark v. Norway)*, Judgment, PCIJ 1933 (Ser A/B, No. 53).

1948 *Corfu Channel case (UK v Albania)*, Preliminary Objections, Judgment, *ICJ Reports* 1948, 15.

1949 *Corfu Channel case (UK v Albania)* (Merits), Judgment, *ICJ Reports* 1949, 4.

1951 *Fisheries Case (United Kingdom* v. *Norway)*, *ICJ Reports* 1951, 116.

1962 *Case concerning the Temple of Preah Vihear (Cambodia v. Thailand)*, Judgment, *ICJ Reports* 1962, 6.

1968 *The Indo-Pakistan Western Boundary (Rann of Kutch) between India and Pakistan (India, Pakistan)*, UNRIAA, vol. 17, 1968, 1.

1969 *North Sea Continental Shelf (Federal Republic of Germany v Denmark)*, Merits, Judgment, *ICJ Reports* 1969, 3.

1981 *Dubai-Sharjah Border Arbitration* (*Dubai/Sharjah*), Award, 19 October 1982, 91 ILM 543.

1986 *Military and Paramilitary Activities in and against Nicaragua* (*Nicaragua v. United States of America*), Merits, Judgment, ICJ Reports 1986, 14.

1998 *Territorial Sovereignty and Scope of the Dispute* (*Eritrea and Yemen*), UNRIAA, vol. 22, 1998, 209.

2001 *ICTY: Prosecutor v. Radislav Krstić*, Case No.: IT-98-33-T, Trial Chamber Judgment, 2 August 2001.

2001 *Maritime Delimitation and Territorial Questions between Qatar and Bahrain* (*Qatar* v. *Bahrain*), Merits, Judgment, *ICJ Reports* 2001, 40.

2002 *Sovereignty over Pulau Ligitan and Pulau Sipadan* (*Indonesia/Malaysia*), Judgment, ICJ *Reports* 2002, 625.

2004 *Legal Consequences of the Construction of a Wall in the Occupied Palestinian Territory*, Advisory Opinion, *ICJ Reports* 2004, 136, at 167.

2007 *Application of the Convention on the Prevention and Punishment of the Crime of Genocide* (*Bosnia and Herzegovina* v. *Serbia and Montenegro*), Judgment, *ICJ Reports* 2007, 43.

2007 *Territorial and Maritime Dispute between Nicaragua and Honduras in the Caribbean Sea* (*Nicaragua v. Honduras*), Judgment, *ICJ Reports* 2007, 659.

2009 *Award in the Arbitration regarding the delimitation of the Abyei Area between the Government of Sudan and the Sudan People's Liberation Movement/Army*, UNRIAA, vol. 30, 2009, 145.

2009 *Maritime Delimitation in the Black Sea* (*Romania v. Ukraine*), Judgment, *ICJ Reports* 2009, 61.

2010 R.M.S. Titanic, *Inc. v. Wrecked and Abandoned Vessel*, 742 F. Supp. 2d 784 (E.D. Va. 2010).

2011 R.M.S. Titanic, *Inc. v. Wrecked & Abandoned Vessel*, 804 F. Supp. 2d 508 (E.D. Va. 2011).

2011 *Responsibilities and obligations of States with respect to activities in the Area*, Advisory Opinion, 1 February 2011, *ITLOS Reports* 2011.

2012 *Territorial and Maritime Dispute* (*Nicaragua* v. *Colombia*), Judgment, *ICJ Reports* 2012, 624.

2013 *Saint Vincent and the Grenadines* v. *Kingdom of Spain*), Judgment, *ITLOS Reports* 2013.

2013 *Request for Interpretation of the Judgment of 15 June 1962 in the Case concerning the* Temple of Preah Vihear (Cambodia v. Thailand) (*Cambodia v. Thailand*), Judgment, ICJ Reports 2013, 281.

2014 *In the Matter of the Bay of Bengal Maritime Boundary Arbitration* (*The People's Republic of Bangladesh/The Republic of India*), Award of 7 July 2014 (available at: <https://www.pcacases.com/web/sendAttach/383>).

2015 *The South China Sea Arbitration* (*The Republic of Philippines* v. *The People's Republic of China*), Award on Jurisdiction and Admissibility, 29 October 2015 (available at: <https://pcacases.com/web/sendAttach/2579>).

2016 *The South China Sea Arbitration* (*The Republic of Philippines* v. *The People's Republic of China*), Award of 12 July 2016 (available at: <https://pcacases.com/web/sendAttach/2086>).

2016 *The Prosecutor v. Ahmad Al Faqi Al Mahdi*, Case No. ICC-01/12–01/15, Trial Chamber VIII Judgment, 27 September 2016.

2018 *Maritime Delimitation in the Caribbean Sea and the Pacific Ocean* (*Costa Rica v. Nicaragua*) *and Land Boundary in the Northern Part of Isla Portillos* (*Costa Rica v. Nicaragua*), Judgment, ICJ *Reports* 2018, 139.

2019 *Case concerning the detention of three Ukrainian naval vessels* (*Ukraine v. Russian Federation*), *Provisional Measures*, Order of 25 May 2019 *ITLOS Reports* 2019.

2020 *Dispute Concerning Coastal State Rights in the Black Sea, Sea of Azov, and Kerch Strait* (*Ukraine/Russia*), Preliminary Objections, Award of 21 February 2020 (available at: <https://pcacases.com/web/sendAttach/9272>).

2020 European Court of Human Rights, *Ukraine v. Russia* (*re Crimea*), Decision on Admissibility, 16 December 2020, Applications nos. 20958/14 and 38334/18.

Other Resources

'A new law to protect underwater cultural heritage', *Russkiy Mir Foundation*, 28 March 2017, at: <https://russkiymir.ru/en/news/222350/>.

'Ancient Greek artifact unearthed at Crimean bridge construction site', *TASS Russian News Agency*, 22 March 2017, at: <https://tass.com/society/936787>.

'Breaking News: Odyssey Explorer Searched by Cypriot Authorities and Cargo Seized', *The Pipeline*, 24 December 2015, at: <https://thepipeline.info/blog/2015/12/24/breaking-news-odyssey-explorer-searched-by-cypriot-authorities-and-cargo-seized/>.

'Canada launches new Arctic search for Franklin's lost ships', *CBC News*, 15 August 2008, at: <https://www.cbc.ca/news/canada/north/canada-launches-new-arctic-search-for-franklin-s-lost-ships-1.702857>.

'Commentary: China's decision to join COVAX will strengthen global vaccine cooperation', *XinhuaNet*, 11 October 2020, at: <http://www.xinhuanet.com/english/2020-10/11/c_139432236.htm>.

'Donald Trump menace l'Iran de frapper 52 sites "de très haut niveau"', *Le Monde/AFP*, 4 January 2020, at: <https://www.lemonde.fr/international/article/2020/01/04/deux-attaques-quasi-simultanees-contre-des-interets-des-etats-unis-en-irak_6024811_3210.html>.

'Facelift Or Farce? "Restoration" Of Palace Shocks Crimean Tatars', *Radio Free Europe/Radio Liberty*, 18 February 2018, at: <https://www.rferl.org/a/crimea-khan-s-palace-restoration-bakhchisary-shock-tatars-persecution-unesco/29046866.html>.

'Franklin ship discovery: Stephen Harper's full statement', *CBC News*, 9 September 2014, at: <https://www.cbc.ca/news/politics/franklin-ship-discovery-stephen-harper-s-full-statement-1.2760566>.

'Indonesia reverses course, to allow treasure hunting by private investors and foreigners again', *Southeast Asian Archaeology*, 3 March 2021, at: <https://www.southeastasianarchaeology.com/2021/03/05/indonesia-reverses-course-to-allow-treasure-hunting-by-private-investors-and-foreigners-again/>.

'Interview with Li Xiaojie: Underwater Archaeology in the South China Sea can demonstrate sovereignty', *Ifeng*, 22 June 2015, at: <http://finance.ifeng.com/a/20150606/13759861_0.shtml>.

'Malaysia firms plunder sunken wrecks for rare steel used to make sensitive medical, scientific equipment', *The Strait Times*, 27 February 2018, at: <https://www.straitstimes.com/asia/se-asia/malaysia-firms-plunder-sunken-wrecks-for-rare-steel-used-to-make-sensitive-medical>.

'New footage offers look into HMS Erebus wreck', *The Globe and Mail*, 16 April 2015, at: <https://www.theglobeandmail.com/news/national/new-footage-offers-look-into-hms-erebus-wreck/article23993670/>.

'Philippines asks Chinese flotilla to leave disputed reef', *DW*, 21 March 2021, at: <https://www.dw.com/en/philippines-asks-chinese-flotilla-to-leave-disputed-reef/a-56943127>.

'Russian archaeologists appropriate over a million Crimean artifacts', *Ukrinform*, 30 May 2019, at: <https://www.ukrinform.net/rubric-society/2711132-russian-archaeologists-appropriate-over-a-million-crimean-artifacts.html>.

'Stolen Heritage: How Russia is Destroying Crimean Archaeological Sites', *Hromadske International*, 4 January 2018, at: <https://en.hromadske.ua/posts/stolen-heritage-how-russia-is-destroying-crimean-archaeological-sites>.

'The expedition of experts to study the historical and cultural monuments of the south coast of the Crimea has finished', *The Hermitage News*, 8 May 2018, at: <https://www.hermitagemuseum.org/wps/portal/hermitage/news/news-item/news/2018/news_106_18/?lng=>.

Alberge, D., 'Mediterranean shipwrecks reveal "birth of globalization" in trade', *The Guardian*, 18 April 2020, at: <https://www.theguardian.com/science/2020/apr/18/mediterranean-shipwrecks-reveal-birth-of-globalisation-in-trade>.

Australasian Institute for Maritime Archaeology (AIMA) *Code of Ethics* (source: <https://www.aima-underwater.org.au/files/AIMA_Documents/AIMA_Code_of_Ethics.pdf>).

Beeby, D., 'Inuit press claim for co-ownership of Franklin artifacts', *CBC News*, 24 July 2016, at: <https://www.cbc.ca/news/politics/franklin-hms-erebus-inuit-parks-canada-hms-terror-1.3689503>.

Beltrán-García, S., 'Trump's threat to destroy Iranian heritage would be a war crime', *The Guardian*, 6 January 2020, at: <https://www.theguardian.com/artanddesign/2020/jan/06/trump-threat-destruction-iran-heritage-war-crime>.

Boswell, R., 'Finding lost ships will help claim on Arctic: gov't', *Edmonton Journal*, 16 August 2008, at: <https://www.pressreader.com/canada/edmonton-journal/20080816/281500747039104>.

Broad, W. J., 'Secret Sub to Scan Sea Floor for Roman Wrecks', *The New York Times*, 7 February 1995, at: <https://www.nytimes.com/1995/02/07/science/secret-sub-to-scan-sea-floor-for-roman-wrecks.html>.

Campbell, P. B., 'Could Shipwrecks Lead the World to War?', *The New York Times*, 18 December 2015, at: <https://www.nytimes.com/2015/12/19/opinion/could-shipwrecks-lead-the-world-to-war.html>.

Cecco, L., 'Mike Pompeo rejects Canada's claims to Northwest Passage as "illegitimate"', *The Guardian*, 7 May 2019, at: <https://www.theguardian.com/us-news/2019/may/07/mike-pompeo-canada-northwest-passage-illegitimate>.

Chan, M., 'Beijing's plans for South China Sea air defence identification zones cover Pratas, Paracel and Spratly islands, PLA Source says', *South China Morning Post*, 31 May 2020, at: <https://www.scmp.com/news/china/military/article/3086679/beijings-plans-south-china-sea-air-defence-identification-zone>.

Chatham House, 'Crimea's Occupation Exemplifies the Threat of Attacks on Cultural Heritage', 4 February 2020 (available at: <https://www.chathamhouse.org/2020/02/crimeas-occupation-exemplifies-threat-attacks-cultural-heritage>).

Coynash, H. (Human Rights Protection Group), 'Crimea: Destroying Built Heritage, Erasing the Past', *Habitat International Coalition*, 13 March 2019, at: <http://www.hlrn.org/activitydetails.php?id=pmtmZg==#.YDDpFSorxfF>.

Coynash, H. (Human Rights Protection Group), 'Ukraine moves to fight Russia's destruction of cultural heritage in occupied Crimea', *The Ukrainian Weekly*, 22 May 2020, at: <http://www.ukrweekly.com/uwwp/ukraine-moves-to-fight-russias-destruction-of-cultural-heritage-in-occupied-crimea/>.

Coynash, H., 'Ukraine fights destruction of cultural heritage in Crimea', *Kyiv Post*, 4 May 2020, at: <https://www.kyivpost.com/article/opinion/op-ed/halya-coynash-ukraine-takes-vital-move-to-fight-destruction-of-cultural-heritage-in-crimea.html>.

Delgado, J. P., Royal, J. and Anastasi, A., 'Revisiting and [*sic*] Early Naval Incident of the Cold War: Archaeological Identification of the Bow of HMS *Volage* Sunk During the Corfu Channel Incident of October 22, 1946' (Source: <https://rpmnautical.org/wp-content/uploads/2016/10/rpm_publications-2010-volage.pdf>).

Erickson, A. S. and Bond, K., 'Archaeology and the South China Sea: A new maritime archaeology vessel is another component in China's strategy for the South China Sea', *The Diplomat*, 20 July 2015, at: <https://thediplomat.com/2015/07/archaeology-and-the-south-china-sea/>.

Focke Museum, Graben für *Germanien*, 10 March–8 September 2013 (source: <https://www.focke-museum.de/vorlage/akkordeon-graben-fuer-germanien/>).

Gillaume, G., 'Rocks in the Law of the Sea: Some comments on the South China Sea Arbitration Award', EJIL *Talk!*, 25 February 2021, at: <https://www.ejiltalk.org/ricks-in-the-law-of-the-sea-some-comments-on-the-south-china-sea-arbitration-award/>.

Gohier, P., 'Hot on Sir John Franklin's tail', *Macleans*, 29 July 2010, at: <https://www.macleans.ca/news/canada/hot-on-sir-john-franklins-tail/>.

Green, C., 'How a map unearthed under a Newcastle housing estate may hold crucial evidence to land dispute between China and the Philippines', *The Independent*, 13 June 2015, at: <https://www.independent.co.uk/news/uk/home-news/china-and-philippines-diplomatic-row-ignited-after-old-map-found-washed-under-newcastle-housing-estate-10317024.html>.

Greenberg, J. 'Museum exhibit becomes front in Israeli-Palestinian struggle', *The Washington Post*, 13 February 2013, at: <https://www.washingtonpost.com/world/middleeast/museum-exhibit-becomes-front-in-israeli-palestinian-struggle/2013/02/13/dca47284-7614-11e2-95e4-6148e45d7adbstory.html>.

Holmes, O., Ulmanu, M. and Roberts, S., 'The world's biggest grave robbery: Asia's disappearing WWII shipwrecks', *The Guardian*, 3 November 2017, at: <https://www.theguardian.com/world/ng-interactive/2017/nov/03/worlds-biggest-grave-robbery-asias-disappearing-ww2-shipwrecks>.

ICC Canada President, 'Inuit and Canada Share Northwest Passage Sovereignty', Press Release, at: <https://www.inuitcircumpolar.com/press-releases/inuit-and-canada-share-northwest-passage-sovereignty-icc-canada-president/>.

ICOMOS, Charter on the Protection and Management of Underwater Cultural Heritage, ratified by the 11th ICOMOS General Assembly in Sofia, Bulgaria, October 1996, available at: <https://www.icomos.org/18thapril/underwater-eng.pdf>.

International Council of Museums (ICOM) *Code of Professional Ethics* (available at: <https://icom.museum/wp-content/uploads/2018/07/ICOM-code-En-web.pdf>).

Liu, L., 'A Chinese perspective on the international legal scheme for the protection of underwater cultural heritage' (2014), at <http://www.themua.org/collections/files/original/7aa041be256dde0ecdb7d04bccec34a3.pdf>.

Millan, L., 'First Arctic Navigation in February Sends a Worrying Climate Signal', *Bloomberg*, 22 February 2021, at: <https://www.bloomberg.com/news/articles/2021-02-22/first-arctic-navigation-in-february-sends-a-worrying-climate-signal>.

Nardi, C., 'Trove of artifacts from HMS Erebus help shed light on last days of doomed Franklin expedition', *National Post*, 21 February 2020, at: <https://nationalpost.com/news/trove-of-artifacts-from-hms-erebus-help-shed-light-on-last-days-of-doomed-franklin-expedition>.

Naylord, H., 'King Herod exhibit "latest example of Israeli exploitation"', *The National*, 23 February 2013, at: <https://www.thenational.ae/world/mena/king-herod-exhibit-latest-example-of-israeli-exploitation-1.306231>.

Page, J., 'Chinese Territorial Strife Hits Archaeology', *The Wall Street Journal*, 2 December 2013, at: <https://www.wsj.com/articles/SB10001424052702304470504579164873258159410>.

Panda, A., 'China's HD-981 Oil Rig Returns, Near Disputed South China Sea Waters', *The Diplomat*, 27 June 2015, at: <https://thediplomat.com/2015/06/chinas-hd-981-oil-rig-returns-to-disputed-south-china-sea-waters/>.

Rakoczy, A., 'Battle over shipwreck treasure: "Cultural heritage is not ours to sell"', *Cyprus Mail*, 10 May 2020, at: <https://cyprus-mail.com/2020/05/10/battle-over-shipwreck-treasure-cultural-heritage-is-not-ours-to-sell/>.

Roach, J., 'Titanic Was Found During Secret Cold War Navy Mission', *National Geographic*, 21 November 2017, at: <https://www.nationalgeographic.com/history/article/titanic-nuclear-submarine-scorpion-thresher-ballard>.

Ryall, J., 'Scavengers pillage wartime wrecks in Southeast Asia', *DW*, 29 May 2017, at: <https://www.dw.com/en/scavengers-pillage-wartime-wrecks-in-southeast-asia/a-39027260>.

Shandra, A., 'Crimea's occupied cultural heritage', *Euromaidan Press*, 10 September 2019, at: <http://euromaidanpress.com/2016/09/10/crimeas-occupied-cultural-heritage/>.

The Israel Museum, Herod the *Great: The King's Final Journey*, 2 February 2013–4 Mar 2014 (source: <https://www.imj.org.il/en/exhibitions/herod-great>).

Theodoulou, N., 'Wrecks found between Cyprus and Lebanon "equivalent to finding new planet"', *Cyprus Mail*, 21 April 2020, at: <https://cyprus-mail.com/2020/04/21/wrecks-found-between-cyprus-and-lebanon-equivalent-to-finding-new-planet/>.

UNESCO, 'Evaluation of UNESCO's standard-setting work of the Culture Sector, part VI – 2001 Convention on the Protection of Underwater Cultural Heritage', UNESCO Doc. IOS/EVS/PI/174 REV, at 23–24 (available at: <https://unesdoc.unesco.org/ark:/48223/pf0000368446?posInSet=2&queryId=N-99620a76-e942-40ee-b421-74cb017adfb5>).

Watson, P., 'Ship found in Arctic 168 years after doomed Northwest Passage attempt', *The Guardian*, 12 September 2016, at: <https://www.theguardian.com/world/2016/sep/12/hms-terror-wreck-found-arctic-nearly-170-years-northwest-passage-attempt>.

Xiaoyan, W., 'China's "Sea Power Nation" Strategy', Institute for Security and Development Policy (2014) (available at: <https://isdp.eu/content/uploads/images/stories/isdp-main-pdf/2014-wu-chinas-sea-power-nation-strategy.pdf>).

Yusha, Z., 'China and Russia help address vaccine shortage in developing nations given Western countries' absence', *Global Times* 25 February 2021, at: <https://www.globaltimes.cn/page/202102/1216608.shtml>.

All websites were last accessed on 1 July 2021.

www.ingramcontent.com/pod-product-compliance
Lightning Source LLC
Chambersburg PA
CBHW071350230926
51846CB00002B/500
* 9 7 8 9 0 0 4 5 0 4 4 6 2 *